The Nation's Homeopath

Praise for *The Nation's Homeopath*

'Dr Batra leveraged high-quality homoeopathy in a manner that made it affordable for and available to all, while simultaneously giving back to homoeopathy itself through investment in research, teaching, awareness building and charity. *The Nation's Homoeopath* is an endearing tale of the seventy years that this passionate and compassionate ambassador of this magical and transformative science has toiled, single-mindedly pursuing his dream to do good for everyone.'

– Rajiv Bajaj, MD, Bajaj Auto

'An inspirational and honestly narrated story about a man who revolutionized and then pinned the word "homeopathy" on the global map. Part-doctor and part-entrepreneur, Dr Mukesh Batra is India's first "doc-preneur" and his tale is truly fascinating.'

– Ashwin Sanghi, bestselling author

'A casual visit to a doctor's clinic for some medicine forty years back, through great filmmaker and actor Manoj Kumar, turned into a lifelong friendship. Dr Mukesh Batra has become a household name all over the country and beyond in the field of homeopathy, thanks to his deep knowledge and commitment. Just as his sweet pills are a must-have to heal, so is *The Nation's Homeopath* a must-read.'

– Shatrughan Sinha, actor, former Union Health Minister

'*The Nation's Homeopath* is delightful, and I found myself enjoying every chapter. It is unexpectedly candid and replete with several life lessons written in a pragmatic way that makes them accessible to the reader. I believe in homeopathy but even if you don't, do read the book. I'm sure you will enjoy it as much as I did.'

– Shabana Azmi, actress and social activist

'*The Nation's Homeopath* is an explicit autobiography of a kind, highly decorated doctor, whose vision, determination, integrity and compassion have made him an icon within his profession. A life well-lived indeed.'

– Professor Barry Stevens, founder,
The Trichological Society, London, UK

'Being a medical doctor yet a firm supporter of the complementary and alternative medical practices, I have always admired Dr Batra for the passion with which he has spread homeopathy all over the world. He has touched the lives of many with homeopathy through his charitable and humanitarian works.

His autobiography will inspire the young and old alike to lead a more meaningful life. The book is well-written with anecdotes from his life, mistakes made and lessons learnt. I strongly recommend *The Nation's Homeopath* for a truly inspiring read.'

– Swami Shailendra Saraswati, doctor, spiritual leader
and Osho's brother

The Nation's Homeopath

How Dr Batra's®
Became the World's
Largest Chain of
Homeopathy Clinics

DR MUKESH BATRA

HARPER
BUSINESS
An Imprint of HarperCollins *Publishers*

First published in India in 2021 by Harper Business
An imprint of HarperCollins *Publishers*
A-75, Sector 57, Noida, Uttar Pradesh 201301, India
www.harpercollins.co.in

2 4 6 8 10 9 7 5 3

P-ISBN: 978-93-5422-726-4
E-ISBN: 978-93-5422-610-6

Typeset in 11.5/15 ITC Galliard at
Manipal Technologies Ltd, Manipal

Printed and bound at
Thomson Press (India) Ltd

Contents

1

A Homeopath Is Born

My story begins in the blood-and-tears-soaked backdrop of World War II, the global nightmare that lasted six years, killing close to fifty million people and displacing millions of others. Rat-a-tat gunfire and exploding bombs, severed limbs and flattened cities, and an absence of anything life-affirming, defined those years. There was no home untouched by the war, including that of my maternal grandfather, Baburao Sirpal—a man who played a pivotal role in my life. We called him Papaji.

Papaji was a tall, slim and handsome man who brooked no nonsense. He owned the largest sports goods store in Rangoon, Burma. It was common then for Indians to move to Burma for a better life. The country was beautiful, bursting with tropical verdancy punctuated by golden domes of pagodas, and with bountiful markets by rivers like the Irrawaddy. The people were gentle and peace-loving.

As Burma was under British rule, Indians anglicized their names. Thus, Baburao Sirpal, Papaji, became B.R. Sir Paul, just as Makkad changed to Maker and Kakkar to Kaicker. Only my grandmother remained Durga, inappropriately, as she was always dressed in a white sari and was short and frail.

Papaji, though strict, lavished attention on his daughters. My mother, Kaushalya or Mary, grew up with a convent education, wore a longyi like Aung San Suu Kyi and spent her vacations at the family's sprawling weekend home in Mandalay, Burma's second important city. My mother always spoke fondly about their Mandalay visits. On her eighteenth birthday, Papaji gifted her with a Cadillac, which she crashed on her first drive out.

It was a happy and affluent family life until 1942, when the Japanese came a-calling as a fallout of World War II. Like an ostrich with its head buried in the sand, Papaji did not take the invasion seriously, thinking that his wealth and contacts would protect him. It was only when Japanese tanks rumbled down the streets and the city began to empty that he realized that he, too, had to flee to India. What was still busy and bustling was the port, where the last ship was getting ready to sail.

Papaji packed as many family valuables as he could into large steel trunks and brought them to the docks. He bought first-class tickets for the family—look at the pride and optimism!—while there were still a few hours for departure. At the docks, the loaders, taking advantage of the situation, asked for Rs 100 per trunk. Papaji blew a fuse. A hundred bucks in the 1940s was perhaps equivalent to Rs 10,000 in today's value. 'I have so many servants at home,' he hollered. 'I don't need you guys. I'll call my staff from home to load.'

However, pandemonium at the docks increased. The throngs, shoving and screaming, their survival at stake, started forcing themselves on to the ship regardless of whether they had a ticket or not. And then well before the official departure time, the ship hooted its last call. Punctuality is not a priority when a city is under attack. Papaji and his family were pushed aboard just as the ship withdrew the gangway to set off on its twenty-four-hour journey to India.

On board there was mayhem. Papaji and his family could not even get a cabin, forget a first-class one. They lay on the floor of the cold, open deck with no blankets and with hundreds of other people crying around them. Imagine leaving behind your life's earnings in a city fading in the distance, together with all the happy memories, including a Cadillac that would never again unite with its original, longyi-wearing owner.

The voyage from Rangoon to Sialkot was a long one for Papaji and his family, and not the last odyssey either. After the ship took them to Chennai (then Madras), they took a train all the way up and west to Sialkot, as it was a hub for the sports goods industry. Papaji built his business up again—rupee by rupee—in undivided India. But there was more pain and displacement to come.

It came to light that Papaji's sister had not made it to the ship in Rangoon. Having to fend for herself, she had wrapped all her jewellery around her body, under her clothes, and walked. She walked from Burma to Amritsar through Bangladesh (then East Pakistan). Her feet were shredded by the time she reached Punjab.

Then Partition happened. Papaji and his family walked thousands of miles from Sialkot to the newly carved Indian territories. Along the way they saw people being slaughtered, they saw babies and children crying, and so much other suffering. The family made it to Delhi.

My mother eventually studied medicine at Lady Hardinge Medical College and moved to Lucknow after marrying my dad, Dr M.C. Batra, a homeopath. Papaji settled in Agra and built his life from scratch for the third time, this instance with a leather goods business. First sports and now leather, both demanding resilience and toil, were apt metaphors for my grandfather's life.

And on 1 July 1951, I was born in Lucknow, the son of a mother who was an allopathic doctor and a father who was a homeopath, making me a product of mixopathy.

2

The Road to Agra

I WAS THE OLDEST OF THREE BOYS. MY YOUNGER BROTHER WAS Rakesh and my youngest brother Navkesh, a name that made no sense. But names didn't have to in those days. Parents had too much on their plates to worry about their kids' names. We only had to sound like brothers, which Mukesh, Rakesh and Navkesh certainly did. And at least we were not called Mogambo or something, like Amrish Puri in the film *Mr India* (1987).

We lived on the upper floor of a rickety old building in Lucknow's fashionable Hazratganj area named after Nawab Amjad Ali Shah, who was respectfully addressed as 'Hazrat'. The buzz around Hazratganj did not change the fact that our building was in poor condition. My first close call with death occurred here, when I was a baby. My uncle saw me crawling towards the balcony and pulled me away, perhaps driven by some intuition. Seconds later, the balcony crashed three storeys to the ground. Events since have led me to believe I have a cat's nine lives (and hopefully the same feline grace). My life, at such times, has seemed like a 1970s' movie, except two of these events took place in the 1950s.

The second close call occurred when I got lost in a mela. It was 1954 and my parents had taken me to the Maha Kumbh in Prayagraj (then Allahabad). I was three. Disorderly crowds in an open space can be a recipe for disaster. Soon enough, a stampede ensued. People ran over and around me like galloping horses. Nearly 800 people died in the crush, and I could easily have been one of them. Luckily a friend of my father's, a strapping homeopath named Dr Sindhi, found me and hoisted me upon his shoulders. He carried me through the surge of people panicking on all sides.

Not much later, my parents packed me off to Agra to live with Papaji and Mataji, which is how we addressed my grandmother. They had been alone after marrying off their two daughters: my mom and her sister Savitri (Savy). They lived in Hing ki Mandi, a congested area. Agra was a blue-collar industrial town, a hub of the leather and marble trades. Save for the Taj Mahal and Fatehpur Sikri, it lacked the sophistication of Lucknow.

My academic year was spent in Agra, at St. Anthony School in Cantt (the cantonment area), and holidays in Lucknow. This meant a once-in-a-year round trip between the two towns. I would be sent on the train journey accompanied by anyone travelling in the same direction, strangers included.

Sometimes, it was an eighty-year-old homeopathic doctor friend of my father's, Dr Sarkar, who frequently went to Lucknow on work. The old-style first-class compartments had no interconnecting paths between carriages. There were just a few berths and a toilet. This was scary because at the age of four or five, on my first trip, I was put on a train with an old man (Dr Sarkar) whom I hardly knew. The train would make a long halt at Tundla station, where the engines were changed, and I remember feeling afraid. Other passengers would wonder how a small child could travel with a much older person. The experience stuck with me. As an adult, I rarely felt lonely, perhaps because loneliness had been my companion since the start.

For most people, childhood train journeys are happy memories—of snacks from different stations, gentle parental admonishment, and games and fights with siblings or other kids in the compartment. My experience was different. Often, there was no one to accompany me on the journey back to Agra after my holidays. At such times, my mother would tell any passenger on the train to keep an eye on me.

One time, my mom climbed aboard at Lucknow to settle me in my seat and the train started moving. She couldn't get off in time and I remember her screaming for help and trying to pull the chain. The train did not stop because, of course, the chains never worked when you needed them to. She got down at the next station with virtually no money with her and somehow made her way home. Can you imagine being about five years old and seeing your mother screaming and pulling the chain? I was traumatized.

Once I reached Agra, however, I was happy to see my grandparents' private cyclerickshaw waiting to take me home, as always. The rickshaw was a luxury in those times, and a marker of Papaji's status. He was not affluent the way he had been in Rangoon. But he was well-off. And his personality elicited the same fear and respect it had in his prime.

The rickshaw also took me to school every day. Cantt was quite far from home. On uphill stretches, my friends and I would have to get off and push this strange love child of a bicycle and a horse carriage. Meanwhile, the rickshawallah—a lungi- and banyan-wearing man—would rise from the seat and pedal with all his might to get some momentum going. My favourite part was standing on the bar behind the rickshaw and holding on to its hood, especially when it raced down a slope. Now when I think of it, I see it as my personal *Titanic* moment.

3

The Smell of Asafoetida

HING KI MANDI HAD EARNED ITS NAME IN THE MUGHAL DAYS when it became the centre of the asafoetida trade. After Partition many of the original Muslim traders relocated to Pakistan and their place was taken by businessmen who migrated to India at the same time, like Papaji. These men had made the area a footwear hub and it was now famous for its handcrafted shoes.

Hing ki Mandi unfolded in layers. First, there was an assault upon the senses at the street level. There were buildings bursting at the seams on both sides of a narrow road. Grime and sludge snaked across footpaths, and pigs competed with people for the limited walking space. Yet, it was vibrant. You could smell the spirit of survival. Every morning, the street hummed with men pushing loaded handcarts, each with a call of their own to entice customers. Even the laundry guy came with a cart. He pressed clothes with a steam iron almost as big as a briefcase, its insides crackling with red coal and ash.

Most residents had a shop below and a house above, the classic '*neechey dukaan upar makaan*' formula. We were no different. Our house was up a dark and dusty stairway. Mataji, my grandmother, had tried to make the space as homely as she could. Yet, our living style was basic. There was a curtained shelf for clothes, no cupboards.

None of this bothered me. I took everything as it came. The only painful memory of those years was when the watchman of the building took me into a bathroom and made me masturbate him. I was seven or eight. I did not tell Papaji. He would have killed the watchman. And then he would have thrashed me for not raising an alarm.

After about four years in that cramped house, we moved into a large kothi in Lajpat Kunj. We were able to exhale. Oh, the sheer size of the place. Just the gate of the house was a couple of hundred metres from the main structure.

The kothi had a front lawn where we grew vegetables on one patch. At the back, Papaji set up a small factory to make shoes. He had about twenty karigars (craftsmen) making handmade shoes to export to different countries like Russia and Eastern European nations like Romania and the erstwhile Czechoslovakia. Papaji would get correspondence from his partners in these countries. The postage stamps on the letters had a whiff of 'foreign' about them and triggered my imagination, transporting me to distant lands. It helped that the stamps came in the most unusual shapes. I remember they were triangular, and not the customary square or rectangular shapes that we were used to in India.

Today I no longer use leather products and have given up non-vegetarian food. But as a child my staple meals were mutton–chawal made by Mataji. The prize was always the marrow, loosened inside the bone with a matchstick or pin, and then sucked out with a slurp.

Evenings brought with them calls for azaan, and the arrival of my friends. Our vast front yard coupled with my arsenal of sports kits made our kothi a magnet for children, most of them older than me. Papaji, with his sports connections, had ensured I had my own cricket bat, football, badminton racquet and anything else I wanted. In cricket, I would get out on the first ball and the rest of the boys would play forever. We also played Indian games like pithu, or used a catapult (we called it catty) to raid guava or mango trees. Some of the boys became my good friends and I am still in touch with them.

At times my cousins from London (Aunt Savy's kids) visited us during their holidays. They were Honey and Bunny, and my nickname was Sunny. Together, we were the profoundly named trio—Sunny, Honey and Bunny. Often, we wore oversized clothes cut from the same bale of cloth or an old curtain. The finishing touch was oiled hair parted in the middle and combed. So, liberally oiled hair is not a Malayali quirk.

We hated the oil. It cramped our style. But it's not that there were too many girls around for us to impress. The only girls we knew were sisters of our male friends. If they were older, we called them 'didi', and if they were younger, they were 'chhoti didi'. There you go.

While our play area was spacious, it wasn't without hazards. It was still 1950s' India, after all. On a patch of lawn was a huge pit dug to dump household waste. Over time, the garbage would turn into manure which was then used to fertilize our vegetable crops and fruit trees. But the pit also attracted snakes, including pythons. Mataji stepped on a garden snake once, thinking it was a pipe.

However, residents rarely killed the snakes as the reptiles ate the rats and maintained the ecological balance. Besides, they were seen as avatars of Shiva. If they were at times deemed too much of a threat, they would be caught and released in nearby vegetation. I do not remember feeling any terror about snakes. We were children, living moment to moment, too busy playing and racing down slopes in a rickshaw to let a mere python bother us.

4

Unbreakable Glass, Broken Lady

DESPITE HAVING FRIENDS AT SCHOOL AND IN THE NEIGHBOURHOOD, I began to grow lonely in Agra. I felt abandoned by my parents and cried most nights. In the winters, when we slept outside on cots with quilts, the dew would mix with my tears and my face would be wet by morning. But my parents had done what they thought was best for their child. They were busy growing their respective medical practices. In Agra, they thought, my grandparents would give me undivided attention and love. Which, they did.

Mornings were better. The rooster would crow. My eyes would open and adjust to the light. Running my tongue around my lips I would catch some of the saltiness of dried tears. I would get up, drawing strength from the optimism of the early sun. By now Papaji would be out in the yard shaving, face pink and long legs stretched out, a man worth admiring, but one you also loathed for the way he sometimes treated people, including Mataji.

Our black cocker spaniel named Kaalu would lie beside him. On Papaji's lap would be a towel, and close at hand a mug of water, a shaving brush, a cake of soap and a plain mirror that he held in his hand. There were no concaves and convexes at that time—life and mirrors were just plain. Working the brush into the soap to whip up lather on his face and talk through it, as Papaji did, was an art. The blade screwed into an open-and-shut metal razor and delivered a clean enough shave with some manly nicks and cuts. Papaji would have looked good on an Old Spice commercial, surfing the waves to the tune of the soaring '*Carmina Burana*' tune. But back then he didn't use a modern aftershave lotion. A stick of alum or fitkari served as an antiseptic. And it stung. If women had their inconveniences, men had their daily shaves.

On Sundays, Papaji played rummy with his friends for hours and the forfeit was one paisa per point. It was Mataji's job to make food for them and it was a kind of picnic for everyone, except perhaps Mataji. I was allowed to peep at Papaji's cards and even hold them. On occasion, I played his turn when he had a bio-break. It was exciting to sit at the card table at the age of eight or nine with the grown-ups. And if I won for Papaji, it was a very big thing, even if the amount was only a few paise.

Papaji was also fond of his drink. It was a specific two pegs every evening of his favourite whisky, Solan No. 1. Two pegs are not excessive but he would still become violent and frequently smash his glass on the floor. Mataji would quietly sweep up the pieces of glass. I was witness to this and decided to never have alcohol. I don't serve it at my parties either, even when I'm hosting actors or politicians.

My aunt Savy, who lived in London with her husband, heard of Papaji's habit of slamming glasses. From the faraway wonderland called England she sent something that reduced some of Mataji's misery, unbreakable glass. Throw it all you want. In this evolving tragicomedy of my grandparents' conjugality, all we had to do in the morning was to pick up the glass, wipe it and set it down, so that it could be thrown again in the evening.

Mataji suffered, really suffered, because of Papaji's aggressive temperament and the patriarchal customs of that era. She had only her satsang and prayers to lean on. I would sometimes accompany her to the satsangs, where we sat on the floor listening to the Ramayana and Mahabharata or singing bhajans, with only the prasad to look forward to at the end of the gathering. These were our only outings.

There were cinema halls in Agra, but Papaji believed films were a corrupting influence. The rare movie we were allowed to watch was a moral tale, like *The Ten Commandments* (1956), which I saw with a visiting cousin. Papaji must have tossed glasses in his grave when I later became passionate about movies and music, and served on the Censor Board as well as the Filmfare Awards jury.

We did have a radio at home but the only thing we were allowed to hear was news and cricket commentary. The 1950s were a milestone period for Indian cricket. Towards the end of the decade in Kanpur, and not that far from our kothi in Agra, India scored its first Test win over Australia. Jasu Patel was the hero of the match, taking a record nine for sixty-nine with his off-spin.

The country's occasional success in sports brought excitement to us boys. To Mataji, it made no difference. While my grandparents provided me with everything a child could want, they were quite austere themselves. Mataji's sole cosmetic indulgence, if it can even be called that, was Loma hair oil. All elderly ladies used it as it turned grey hair gold. De facto, Loma became one of the earliest hair colours in India. Most of the women in the region were born in Punjab and had a fair complexion. Their newly acquired blonde tresses made them look like foreigners. What a change from the mustard oil used on us children. Mustard oil was used in everything in the north. It was used in cooking, for a body massage and on the hair. They might as well have fried us in it too.

5

A Mausoleum and a Pet Cemetery

I SOMETIMES FEEL GOD HATCHED SIMILAR PLANS FOR MADHUBALA and Agra. To Madhubala he perhaps said, 'Your life will have tragedy and sickness, but I will bless you with such rare beauty that it will make you immortal.' To Agra he said, 'You will have dust and poverty and the smell of leather, but I will give you the Taj Mahal.'

We had one thing going for us. But what a thing it was. The Taj Mahal was bigger and grander than photographs can ever suggest—soaring 561 feet towards the sky, taller than the Qutb Minar. The Taj and its sprawling gardens had a mystique so powerful that I never tired of it. Every season, every time of day, revealed a new facet of the monument.

The Taj Mahal was built between 1631 and 1648, give or take a few years, depending upon different historical accounts. When I lived in Agra, the Taj had just completed its third centenary. We were aware of all the stories around it. To a young mind, the scale of the structure, the logistics, the emotion as well as the rumoured cruelty behind it, were mind-boggling.

How on earth did Shah Jahan and the force he employed, led by his chief architect Ustad Ahmad Lahori, create something so huge and complicated? Was the story of the workers' arms being chopped off by Shah Jahan after the completion of the mausoleum, a myth or fact? I also failed to understand, at least in the naiveté of youth, how a man so much in love with his wife, Mumtaz Mahal, could have had other wives.

These curiosities made me only too happy to be the designated Taj guide for relatives visiting Agra. On nights when the moon was in its element, the Taj would be bathed in silver white light. We would spread durries on the lawn and take out the picnic hamper—aloo parathas, achaar, sabzi—and absorb the beauty around us. Back then, you could go down to the graves. There was no electricity, though. You needed candles, which made it more thrilling and borderline spooky.

I did not count the number of times I visited the Taj. But I must have taken nearly a hundred pictures on that marble bench with the dome in the background. Every celebrity who visits the Taj takes a picture on the bench. And in my view it was the iconic photo of the unlucky-in-love Lady Di, sitting alone, that made that spot more popular than anyone else.

Agra had three other things travellers sought—the savoury dal moth, the sweet petha and a mini Taj replica for home. The snacks had to be from a shop called Panchhi. I don't care for petha any more as I find it too sweet. Back then I didn't mind it, though I knew that the process to make it wasn't hygienic. A pumpkin was hit repeatedly against a roadside pole and pulled apart until it became a gelatinous pulp. This would be sugared, flavoured and sugared some more. Petha came in different varieties like rose and orange. And as the joke about Indian street food goes, the fungus on the mithaiwallah's hand perhaps imparted its flavour too.

My quiet existence was punctuated with some highs, like visits to the Taj, and some lows, but it took a brutal tragedy to shake me to the core. Without my parents and brothers in Agra, Kaalu was my lifeline. Papaji knew this. Yet, when a doctor in the neighbourhood complained that Kaalu had rabies and had become a risk, Papaji agreed for the dog to be put down. Papaji must have known I would never allow it. So he did it behind my back.

I had gone to school and when I returned, Kaalu wasn't there to greet me as usual—with wagging tail and soulful eyes. I went around the compound thinking he must be burying a bone or up to some mischief. It was all quiet.

Mataji called me inside. She told me what had transpired. My heart sank and big tears welled up. While I was at school, laughing along with friends, my dog had died a most painful death by air-gun pellets. The horror of that realization broke me. Air rifles are meant for sport, not to kill. How many times must Papaji or his henchman have shot Kaalu to kill him? What kind of a person could have been capable of such cruelty?

I imagined the scene over and over again, trying to feel Kaalu's pain, as if trying to punish myself for not being there to save him. Then I insisted they take me to the field where he had been shot. Papaji, for once, allowed it.

At first, I did not even see the body. All I saw was a flock of vultures tearing pieces of flesh off a carcass. My brain froze, unwilling to make sense of what my eyes were seeing. Yet, out of duty, my feet drew me closer. It was my dear Kaalu's mangled body, intestines spilling out, eyes scratched out, and his once warm fur sticky with blood.

We accorded him whatever little dignity we could by burying him, and with it, a part of my innocence.

6

The Departed

My time in Agra made me the man I am. Seeing how Mataji was treated made me sensitive towards the women in my life. For instance, I have always believed that women should be financially independent. I ensure that every woman in my life, my daughters-in-law included, are made financially independent so that they don't have to suffer fools or injustice.

The second thing I learned from my student years was to speak the truth. I made this decision after an innocuous incident where I told a lie and got caught. It was the rare time I had done badly in Mrs Bhatia's Hindi test. She gave me a note for my grandfather. I was so fearful of my grandfather that I did not show the letter to him or Mataji. But at school, I told Mrs Bhatia that I had done the needful. And then the fear of getting caught took hold of me. For a few days, I was a nervous wreck.

I did get caught. Aunt Savy, who had come for a visit, bumped into Mrs Bhatia at school and that was that. Chastened, I swore not to lie again.

Coincidentally, it was Aunt Savy who realized how lonely I was and was responsible for finally reuniting me with my parents in Mumbai (then Bombay), where they lived after my father's transfer. Aunt Savy was attuned to my moods and my feelings, even if I never said anything to her. She just knew.

I felt relief at the prospect of being back with my parents, but I also felt guilty about leaving my grandparents. While I was moving on with my life, they would be left to theirs, with only our new dog Bina for company.

After I left, Papaji sold the large kothi and moved into a smaller bungalow. Bina could not acclimatize to the small space and died shortly after that. Meanwhile, even as my grandparents were trying to get used to being without me, the manager of Papaji's business cheated him of his money and vanished. Some international payments that Papaji had expected did not come through. Proud and fierce Papaji began to unravel after that.

He began to visit wine shops in the neighbourhood and would leave large sums of money there as a deposit, so that he could pick up his tipple without having to go through the chore of paying. Finally, he was left with nothing but a numbing loneliness. He came to Mumbai to visit us occasionally. I was happy to be with him and have him sleep in my bedroom. But we hardly spoke. As much as I felt for him, we had moved beyond the common language of my childhood.

Alzheimer's set in soon for Papaji. One day, he disappeared from our home and was found a few days later sitting on a bench in Juhu, unshaven and lost. We brought him home, and after he had rested a few days, we took him back to Agra. In a smaller town and familiar surroundings, the chances of him wandering off too far were slimmer.

I was in my second year of homeopathy college in Mumbai when I got the news that Papaji had passed away. I was heartbroken. I ran to the washroom and cried my eyes out. There was no money for all of us to fly for his funeral. The train would have taken too long. I felt his death deeply. Papaji and Kaalu, the two pillars of my childhood, had died without me by their side.

Papaji's death left Mataji alone. She divided her year between staying with Aunt Savy and us. She was happy to be near me but her suffering continued, although in a different form—she got breast cancer and had a mastectomy. Mataji was so old and frail, she must have weighed 32 kg. I saw her dying right in front of my eyes. I remember every moment in slow motion: the body lying on the floor, her last breath long gone and the realization of the impermanence of life washing over me. We cremated Mataji at Banganga and then took the ashes to Nashik. We went out into the waters in a makeshift woven basket and let go of her ashes. I had performed her last rites as she had no sons and I was her eldest grandson.

My grandparents have been gone for a long time now. But what they did for me, what they taught me in ways good and bad, built the foundation of my value system. Papaji's rebuilding of his life three times in different cities amidst political strife, showed me what a man could do with sheer will. His vanity and aggression taught me never to be egoistic and not to touch drink. Mataji taught me quiet dignity. She fed me and took me to satsangs where I imbibed life lessons from mythology and spirituality. In my heart, there will always be a special place for my grandparents, not just a small corner but a large kothi.

7

Tackling Mumbai

I HAD COMPLETED FIFTH STANDARD IN AGRA, WHEN IT WAS DECIDED that I should rejoin my parents in Mumbai. They had moved there a few years earlier, Rakesh and Navkesh in tow, after my father got a promotion. And thus the great chess player up above, pitchforked me from bucolic Lajpat Kunj to noisy, grey Grant Road, where a train station, bakeries, electronic shops and the red-light district coexisted within baffling proximity.

Our home was a two-bedroom apartment squeezed into Navyug Mansion on Sleater Road, Grant Road West, right outside the station. My uncle Ram Batra, a builder and a prominent name in Mumbai, had constructed Navyug Mansion. Navyug, meaning 'new era', was aptly named considering my family started a new innings there.

It took me a while to find my feet in my new surroundings. Make no mistake, I was happy to be back with my immediate family, to be rid of loneliness, to at last wake up without tear-stained cheeks. But life is often like a video game. You see off one set of challenges, and another set appears. In Grant Road, yellow and brown local trains with people packed in like chickens for slaughter, clattered past the house the entire day and till late in the night. No wonder they call Mumbai the city that never sleeps.

The landscape was mostly concrete. The woofs of Kaalu that I was used to in Agra were replaced by the sound of traffic. In 23 Lajpat Kunj, I had the whole kothi to myself, but here I was sharing a room with two brothers, and with one of whom I developed a slight sibling rivalry (Rakesh, who was seven). Navkesh was about four, just a toddler. Today, though, the three of us are very close. We did have another two-bedroom flat next door, which sounds a lot by urban standards, but that apartment was used by my parents for their respective clinics.

I missed Agra—its space, peace and greenery. More so because I was not naturally the outgoing 'Mumbai' type either. Nor had I yet developed an interest in films, which meant that the presence of Bollywood and film stars in the city made no difference to my life at that point.

Mornings inevitably meant competing with Rakesh for the bathroom and our mother's attention too. As for Mumbai colloquialisms and Bambaiya Hindi, they made me wince. '*Tu aayega, tu jaayega*?' Really?

Was this how a great city spoke? I couldn't believe it when children in Mumbai sometimes addressed their elders as 'tu'. Where I came from, even elders addressed children as 'aap'. Once, I reprimanded a stranger for not addressing me properly. '*Hum aapko aap kahe ja rahe hain, aur aap hume tum bula rahe hain.*' Imagine the scene, a little boy wagging his finger at an older stranger on the subject of cultured manners in the middle of a Mumbai street: 'I keep using "aap" to address you and you use "tum" for me?'

In this time of change and adjustment in my life, there were islands of fun. During the rains, our area, low lying and with a British-era drainage system, would get so flooded that we would dive into the chai-coloured water from the first floor and not hurt ourselves. Cars parked in the compound would end up floating and bobbing ten buildings away. Once the water receded, we would play 'Spot the Car'.

Television reception in those days was as patchy as mobile networks today. A gust of wind, and the screen would go crazy. This, while the entire neighbourhood was gathered in your living room, crowded around that one black-and-white TV set. Then, with all the elegance of a neurosurgeon, you would have to delicately move the antenna while everyone held their breath. A clear picture elicited as many cheers as an Olympic medal.

Occasionally, our parents allowed us the decadent mawa cakes from Merwan's Bakery on the other side of Grant Road station. Its owner, Bomi Hormazji Irani, was always around. And he would often be scolding the waiters. Having witnessed Papaji's anger, at first I thought Mr Irani was truly angry at his staff. Then I realized there was a bit of theatrics to it, so that the establishment could live up to its eccentric reputation and give the customers a bit of a show.

Repairs were made to the café frequently over the years, but it retained much of its original look with marble-topped tables, Minton-tiled flooring, rickety wooden chairs and a gruff person at the counter. The more cantankerous the guy was, the fluffier the cakes. Perhaps that was the secret of their success.

Grant Road did not have many green patches, but it had August Kranti Maidan, not far from our home. A Konkani nanny looked after us while our parents were at work. It was her duty to feed us the whole day—and as three children in various stages of growth spurts, I now realize what a challenge she must have faced. But we needed fresh air and the closest spot for it was the iconic Gowalia Tank. And the three of us would go there with her.

It was from here that Mahatma Gandhi had issued his Quit India call to the British on 8 August 1942. With the fervour of Independence not yet subsumed by the travails of post-independence India, we would enact Gandhi's speech. Rakesh and I fought to be the Mahatma while Navkesh, having no choice in the matter, had to be one of the listeners who punched his hand in the air and shouted 'Jai Hind!' and 'Vande Mataram!'.

8

Campion Calls

WHEN I WALKED OUT OF THE BLACK IRON GATE OF ST. ANTHONY'S in Agra Cantt for the last time, I had no idea that my next school day would be in Mumbai.

Campion School was a neat white box of a building with a red trim, standing somewhat inconspicuously on a leafy street near Colaba. It was at the epicentre of one of the city's great precincts. We were in the same radius as Oval Maidan, Regal Cinema, Cooperage Football Ground and the Gateway of India.

It was a prestigious school, not easy to get into. But they recognized a good family background when they saw one. We were middle class, but my parents were doctors, and that must have counted for something.

Among those whose laughter and tears rang out in the halls of Campion were sons of industrialists, bureaucrats and film personalities. A big imported car would drop two impossibly pink and fair boys off at the school gate. Their names were Randhir and Rishi Kapoor. Randhir was my senior, while Rishi was one year junior, as was Shashi Tharoor. You could understand his English then. Most others, however well off, were dropped off in Ambassadors or Fiats, as it was still an India where foreign cars were difficult to acquire.

With his light eyes and complexion, Randhir was princely but also goofy. He was already close to six-feet tall. Rishi, may his soul rest in peace, was chubby and cheerful. Frankly, the Kapoor kids came to school for fun and basic education at best. 'We only need to study enough to learn to sign autographs,' they'd say.

We had some exemplary teachers. Many of them came from well-to-do homes. Salary was not their primary motivation, they were driven by the motivation to teach. Private tutoring was not encouraged and our teachers gave their best to every student in class. A Jesuit brother from the school even visited the home of each student at least once a year, to make sure that children were well adjusted at home. Moral science was not a subject; it was a way of life.

I was a front-bencher by nature and due to my height. The spirit of rebellion had not yet set in. I had no problem following instructions of authority figures. My Hindi and drama teachers in particular were fond of me due to my Agra and Lucknow connection, and my increasing interest and participation in plays and elocution. One of my Hindi teachers, Mr Bhatia, went the extra mile to teach me Hindi elocution by giving me lessons at his Malabar Hill home. He was a warm man and never let me leave without a snack. We had examples of humanity and selfless teaching before our eyes every day. This would serve as an inspiration in my later years as a doctor. Could I give to society and patients the same love and care that I received from my teachers? That was a standard I always measured myself by.

There are few things that come close to the unadulterated excitement of school or college competitions. The high of youth combined with the first sense of being good at something is a delicious cocktail. You may win only a cheap trophy or medal at the end of it, but the confidence that it gives you can set you up for bigger things in life.

I remember the debate finals from one year. I was probably in ninth or tenth standard. The battle of wits and oratory was fought between two houses, represented by me on one side and on the other by a boy who went on to become a famous politician.

We won the competition. When I returned to class, there was applause. Even in moments of triumph, I was not one for wild gesticulation. I calmly accepted the congratulations and sat down on my desk. But I did feel self-belief coursing through me. This form of R&R—or reward and recognition—is a management practice that left an indelible mark upon me and served me well in my later years as an entrepreneur.

Our pranks, fuelled by rising testosterone, were no less enjoyable. Some boys would sing 'Campion Calls', our school anthem, as 'Campion Balls'. At school camps, I learned both discipline and leadership, but more than that I learned how to play tricks on my classmates using whatever was at hand. If it was boot polish, it went on the face. And if it was toothpaste, it went inside the pyjamas of unsuspecting innocents. We always returned from these camps having made friends but losing our voices.

There were other gains too, like loyalty. For instance, there was a boy in my class named Pestonji, who once sat on the last bench near a window that was right above the principal's office. Pestonji tied his school bag with a rope, lowered it into the Big Chief's office and swung the rope so the bag whacked the principal on his back. The entire class got a thrashing. But no one ratted on Pestonji. We lived by the mafia's code of omerta.

'Spare the rod and spoil the child' was the credo of our time. In other words, teachers had carte blanche to hit us. In fact, every teacher was thoughtfully provided a ruler and a cane, just as cops are issued a lathi or a gun when they join the police force. Both ruler and cane were used frequently. For the smallest of mistakes, we were whacked on our knuckles or bent over the table and caned on our bottoms till the corrections were ingrained in our minds. Dusters and chalks were used as flying missiles to hit students talking at the back of the class. In geography class, if you got something wrong, our cigar-smoking teacher Menezes—Manju in short—pinched you in the stomach so badly that it left a world map of a bruise on you. He called it an operation which it truly was, but without the anaesthesia.

Manhood was approaching fast. My first adult movie (not that kind of adult) was Sidney Poitier's *To Sir, With Love* (1967). I was fourteen. The school had arranged a show for us at Eros, Mumbai's art deco cinema hall. Those were the days of the grandeur of single-screen cinemas. Going to a movie was like going to the opera. It was an occasion.

Viewers were allowed to bring their own snacks to the cinema back then. But this was a school event. Each student got a chicken or veg roll, oily wafers that stained the white paper bags they came in, and a Softy ice cream. I had no inkling then that twenty years later, I would visit the same cinema hall every Wednesday for five years as a member of the Film Advisory Committee of the Censor Board.

In the tradition of schools in the West, the academic year at Campion ended with an evening ball on the school's terrace, with the wind blowing and the lights of the boats near Gateway twinkling in the distance. To the west was the dazzling view of Malabar Hill. It was the most awaited of all programmes in the calendar. We spent many restless hours before the ball deciding what clothes to wear and how to style our hair. Being a boys' school, there were no girls to dance with. But there was street cred to be gained from turning out well. Music by Cliff Richards, Elvis Presley and The Beatles was played on vinyl discs. There were no DJs at the time, only DGs—dangerous guys—waiting to let loose. Common dances were the foxtrot for slow numbers, and the twist for fast ones.

The boys who danced got most of the spotlight. But sitting quietly in a corner when everyone else was on the floor could get you noticed too. I caught the eye of a beautiful young teacher of the junior grades who beckoned me to dance with her. So far, was the closest I'd got to a woman other than my mother or grandmother. My pulse quickened as I held her by her slim waist and felt the warmth emanating from her body. Her smile put me at ease as well as made me enamoured of her. At the end of the evening, she asked me to drop her home, which I did. When I kissed her goodbye on her cheek, I realized I was leaving my childhood years behind.

9

Flat Cola

MY BATCH IN SCHOOL WAS AMONGST THE FIRST TO STUDY IN THE board that we now know as ICSE (Indian Certificate of Secondary Education). Prior to that, it had had the stately title of Senior Cambridge.

It is said that students' papers used to go to Cambridge for corrections. One year, the ship carrying the papers sank and all the students were adjudged as passed. Even when we were at Campion it was believed our English language test papers went to Cambridge. We hoped for history to repeat itself. But the ships sailed through just fine.

Jokes aside, there were two good things about the Cambridge system. First, it laid emphasis on analytical thinking and not just rote learning. If an answer to a physics problem was wrong, but your method of working it out was right, you still got 60 per cent marks. Developing analytical thought helped me a lot in problem-solving during my later years. Second, as the school-leaving exams would get over in December and first year of college started in June of the coming year, we got a well-deserved break of six months.

However, any plans of a jolly time with friends, of self-exploration, of romantic pursuits or other teenage preoccupations were nipped in the bud by my father. He did not want me sitting at home. He packed me off to my first job. It was with a travel agency called Hind Musafir at Flora Fountain. I was made an accounts clerk for the princely sum of Rs 100 per month. I loved the posters of global tourist attractions and airplanes all over the office. These were boom years for the travel trade. Travel was not as accessible to everyone as it is today. Taking an exotic journey had glamour around it.

I also liked dressing up in the trendy clothes of that time—bell-bottom trousers and dog-collared shirts—and going to work at Flora Fountain. The area had energy. There were nice eating places around and lots of pretty girls. And still, I quit my job after just three months. Accounts did not suit my temperament at all, and there was only so much I could marvel at the Pan Am ads.

Nothing is ever wasted though. The three months at Hind Musafir gave me confidence and the taste of financial independence. If I could earn from a subject that I knew so little about, I could earn much more from something that I was passionate about. The question was, what was that something? I had no clear idea what I wanted to do. There were boys who wanted to become cricket players, actors, pilots. I liked a bit of various things but did not have one particular ambition. So I thought I would chill for a while at home, to use today's lingo, and mull it over.

My dad sent me to work again, this time it involved distributing Coca-Cola. The bottles were cold, but this wasn't the chilling I had in mind. This is how it panned out. My father set up an ancillary business in my name, aptly called Mukesh Bros. During those days of the licence raj, the best way to make money was to get an agency. While others got the lucrative petrol pumps and gas agencies, a Coke agency came my way. This was in the late 1960s, much before the battle between Indian socialism and American capitalism had reached its peak. George Fernandes, the firebrand industries minister and trade unionist, had yet to knock the fizz out of Coca-Cola and send it back to the US.

There was a Coke plant in Worli. And its owner was a sardarji, whose wife my father had treated. In gratitude, they gave the Malabar Hill agency to Mukesh Bros. We hired a manager and loaders. Next, we needed a truck. And we had to pay for it ourselves. My father's budget, however, allowed only for a second-hand truck, so that is what we bought.

We might as well have bought a bullock cart.

The truck would stop frequently on the steep roads of Malabar Hill. I would get out of my seat next to the driver and push the fully loaded truck uphill, with the help of loaders and passers-by. 'Coca-Cola or Dhakka Cola?' a man remarked on one such occasion.

The logistics made things harder. Each wooden crate had two dozen glass bottles. Our job was to deliver several such crates at shops, clubs and housing societies in Malabar Hill. Many buildings were high-rises, and outsiders were not always allowed to use the lifts. In such cases, the loaders would carry the crates up many flights of stairs.

Anyone who needed Coca-Cola in Malabar Hill had to buy it through us. This looked like a profitable monopoly on paper, but was totally different in practice. We got a commission of just one rupee on the delivery of twenty-four bottles. That's not all. The bottles chipped and cracked easily. Fifty paise was deducted from our commission for every chipped bottle we returned to the company. Two chipped bottles meant no commission. More chipped bottles, and you were paying the company instead of the other way around.

Mukesh Bros soon shut down. It was my first lesson in failed entrepreneurship. Many more were to come later. And when Fernandes sent Coke scooting, I almost put up a poster of his on my wall.

10
College Capers

AT LAST, AFTER MY TWO STABS AT WORKING, MY FATHER FELT I deserved to spend the rest of my holiday like a holiday. He sent me to Delhi, where I stayed for a month with the family of his friend, Dr Bhutani.

I went to Delhi on the bright orange Rajdhani Express, a status symbol next only to flying. It was a twenty-hour train trip in air-conditioned comfort and 'Vatanakulit' would be written in red Devanagari script on the bogies. Twenty hours for a 1400-km haul was considered quick those days. And even VIPs or politicians who did not get a seat on a flight would take the Rajdhani.

Dr Bhutani was a Walter Matthau lookalike—tall, slightly hunched, wearing black-framed spectacles. He was a homeopath who gave up his practice to become a successful businessman. When my father and he got together over a glass of whisky in the evenings, you could hear their laughter till the next kothi. Their jokes were normally in Multani, as they were both born in Multan, Pakistan. We understood the jokes only partially but laughed nonetheless, because the laughter was infectious.

In Delhi, my day would start early, with a substantial Punjabi breakfast of stuffed or plain parathas with yogurt and leftover sabzi. Before Amul '*Doodh peeta hai India*', we got our daily supply of milk straight from the local cowshed. Afternoons were spent reading or lazing around. Evenings were more interesting. I would take the family scooter—a two-tone Lambretta—for a spin.

I returned from Delhi refreshed and rested. Overall, the holidays were spent well, first getting an initiation into the ways of the working world, followed by leisure and travel. It was now time to get back on the academic road again. The next step on this route was Jai Hind College on 'A' Road in Churchgate, with Marine Drive and the Arabian Sea just a few yards away. Marine Drive offered stunning views of the setting sun every evening. The great orange ball would disappear into the silvery ocean, with the buildings of Malabar Hill silhouetted against the sky. But where I was in life, it was a time of sunrise. I couldn't wait for college to start and seize the day.

Jai Hind was a college of the Sindhis, by the Sindhis and for the Sindhis. Almost everything in post-independence India had some connection to the freedom struggle or Partition. Jai Hind was a child of Partition. It was started by some professors from Karachi's D.J. Sind College and some other educationists such as the college's founder principal, T.M. Advani, under the banner of the Sind Educationists' Association.

Most professors at Jai Hind wore white bush shirts, white trousers and white shoes. I was lucky to get admission there as it was considered one of the best science colleges in those days. And the joke was that Sindhi culture also taught you a bit about making money.

However, coming from Campion, Jai Hind initially posed a culture shock. I went from a class of polished students to a circus of 150 students of different levels of sophistication. At Campion the teachers 'spoke' propah English. At Jai Hind, the instructors stumbled along in local dialects, making it hard to decipher them. It was a case of 'B' for 'Bhegetables', as the joke went.

The professors were not short on skill, though. I vividly remember the popular Prof. Lahiri, who taught mathematics. He was proficient in hypnosis and often gave shows where he made students do ridiculous things on stage. One of his tricks was to make people believe they were driving a car at full speed and were about to crash. Soon enough, the stage was full of students screaming and slamming imaginary brakes. Students would meet him after the show and he would help them give up smoking and alcohol through free sessions of hypnosis.

The other big thrill about my first year in college was standing for elections for the position of class representative. Unlike school, you weren't assigned the role. Being the teacher's pet made no difference here. College elections called for the manly arts of throwing your hat in the ring, networking, power-broking and winning on your own merit. I would even say it was an early lesson in forming and then leading a company.

The same skill that enabled me to win debates in school helped me in student politics. I could lend people an ear. I could put them at ease. After personally canvassing for votes from all my classmates, but without bribing them with the canteen's famous heart-shaped veg cutlets with chhole and chutney, I got elected. I felt like Kennedy.

Even though I was a class representative, I spent more time outside class, or being an 'outstanding' student, as the joke went. And like all colleges, Jai Hind's nerve centre was the canteen. Today the cafeteria looks like a gleaming food court in a mall. Back then it had the feel of a basic Irani café. Even if you didn't have money to eat or drink anything, you could still hang out there with friends from class, seniors and outsiders who were there just to ogle at the girls. The only thing we did not fool around with were science practicals, held between 7 and 10 a.m. After that were theory classes. No one cared about those.

The freedom from daily class attendance was a joy. And it left me free to pursue my increasing interest in films. We were spoilt for choice in terms of movie theatres. Eros, Regal, Liberty, Sterling, New Excelsior—the best cinemas in town were either walking distance or a short bus ride away. Morning shows ran to packed houses mainly due to college students, some of whom got a chance to cosy up with their girlfriends in the cool privacy of the theatre. I would go with my friends Arun and Babloo.

The magic of the black-and-white era, the pathos of Guru Dutt, the romance of Dev Anand, the simplicity of Raj Kapoor and the poetic tragedies of Dilip Saab unfolded daily before our eyes. Tickets were a rupee and 75 paise each. I used my pocket money of Rs 10 per week judiciously to see as many films as I could. This was my first lesson in financial planning. Use your money for things you really want. After college we'd catch the bus back home, to be welcomed by the warmth of our mothers, who always felt sorry for the hard day we had had buried in books.

My success in class elections in my first year emboldened me to stand for college elections in my second year. This meant a month-long campaign in all divisions of the college. Freshers and seniors from the science, arts and commerce streams all had to vote. A tricky ritual for candidates was the visit from the dadas or bhais from other colleges to 'request' you to step down in favour of their candidates. But I was made of sterner stuff. I became the joint magazine secretary, an important portfolio at that time. The responsibility of producing the college magazine sharpened my writing skills and increased my clout on campus.

It was in this eventful background that I turned eighteen. With cousins and friends for company, I celebrated my birthday at Cream Centre in Chowpatty. We had chhole bhature and ice cream. I could now apply for a driving licence. Life was moving into another gear.

11

An Accidental Homeopath

LIKE MOST EIGHTEEN-YEAR-OLDS OF MY TIME, I DIDN'T KNOW WHAT career to opt for. '*Dekh lenge* (We'll see),' I'd think. It was not an unreasonable approach. For a teenager, it was acceptable to go through early college years without a final destination in mind. After college came the time to make a decision.

I was fascinated by the glamour of the hospitality industry. To get a first-hand experience, I was sent to meet a family friend, Ravi Ghai, who owned the Natraj Hotel, now The Intercontinental, on Marine Drive. The Ghais were also the proprietors of Kwality ice cream and restaurants.

Ravi was a young man himself, a second-generation owner. He had recently returned to India after graduating in hotel administration from Cornell University. He enjoyed golf, horses and cigars. Ravi cut a sharp figure and generously gave me his time and advice.

After we shook hands in the foyer, Ravi took me to the kitchen and the housekeeping departments and showed me the grubby, behind-the-scenes picture of the business. Huge mounds of vegetables and several pink-white slabs of frozen meats were being washed, cut or thawed by the kitchen staff. Behind a wall, dozens of dishes were being washed. This was restaurant standard washing with no margin for error. The crockery had to be spotless. The dishes and cutlery were among the first things a customer saw, even a small stain would be enough to cause a public relations disaster.

Next, we rode up the elevator to see the rooms being cleaned and beds being made. Once again, there was no scope for even a slight mistake. The sheets had to be clean and smell fresh. The floor had to shine. Ravi turned to me and said the words that drove home the message. 'You will be married to your hotel.'

I had seen my parents working as doctors with very little family time. I didn't want that for myself. I thanked Ravi and walked out of Natraj into the sun-blasted street. The hotel industry was off my list. I realized that hotels were like icebergs. We only saw the tip and not the gigantic mass that lay beneath. In a different way, medicine was like that too. You think a doctor gives you only ten or twenty minutes during a consultation and charges a hefty fee. But behind those few minutes are years of study and knowledge.

Another career that appealed to me was the armed forces, but as a medical doctor. A senior friend from the Armed Forces Medical College in Pune waxed eloquent about the wonderful army life—a good salary, free rations, housing and a uniform to woo a pretty maiden. It sounded like a great deal.

I went to take an entrance exam at INS Ashwini, the naval hospital in Navy Nagar. I got through the theory papers and made it to the final interview before a panel of top military brass with curly moustaches, booming voices and starched uniforms. Medicine apart, I was asked out-of-the-box questions. 'How many steps did you climb to reach this room?' 'Did the water cistern down the corridor open to the left or the right?'

I don't know if it was because I was vertically challenged, had glasses or had simply blown the final interview, I didn't hear back from the forces.

The army's loss was homeopathy's gain.

Homeopathy came to India through an Austrian doctor, Dr Johann Martin Honigberger. A combination of circumstances placed Honigberger in Lahore and other parts of erstwhile Punjab in the mid-nineteenth century. Initially, he treated soldiers of the East India Company, and then Maharaja Ranjit Singhji for the paralysis of his vocal chords. It took almost 150 years after that for homeopathy to be officially recognized as a system of medicine in India, thanks to an act of Parliament in 1973.

By 1969, when I finished my graduation at Jai Hind, homeopathy was still finding its feet in the country. The homeopathic college in Mumbai had moved from Sion to a larger property in Vile Parle West and the trustees were looking for students from good families. Dr Edul Behram, one of the trustees, visited us at home and invited me to join the college. To be asked to join a college seemed special. Since my father was a homeopath, I also thought it would be an easy option.

The flip side was that my dad was the principal of the college and I would now be under his strict watch at home and at college. The two years of freedom that I had enjoyed at Jai Hind would soon be lost. But it had to be done. By this time, we had moved from Grant Road to one of the lowest floors in one of the tallest buildings in India, Land's End in Malabar Hill. It had twenty-eight floors and our home was on the first floor, closer to land than sky.

Land's End was almost the last building on the winding, tree-lined Dongersey Road. Near the building was a large bungalow called Cosy Corner. It belonged to the wealthy Cama family, which owned the largest-circulating Gujarati newspaper, *Bombay Samachar*. Their famous collection of vintage cars had started growing by then and you could catch a glimpse of a Ford, Mercedes or Cadillac in their yard.

Behind our building was the Saint Elizabeth Nursing Home where, much later, both my sons were born. The area also had the odd rough edge. Near our home was a dark alley where almost every day drunks would get into brawls.

From Malabar Hill to college in Vile Parle was a long trip in terms of distance as well as culture. I'd take a bus to Grant Road station, then a train to Andheri and again a bus to Vile Parle. It was a two-hour commute one way. Public transport was crowded, even in the 1970s. An empty seat was rare and coveted. It was easier to get a seat on the way back from college. Sitting by the window and having the breeze blow into your face as the train picked up speed, often lulled you to sleep. One day, I found myself being woken up rudely by a train attendant. I had overslept and reached the yard, where trains were serviced. It was a long walk to the nearest bus stop.

Another day, when I was in a hurry to get to college, I crossed the railway tracks at Mumbai Central station. The railway police caught me and I was taken to a magistrate's court nearby. With me in the court were petty thieves, sex workers and the sort. Standing in line for my turn, I imagined the typical courtroom scene from a Hindi movie, '*Champabai*, *Chhotubevda*, *Mukesh Batra hazir hon*!' I was let off with a warning and a fine of Rs 100.

Not only had I missed my class but I was out of money too. Home was 4 km away and I had no choice but to take the No. 11 bus, i.e., walk back.

12

A Rebel with Many Causes

The homeopathic college at Irla, Vile Parle, though operational, was still under construction. The roofs of some classrooms leaked in the monsoons, causing us to huddle together in the dry corners. And the college canteen had a thatched top, Goa shack style.

We called it 'Sun and Sand', after the famous hotel round the corner in Juhu. The canteen had sunlight pouring in from the top and sand on the tables. But it was a unifier as it provided food and shelter to students from all kinds of backgrounds. While our college had some students from higher-income homes, most were from poor families in smaller cities. The parents of some of them had mortgaged land and jewellery so that their children could become doctors.

While the infrastructure was poor, we had some good teachers and opportunities for hands-on learning. The college had its own outpatient department (OPD). Besides, we were attached to Cooper Hospital next door for clinical work.

The programme was a licentiate course of four and a half years. The first term was eighteen months long and mainly covered anatomy and physiology, together with some homeopathic subjects. The most difficult subject of the year was anatomy. It entailed studying the bones on skeletons and dissecting cadavers. Cadavers were dead human bodies placed in tanks of formalin. Just being around formalin stung your eyes more than chopping a thousand onions.

During practicals, the body was taken out of the tank. Through squinting, watery eyes, we observed parts being cut with a surgical knife for the study of muscles and ligaments. Not something the weak of heart could stomach. It was common to skip lunch on such days. Some students also threw up.

In college politics, however, courage never failed me. In my first year, I fought elections as the cultural secretary. While student elections were not as frenzied as they were at Delhi's Jawaharlal Nehru University (JNU), they were still fiercely fought. As a fresher, you had to take on your seniors and that could be challenging. There were veiled threats from them to step down. One day there was a knife stuck into the tyre of my father's car, a black Italian Fiat. I withheld the pressure and won comfortably. This taught me to hold my own in life.

Later on I became general secretary. I pushed for homeopathy colleges to be allowed to participate in inter-medical college sports and drama competitions. I was good at table tennis and theatre and did well in those events. Many of the matches took place at Grant Medical College, which had a great campus. The atmosphere was like in Karan Johar's teeny-bopper films. Students from all participating colleges would turn up and cheer the players. For us homeopaths, these victories were sweet, because the MBBS students always had an attitude towards us.

I was up to a lot in college, including sharing meals with a girlfriend, while my own lunch from home stayed untouched. My bespectacled father kept an eye and ear on everything even while in his office, which had swinging half doors, the kind you saw in Western movies, from which the hero emerges with a gun in either hand. No such gimmicks for my father. He did not speak a word about my activities at home. He never told me what to do. He let his son make his own luck, good or bad.

Studying in a college where your father is the principal is tricky. It is trickier when you are also active in student politics. One year, the college doubled the fees, causing outrage among the students, especially the underprivileged ones. As their elected representative, I had to lead their protests against the establishment, pitting me and my father in an Amitabh Bachchan vs Dilip Kumar type of clash in the 1982 Hindi blockbuster *Shakti*. Ours was never as dramatic or loud, of course. It wasn't even vocalized. But it wasn't always easy living through it.

At first, the student body tried to reason with the management. A bit of a fee hike was okay, but a 100 per cent increase was brutal. When the management did not relent, we went on strike. Hartal in 1960s' and 1970s' India had a rebellious sex appeal, and now we were those charismatic rebels. Irla Naka became our pulpit, our JNU. The Che Guevaras of the campus, including me, stood here and delivered speeches about rights and injustice. Our nourishment was suitably worker-like, multiple cups of 'paani kam' chai from an Irani café in the neighbourhood.

To gain momentum, we decided to stage a self-immolation. One of our classmates was a gullible girl called Manju, who came forward as a volunteer though she had no idea what immolation meant, such was the thrall of our leadership. We planned it all and assured Manju that there would be no actual fire. She only had to threaten to burn herself on the terrace of the college. Meanwhile, we notified the police and fire brigade.

At the appointed hour, Manju went up to the terrace and did her bit. She screamed, holding up a jerry can of fuel and matchsticks. After a while, the police saw through it. Manju was marched to the police station and released on bail.

We were in no mood to end our agitation. Personally, it was a reversal of temperament for me. I had been compliant during my childhood years. Now, I was going anti-establishment.

We took our fight to Azad Maidan led by a senior student whose name was George Fernandes, not the politician but a namesake. Our George was a member of the Forward Bloc from Kolkata and a hot-blooded leftist. These were the people who had the fever to change the world.

I was not protesting for myself. My father could easily afford my fees. We lived in Malabar Hill for God's sake and I'm sure many students felt I was a bit of a limousine radical. But I was driven by justice and believed my classmates were being exploited.

While demonstrating at Azad Maidan, we found a lawyer called D'Mello. He was an unknown factor, but for a few hundred rupees he agreed to make recommendations that would take our issue to the next level. D'Mello said he would get us a stay order from the court. From Azad Maidan, our group of about a hundred students moved to the court across to file a petition. Imagine a frenzied mob of a hundred students, demanding justice. The judge warned us that we would be held in contempt of court and threw us out. I remember him shouting, 'Order, order, all you students get out! You can't come to my court like this; it is not a fish market. Get out!'

Finally the case was heard. As one of the leaders of the morcha, the petition had been in my name. My opposite number was V.N. Desai, a senior college trustee. I remember the lawyer reading: 'V.N. Desai, eighty-two years, vs Mukesh Batra, nineteen years'. It was absurd. V.N. Desai had been the mayor of Mumbai from 1960 to 1961 and I, a mere teenager, had dragged him out of his peaceful retired years to court. But we didn't have money to continue with the case beyond a point. So we withdrew. Not before the case had created news all over, though.

Finally, we took a morcha to Sachivalaya to meet Health Minister Rafique Zakaria. We were stopped at the gate by cops, who said only three people could go in. Two others and I were allowed inside.

Zakaria was a scholar in Urdu literature. His wife Fatema was the editor of *Femina*. He tried to pacify us with tea and sweet talk. The tehzeeb took me back to Agra, but I was also aware we were not being given any assurances. So we told him we would not leave his chambers unless he gave us a commitment. Once again, look at the nerve. Zakaria then wrote a note on a piece of government paper that I remember to this day: 'This boy has no interest in academic pursuits.'

As luck would have it, many years later I was called upon to treat his wife. When she got better, I reminded him, 'Sir, I am the same kid about whom you wrote this and this is who I am today.'

13

A Soulmate Lost

ONE OF MY JOBS AS CULTURAL SECRETARY IN COLLEGE WAS TO organize the annual day function. Since the film actor Dharmendra lived near our college, we sought an appointment and went over to invite him to be our chief guest. Those days stars did not have as many minders around them and were quite accessible. Still, this was my first brush with Bollywood, after a good ten years or so of living in Mumbai. In Agra I was made to believe that actors roamed around the streets eating bhelpuri.

Garam Dharam lived in a bungalow in Juhu. We were led into his well-furnished drawing room. Sitting in the corner on a sofa was the man himself. He had a presence and was polite. He offered us tea, but refused our invitation due to shooting schedules.

Decades later, I met Dharmendra on a flight to Jaipur. I was sixty-five and he was over eighty. He didn't remember me as a student, but said that his daughter-in-law spoke well of me as a doctor, one who took care of his grandchildren.

Amidst planning the annual day, inter-college competitions and fighting for reduced fees, there was the realization that medical exams were eighteen long months away. My father was keen that I use that time to graduate in another subject. So I went to the USA—the United Sindhi Association in Ulhasnagar. There I enrolled as an arts student at the Talreja College in Camp No. 5. Talreja was affiliated to Poona University. So I was studying medicine at Mumbai and arts at Poona University. As they say, only in India. And I might add, only in Ulhasnagar.

I chose economics and clinical psychology as my subjects at Stanford, I mean Talreja. I knew psychology would help me in understanding my patients. But economics was a different ball game. It was difficult to self-learn diminishing returns and marginal utility from books. Sociology and cultural anthropology were easier.

Studying on my own meant social distancing. I hired a room in a hostel in Ulhasnagar for a month and locked myself in to study. It was hot, about 40 degrees Celsius, and I tried to keep myself cool in a lungi and by taking five showers a day, and also by downing multiple glasses of thandaai from a handcart that sold the stuff downstairs.

When I came back to Mumbai, I said goodbye to my father's four-bedroom Malabar Hill home and moved into a single room at the Kelavani Mandal Hostel, shared with two others. The room consisted of three single beds, covered with thin bed sheets, and two cupboards. The elaborate meals of home, eaten while breathing the same air as the Camas of *Bombay Samachar*, were replaced by cafeteria fare—rice and sweet yellow dal, called 'moda dal', with ghee. It was the same thing almost every day. The best thing in the canteen was fruit salad, which was all water and sugar with two blackening pieces of banana and an apology of a piece of apple. The fruit floated on a pale yellow surface like dead leaves. And yet we would look forward to it.

I was nineteen and living a full, often exhausting life. The scope of study was vast, demanding that we tackle tomes that at times ran beyond a thousand pages. The little spare time I had, I would walk around with my classmate and girlfriend, Nalini. I went home once a week or sometimes once in two weeks.

Even when I went to Malabar Hill I would use some of that time for Rotaract activities. Rotaract was the youth wing of the Rotary Club. I was busy as it was, but from an early age I wanted to do things that involved leadership and contributing to society. The Rotaract meetings would often be held at my parents' home in Malabar Hill. My experience in student activities made me a natural fit at the club and soon I ended up becoming secretary. The next year I became the president and later, the district representative.

Rotaract taught me leadership skills that helped me throughout my career. I made some great friends there. Two people I remember very well are Vani Ganapathy, who was married to Kamal Haasan for some years, and her sister Meera. When our group of friends went on picnics or organized functions, Vani and Meera would perform Bharatanatyam. It wasn't the *Summer of '69* but certainly those were the best days of my life. I still stay in touch with them.

Another lovely soul I met through Rotaract was a dusky girl with beautiful eyes named Nalini, my girlfriend's namesake. She lived on Napean Sea Road. Her surname was Mathur and it was after a few days of knowing her that I realized she was the daughter of Mukesh, the famous singer. Despite her privileged background, she had a kindness about her. She liked my simplicity and we hit it off instantly. It was a pure, warm, platonic friendship. I remember on my nineteenth birthday she gifted me an expensive cologne. It was typical Nalini—generous to a fault.

At the Rotaract Club we had once tried to invite Mukesh for a fundraiser concert. Initially we did not involve Nalini. But when we were rebuffed by someone in his circle, Nalini relayed our request directly to Mukesh. He was extremely fond of Nalini and rarely said no to her. 'It's your friend's function. How can I not go?' he said to her.

The show was at Jai Hind, my alma mater. Mukesh arrived in his car and put us at ease with his decidedly non-starry behaviour. I remember him pulling out his harmonium from the trunk himself, even though we offered to carry it for him. He sang for an hour and did not charge us a rupee. I was touched by his gesture and grateful to Nalini for it.

Mukesh was just around fifty at that time. He seemed set for many more years of fame and fortune. We had absolutely no idea then that this dapper, gracious man, who sang '*Sar pe laal topi Russi, phir bhi dil hai Hindustani*', would meet his own end overseas, and very soon. Mukesh died of a heart attack in Detroit, USA, where he had gone for a concert. He was just fifty-three. Nalini was shattered.

Two years after Mukesh's death, Nalini, not yet fully free of grief, was visiting Delhi. One day, she was out on a morning walk. At age twenty-five, she wanted to get into shape and get married. Behind her, misfortune was lurking. A novice driver lost control of his car and knocked her down. The vehicle continued to move, dragging Nalini along the road. And just like that, Nalini Mathur, the sweetest soul you could meet, was dead too. I got the news on phone. I broke down, trying to console myself that at least she was reunited with her father.

14

How I Was Drawn to Homeopathy

Like the phone, the mirror is a messenger that brings you good news or bad news. One morning as I splashed water on my face and looked at my reflection, I noticed something different. A couple of warts had sprouted on my face. It was a viral infection, I was told, and was asked to the take thuja, a common homeopathy medicine for unwelcome visitors such as warts. I was happy to try anything. It was close to college annual day. As general secretary, I had to give a speech. And I wanted to look good while at it.

But when I took the thuja and went to sleep, I woke up after a while with a start, feeling as though I was falling off the bed. This is a known effect of thuja, and it showed how sensitive I was to it. In medical jargon, I was 'proving' the drug. This is why I feel that homeopathic medicines should only be taken under medical supervision and not as casually as people take them. I experienced thuja working on me, even though adversely.

In a few days, the number of warts on my face increased. My hopes to recover before annual day crashed. When I met my father at college in his office, the one with the swinging doors, he said, 'Why don't you take dulcamara?'

I did as advised. The next morning, when I washed my face, more than twenty warts just came off my skin into the towel. Such a clean operation. Not one scar. One growth around my neck remained and I used to joke that it was my swear wart. I could swear anything by pinching it and it never came off. But after another dose of dulcamara, even that wart went away. That was some fifty years ago and I haven't had a wart on my face since.

Impressed by the first-hand experience of the efficacy of the medicines, I devoured material on homeopathy. My knowledge grew, and with it my reputation. I started teaching other students, including seniors. We also had practical class. Over time, I understood that theory was very different from practice. Theory is the fundamentals of medicine. But true knowledge comes from being by the bedside of patients. It comes from clinical learning.

Importantly, surgery and gynaecology were a part of our curriculum. 'Always at your cervix' was the credo of the folk who brought life into the world. Theory classes would be held during the day, and unlike junior college, you could not miss them. Each class was crucial. Theory was followed by practical class at Cooper Hospital in the evenings. And one of our tasks was to be present during twenty to twenty-five childbirths over a year. Without that we were not eligible to take exams.

After the tiring theory classes in the morning, the evenings and nights were spent at Cooper waiting for babies to pop out. Meeting the target of twenty to twenty-five deliveries may not sound like much in a country known for its population. But it was very difficult. There were only so many hours we could be at the hospital before we staggered back across the road, like zombies in a Ramsay Brothers film, to our hostel. If we were lucky we could catch a couple of hours of sleep. But many times we went straight to college for the lectures. There were quite a few times we went twenty-four hours without sleep.

The second difficulty was that there was no guarantee the baby would emerge in our presence. I have spent entire nights by pregnant women, holding their hand, only for them to deliver after I left.

Occasionally, luck and a toothless pink bundle would smile at me. I was entering the hospital one day when a taxi rushed in bearing a pregnant woman. She had already dilated and there was no time for her to go to a room. I delivered the baby in the taxi. I couldn't stop beaming. I had bought fruit salad for the entire college that day.

Assisting in childbirth also led to one scary experience. Again, it taught me a lot. We were allowed to give a woman an episiotomy—a surgical incision of the perineum and the posterior vaginal wall. This was generally done by a midwife or an obstetrician to quickly enlarge the opening for the baby to pass through. Not everyone put their hand up for the task. But I was confident and gave it a try. Episiotomy involves not just the first cut but also snipping the umbilical cord, then stitching up the wounded part, and then removing the stitches a few days later. It is simple, but it was my first semi-surgical procedure. To my horror, I made a mistake somewhere and the lady got infected.

Luckily, things did not turn out too badly. The woman healed. Nonetheless, my teacher, Dr Bhide, a gynaecologist herself, asked me if I had met the lady and apologized. I said I hadn't. 'You must do it,' she said.

I did as told. The woman was still in the hospital. I said sorry to her and made sure she was comfortable. I walked out of her room clear about a couple of things. One, don't make a mistake. If you do, go back and face it, own it. That has stayed with me all my medical life.

15

My Early Years as a Doctor

In 1974, I was twenty-two and about to embark on my career. On some mornings, I would stand in the balcony at home, admiring the winding paths and green cover of Dongersey Street. Records of the Bombay Natural History Society suggest that the area was once a forest, with tigers. When thirsty, the big cats would prowl to Gowalia Tank for water. (No one was delivering Coca-Cola in Malabar Hill then.) As nice as the view was, I wasn't a *National Geographic* photographer or writer. I was a homeopath, among the youngest to graduate as one, having done very well in my examination in December 1973.

My marriage to Nalini, my girlfriend at the homeopathic college, was also coming up. To my father's disappointment, I had turned down an attractive job offer from my college to become a lecturer there at a salary of Rs 2000 per month. 'You are making a mistake,' he told me in his gentle voice, his lips barely moving under his Raj Kapoor–type moustache. But I was clear I wanted to be a clinician, not an academician.

By the look of it we were an upper-middle-class family, with a four-bedroom apartment in one of the city's prime areas. But my two brothers also lived there. Eventually our wives would come into the picture too. It was clear that we had to quickly start taking care of ourselves.

Even if we'd had a palace with enough space for everyone, I was determined to not piggyback on my father's set-up or his reputation. In medicine, or any other field, it is difficult to inherit your father's legacy. Also, there is the danger of being in your father's shadow and always being perceived as not being as good. It's a battle you can't win, like with mother's cooking—revered, even though it may not always have been great.

It is true I was in the same field as my father, and that some comparison couldn't be avoided. But it would be less if I struck out on my own. Soon enough, I learnt of an exciting opportunity for my internship, which was mandatory. It was almost next door, at a reputed charitable homeopathy clinic in Malabar Hill called Shaligram. The building that had the clinic was owned by the father of a close friend of mine, S.D. Parkash. Surely, it would be a shoo-in for me. All I had to do was get an approval from the old man. I went to see my buddy's dad, thinking it was a mere formality.

I was in for a shock. 'Nobody wants a fresher in medicine,' he said. 'I can't give you the internship.'

This was unexpected and crushing. How could an intern not be a fresher? I pleaded my case. 'I don't want any money, sir. Let me just sit and observe.'

'I don't want money' is a clincher in Malabar Hill, the home of crorepatis. And I got in. In fact, I even got some honorarium, Rs 150 a month.

My job was to be an assistant to the doctor at Shaligram, Dr Subhash Shah, a respected classical homeopath. Classical homeopathy was the way of Hahnemann, the founder of homeopathy. Today, people mix four medicines and give you a cocktail. In classical homeopathy, you give one medicine based on a deep understanding of the person. For a young homeopath like me, there couldn't have been a better internship than under Dr Shah. Life is an opportunity that comes your way and your future depends on what you accept or refuse.

The timings were from 9 a.m. to 2 p.m. Afterwards I would head back home, to the one bit of my father's infrastructure that I used—his home clinic. He had two dispensaries, the other being in Tardeo. He allowed me to use the space at home on the days he was in Tardeo.

I was unknown and hardly anyone came to see me. Those days you needed grey hair to give white pills. Occasionally the building watchman would come for some treatment. There were times when I would take a nap as there was nothing else to do.

Our house cleaner was quite intelligent, and my mother suggested I train him and make him my dispenser for a salary of Rs 100 a month. It was a sound idea. And now I, who was an assistant to someone, had an assistant of my own. His salary of Rs 100 was paid from the Rs 150 I got at Shaligram. It is true that most days his job was just to hear me say, '*Agar koi patient aayega, toh mujhe utha dena* (Wake me up if a patient comes).' But I believed in myself and I knew that at some stage recognition would come my way. I pursued my charitable work with great dedication and no monetary expectation. When you are starting off in a profession, look for experience, not money. If you do a job well you don't need to chase money, money chases you.

16

Actor Calling Doctor

I reckon some of you who are reading this book are young people. You want to make something of your lives. Let me tell you one thing. If you are asked to write something, or speak somewhere, do it.

You may wonder about the point of it. So many people are writing and speaking, what's your two pennies' worth going to achieve? You imagine it will sink into the vast sea of content, and lie ignored on the ocean floor, next to the wreckage of the *Titanic*. But words once spoken or penned are always alive. And there may be some influential person who likes what you said, salvages it from the bottom of the sea and gives your career a shot in the arm.

In 1974, when I had just gotten married and started my practice, I became friends with Sangeeta, the daughter of Madan Mohan, the music director of classics like '*Lag ja gale*' and '*Ruke ruke se kadam*'. Sangeeta worked for *Eve's Weekly*, the women's magazine.

Sangeeta's mother was a patient of my father's, while I treated Sangeeta. Happy with the results, she once said to me, 'Doc, you have taken good care of me. I'm going to ask my editor if you can write an article on homeopathy for *Eve's Weekly*.'

Why not? I thought, and started sharpening my turn of phrase, last used during college plays.

The magazine's editor, however, was not so keen on a piece on homeopathy. Sangeeta then referred me to another publication in the same stable. It was called *Mirror*. I would describe it as a young person's *Reader's Digest*. It was a monthly edited by a man called Rajan Narayan. The *Eve's Weekly* editor was a fashionable and beautiful woman. Rajan was the quintessential jholawala journalist, but there was no doubting his intelligence. And he knew what he wanted. Despite his forbidding appearance, he did not reject the idea of a piece on homeopathy outright. He asked me to give it a shot.

When I took the first draft to him after a few days, Rajan went through it and, with a basketball pro's skill, tossed it into the waste-paper basket. Thereon, multiple drafts received the same welcome. I was disappointed, but also entertained. One day I almost suggested to Rajan that he should be playing with NBA stars instead of being at the *Mirror*. Jokes aside, I did not let his rejections break me. After all, even best-selling author J.K. Rowling was rejected twelve times! That's a lesson for young folk. Don't give up so easily. Keep trying. I kept coming back with a smile and a new draft. Eventually, he took a liking to me and also the article. It was published under the headline 'A Homeopath Is Not a Quack'.

Some days after the piece appeared, I was at home when the phone rang.

In a deep growl, the caller asked, 'Am I speaking to Dr Mukesh Batra?'

When I replied in the affirmative, he asked, 'Am I speaking to the author of "A Homeopath Is Not a Quack"?' I said, 'Yes'.

'This is Manoj Kumar speaking,' the caller said. I put the phone down. Manoj Kumar, the film star whose *Roti Kapda aur Makaan* was 1974's biggest hit? Whose stature was as big as Dilip Kumar's? This had to be a prank. And I, the smart Dr Batra, had refused to fall for it.

After a few minutes the phone rang again. He must have known what was happening and this time he pre-empted me by saying it was truly him, '*Bhai mai sach mey Manoj Kumar bol raha hu.* I want to consult you.'

This time I believed him, and gave him my address. Once I put the phone down, however, I was in a tizzy. The article did not have my picture, just my name. Manoj Kumar probably thought I was a senior doctor when the reality was that I was a rookie, twenty-two years old, with barely any patients. And now this towering film star was on his way to my house-cum-clinic. At least I had the dispenser with me, so my surroundings looked a bit professional.

I had a certain image of him and vice versa, and the first few moments after Manoj Kumar entered our apartment at Land's End were spent aligning the perception with the reality. Once the ice was broken though, we realized both of us had a passion for homeopathy. In fact, Manoj Kumar, Ashok Kumar and Salim Khan were practitioners of homeopathy in Bollywood that time. They also used to dispense medicines.

Manoj Kumar and I hit it off. He began to treat me like a younger brother. In the following years, I spent many hours at his home in Juhu talking medicine, movies and eating vegetarian food sitting on the floor. He never sat at a table, even though his home was well furnished. And the other thing he rarely did was fly. He had a phobia of flights. So if he had to go to Delhi, he would book a first-class ticket on the Rajdhani.

My proximity to Manoj Kumar brought more film folk to my door for treatment. The man known for his signature move of partially covering his face with his palm put me in the spotlight and on the radar in Bollywood, a choosy club that does not easily allow outsiders past its gilded gates.

17

A Covid-style Wedding

I LOVED THE FLOWERS IN NALINI'S HAIR. AND HER FATHER HATED the meat on my plate.

Nalini and I had been dating since college. I loved her, she loved me. We could spend hours walking or discussing songs by Mukesh or her favourite, Hemant da. Long drives were possible because petrol was just Rs 1 per litre and with my pocket money of Rs 10 a week I had plenty of fuel to burn. Our parents knew we were seeing each other. This was all very good. But the fact remained that our backgrounds were very different. She came from a conservative, vegetarian Gujarati family, led by her father Dr Jadhavji Thakkar. He was a cardiologist, radiologist and a pathologist. On the other hand, I came from a meat-eating Punjabi home.

Besides, Dr Thakkar had two older eligible daughters to think about. And he did not want chatter about me and Nalini to dent the family's reputation. So one day, the message that every boy dreads came my way. Nalini's father wanted to 'have a word' with me.

Nalini came to pick me up that day. As we went up the stairs of their building in the Bandra Talao area, she seemed relaxed. I was nervous. When we reached the door, I took a moment to catch my breath. We rang the bell and went inside. Dr Thakkar emerged. Tall by Indian standards, he wore black-framed glasses over a prominent nose. His clothes were white, and white is all he wore.

Dr Thakkar had only two passions, both diametrically opposite to each other. They were medicine and religion. His attire—pure and fuss-free—reflected that. He was no-nonsense, the way patriarchs used to be. Life had also dealt him some inevitable blows, contributing to his taciturn personality. His sister had died a violent death in 1944 in a bomb explosion at Mumbai's Victoria Docks.

Dr Thakkar was courteous to me, yet firm. 'If you are serious about my daughter, you must marry her right away.' He was also squeamish about me being a non-vegetarian. He did not say this to me but had expressed it to Nalini. She made him come around. 'At least he does not drink or womanize,' she told him. To which he apparently said, 'Either he is lying to you or you are lying to me'; so much for confidence in the male species. But there were no lies here. I was loyal to Nalini and I did not drink.

Nalini's father came around to marrying his youngest daughter before his older ones. He was fond of Nalini and wanted her to be happy. Beneath the stern exterior he liked me as well. But he was clear about one thing. This was an unconventional marriage for that era, so he wanted to be subtle about it. The wedding would therefore be low-key, with scope for just about twenty-five guests.

As far as my parents' reaction to Nalini was concerned, it was a mixed bag. I had taken her home in the past and my mother loved her like her own daughter. My father was reasonably fond of her. But he was chauvinistic in his thinking and had some of the boy's father–type '*hum toh ladkewale hain*' attitude in matters of the wedding expenses and gifts. He didn't say anything but that was the mindset then and I could feel it. But I was certain I did not want dowry. All permissions taken, it was time for JMPB—*jhat mangani pat byah*—and the engagement and wedding happened on the same day, 1 May 1974, with only about twenty-five immediate family members in attendance. Life goes in circles. Many years later, small weddings have become the norm during Covid.

The first ceremony was at the Arya Samaj temple in Santacruz West. It was a hot day and my kurta was soaked with sweat within minutes. We egged the pandit on to hurry up with the mantras. No such luck. He turned out to be a stickler. From Arya Samaj, the wedding jingbang headed to the Swami Chinmayananda temple in Powai. Swamiji made a short appearance and blessed us. I don't exactly remember why we got married at two places. Perhaps it was to make sure we remembered our vows.

Lunch was served in the marble ramparts of the temple. It was simple, langar-style fare. The one indulgence was rasgullas. Almost every person from Nalini's family lined up to feed me a rasgulla, while I sat with my head back and mouth open as if in a dentist's chair. I love Indian sweets but after a point I wanted no more. Like with many people on their wedding day, I was in a mixed zone of happiness, anxiety about the future and an undertow of grief over losing my independence. It's not like I wanted to be a playboy, but at age twenty-two, there is some natural doubt about getting tied down.

The reception was held the following evening at the Natraj Hotel, the same place where I had gone to meet Ravi Ghai when I was contemplating a career in hospitality. This time the guest list was larger, comprising nearly 500 people. It was also more raucous. Almost my entire college batch was there. Having been the general secretary, and being the first to get hitched, I had to invite the rascals. They gorged on the dinner and expectedly made nudge-nudge-wink-wink remarks to me about my wedding night, which was also to be spent at the hotel.

After the reception, Nalini and I entered the suite. Relief washed over us. I loosened my tie and took off my suit jacket while Nalini freed herself of the various bits and bobs that hold a bride's hair together. For a few minutes we just sat and absorbed the view of the sea and the inky sky. Hotel rooms free you from the realities of life. This was our momentous night, and we decided to set aside our worries and savour the moment. As we lay on the bed, I felt something under my back. It was a pack of condoms, left for us by well-meaning relatives. Both of us looked at the box, at each other and burst out laughing.

18

Charity Goes a Long Way

When it was time to get married to Nalini, my father-in-law offered her a choice of a diamond necklace or a clinic. It was a no-brainer. Nalini chose the clinic. The place was located in a slum in Wadala. Nalini opened the shutters and started practice. She was a homeopathic doctor but she virtually functioned like a general practioner (GP).

Nalini displayed Olympian levels of energy and time management. From Malabar Hill, she would take a bus or train to get to Wadala. A taxi or my father's Italian Fiat was only for emergencies. She would be at the clinic from 9 a.m. to 1 p.m., seeing patients of all ages. From there, it was back home for lunch and some domestic work. At 5 p.m., she would again be at the clinic until it closed at 9 p.m. or 10 p.m.

The only reason she could safely work in the area was because her brother-in-law's clinic was right next door. He was a respected doctor, and with him around nobody dared to harm Nalini. In fact, both Nalini's family and mine had lots of doctors. There were four doctors on my side and all my in-laws were doctors. Nalini's sisters were also married to doctors. So you can imagine what our get-togethers were like—every family dinner was a medical conference.

Nalini's reputation grew. Soon the clinic was earning her nearly Rs 2000 a month. For many years, she was the one who kept our home running. Food and shelter were taken care of anyway, since we were living in my father's house. This allowed me time to find my own feet. Though I was making very little money of my own, I spared no effort to gain experience. I took any job that came my way, irrespective of the compensation or location. In addition to assisting Dr Shah at Shaligram and seeing the odd patient at home, I took on charitable assignments. At least no one minded my lack of experience there, and I could get some 'match practice' under my belt, to use a sports expression.

One of my stints was in the polar opposite of Malabar Hill—Dharavi, one of the biggest slums on the continent. If Mumbai had an endoscopy, it would mainly consist of visuals of Dharavi. My commute, no less Olympian than Nalini's, took me through three bus changes. The last bus would drop me only up to a certain point in Dharavi. From there to my clinic, through the innards of the neighbourhood, was an obstacle race through muck, sewers, roosters, pigs and humans. You either walked or took a rickshaw, which too was an indulgence. And indulgence was something I rarely allowed myself, not even when I became successful. I got by on a few shirts, a couple of trousers and basic footwear whose use I extracted every bit of.

Dharavi was a challenge even for someone like me, who had none of the South Mumbai snobbery and liked to help people, especially the poor. In the end it was satisfying because it was true service.

In the 1970s, Dharavi wasn't a slum with secretly wealthy people having televisions, air conditioners and mattresses stuffed with cash. Yes, it was a crime den, and there must have been black money circulating, but the leather boom had yet to happen. People were genuinely poor. They were grateful to see a doctor who was polite, who reassured them and gave them medicine. Many of them were happy at the very sight of a doctor. It gave them some hope in their eternal fight against the odds.

My other charity work was at the bullion market in Kalbadevi. A family friend who worked there once said to me that they had an Ayurvedic clinic up and running there and I should start my homeopathic work alongside. His logic seemed to be, '*Chai ki dukaan hai, samosa bhi chalu karo* (We already have a tea shop, let's start samosas too).'

Bring it on, I said. And soon I had a little practice in a rickety-old building in Kalbadevi. I had a wooden table and chair and a cupboard of medicines at my disposal. My fees were Rs 100 per hour. If I went there about once a week, I made an extra Rs 300 or 400 a month, which went a long way in the 1970s.

Back home at night, the contrasts of our life would hit me. From being in tin-roofed rat-infested slums through the day, we came home to sleep in a comfortable bed in Land's End. How long could this go on? The house at Land's End was my father's, not mine. What was my place in the universe? The answer that I got, as always, was that my place in the universe would have to be made by me.

19

Always Start with Something Simple

Beneath the black pendulum clock, seated on the wooden bench in my dispensary, I began to regularly see a famous face or two, patiently awaiting their turn. At times, actors would make surreptitious visits in the dead of the night, dressed in burqas and what not. In this phase of professional growth, a family drama was unfolding on the personal front.

There had been undercurrents of tension between my father and me at Land's End, and now they were bubbling to the surface, though never in a quarrelsome way. It was clear my father was no longer happy to have me and Nalini staying there. He was getting on in years and craved his space. He also felt resentful about my growing list of patients.

I could understand that he felt cramped. The arrival of a new person in the house, in this case Nalini, changes the whole dynamic of the space, however nice that person may be and however large the space may be. But I could not wrap my head around my father feeling envious of my success. Especially when he was still doing well, and was loved by his patients. He was gentle with them. He would hold their hand and comfort them. He was among the very few doctors who offered this winning combination of knowledge and caring.

Perhaps there was a financial reason for his irritability, I initially thought. I told him, 'Don't worry, I will pay for all the assistants and the medicines we use.' But that wasn't enough.

One day he came to the point. 'Maybe it is best you move out,' he said in his usual quiet way.

In India we are brought up to believe that parents love their children unconditionally. We see our parents as embodying the all-sacrificing ideal. But while they may love us, they are individuals with their own needs and flaws. They cannot be taken for granted. The parental house too cannot be taken for granted. When these truths become apparent to us, our long-held image of our family members, of our relationship with them, is shattered. We deal with the shock. But we also grow. With time, we also realize that our parents do us a favour when they nudge us towards building our own roof.

I accepted my father's decision, and Nalini and I started looking for a home and a new place for my practice. We took stock of how much time we had at Land's End, how much money we had (or didn't) and made a tentative schedule.

Call it luck or the hand of a higher power, when you are in difficulty, you are often thrown a lifeline. My first breakthrough was getting a spot to pitch my homeopathy tent in Matru Ashish Building, Napean Sea Road. It was a polyclinic—a co-working space for doctors, owned by a paediatrician. Getting in was not easy. Homeopathy was still not taken seriously, and as usual I was deemed too young, even though I had started wearing zero-powered glasses to look older. It took the recommendation of Dr Merchant, an eminent paediatrician, for me to get a room at the polyclinic. As a young entrepreneur do not be shy to ask for help—it may give you a kick-start.

Napean Sea Road was home to the affluent and the influential. And some of them became my patients or brought their near and dear ones to me. Jennifer Kapoor lived just down the road in Atlas Apartments. At the time, Shashi Kapoor was producing the film *Junoon* (1978). The cast featured Mrs Kapoor and a young Nafisa Ali. But Nafisa had acne, and Mrs Kapoor brought her to me. They had to start shooting soon and I only had a week to treat her. The medicines worked and Nafisa was able to make her film debut.

Another person who lived in Atlas, in a house with a decorated ceiling and artificial pigeons, was the builder Appa Singh Makkar, better known as Maker. He also believed in homeopathy. Also, in those years, he was developing a swampy reclaimed patch of land called Cuffe Parade into a residential and office area. His vision for it was to get decent people from different backgrounds to live there. One day, he offered me a flat on a very sensible, pay-as-you-can terms. I could also practise there. Nalini and I thought it was a good idea. We cobbled together an amount to put down on the flat and eventually moved into Jolly Maker III (Jolly was Maker's partner).

We had done it. We had bought a home in the megacity with our own resources.

Cuffe Parade wasn't glamorous then. Many roads were unpaved. The water and electricity supply was inconsistent. In the evenings it would get dark and desolate. But it was our house. The freedom with which we could come and go, and sit and talk, was worth the growing pains of the area. In any case, we spent most of the waking hours working. After sharing a cup of coffee with Nalini to save costs, I would take a couple of buses to go to Shaligram at 9 a.m. and then to Matru Ashish. I would be there till 6 p.m. My patient list by then included staff of politicians and sometimes politicians themselves. This was because there were many ministerial residences around.

In the evening, I would practise a few more hours at Cuffe Parade at my residence. The set-up there was simple. A little passage inside the door served as a waiting area, beyond which was the drawing room a.k.a. the consultation room. One of my first patients, the architect Keshav Pansare, fixed a curtain-separator between the two areas, thereby ensuring privacy for whoever was within. I learned that some of the simplest solutions trigger the biggest changes. This simple idea showed me that not every solution needs heavy investment.

The drawing room too was an amalgamation of ideas, full of use-reuse innovations which, I am sure, interior designers would have charged big bucks for today. A Chippendale bar donated by a cousin served as a medicine dispensing cabinet, while a simple folding table made up the consulting table. Three chairs and a stool from Chor Bazaar made up the eclectic seating space and a divan served as an examination table. A simple wooden bench was the seating in the waiting area. Frugal innovation is what I have always believed in and I strongly recommend it to budding entrepreneurs.

Despite being such a make-do set-up, my practice thrived. The day ended with a late dinner. Afterwards, we would go to bed, without any nagging thoughts that I was being a burden on my father.

20

Cool AC, Warm Friendships

SLEEPING IN OUR NEW HOME BECAME MORE ENJOYABLE THANKS TO A midnight gift from a friend. One summer night, as Cuffe Parade snored around us, I was told there was a delivery for me. I was surprised. A delivery at this time? Yes, because the man who had sent it functioned like that. He marched to his own clock. And if anybody objected to it, he bellowed, '*Khamosh*!'

Standing at my door was Shatrughan Sinha, with a bunch of mechanics carrying an air conditioner (AC). My firstborn, Akshay, was a baby at the time. Shatru slapped my back and said, 'My friend, you work so hard and you never pamper yourself. But you are a father now and I want all of you to sleep in comfort.'

The workmen went inside and started fixing the AC, the high-pitched whine of their drill piercing the silence of the night. Shatru waited till everything was done and till the room was sufficiently cool. Nalini and I had consciously avoided becoming slaves to creature comforts. But when that first cool draught of air caressed our sweaty brow, it was indeed a blissful experience. We were filled with gratitude for Shatru, and realized that one must allow oneself some pleasure. Every other day, we would give the air-conditioned room the name of a summer holiday destination. Mahabaleshwar today, Switzerland tomorrow, Kashmir the next.

Shatru would drop by often, for medicines, snacks and chit-chat. He almost always came at night, having completed his last shooting shift. The pungent pani puri Nalini made was a favourite of his. We would keep it ready and I would catch a nap while I waited for him. When he arrived I would give him his medicines and the snack specially made for him. 'Spicy pani puri and sweet pills,' he would say and follow that up with a booming guffaw. We would talk into the early hours, and when day was about to break, he'd call it a night.

Lord Ram was a big influence on Shatru, though it was not always apparent in his lifestyle. He named his boys Luv and Kush, after the sons of Ram. His residence was named Ramayan, and his brother was called Lakhan, which is another name for Lakshman. Lakhan was the co-producer of *Prem Geet*, the 1981 Raj Babbar–Anita Raj starrer, which is still remembered for the ghazal '*Honthon se chhu lo tum*', sung by Jagjit Singh. Shatru invited me and my family for the shooting of the song in Shimla.

It was refreshing to leave Mumbai and land in the clean air and quietude of Shimla. We stayed at the original Wildflower Hall, an imposing structure with a wooden roof, large rooms with tall ceilings. We spent five enjoyable days there. During the day we watched the shoot and saw how labour-intensive film-making was. The director would say 'cut' every second minute. To shoot just a small part of the song took hours.

The rest of the time we walked around, absorbing nature that surrounded us in all its majesty. The hotel, due to its architecture and location, acquired a haunted dimension in the evenings. Ghost stories would be exchanged among the film crew. The swashbuckling Shatru was not present at the shoot. But we had no reason to fear any spirits. With one '*Abey chapatganju*!', on the phone he could knock all of them off.

I have often wondered why some B-town folk opened up so much to me. Sure, my treatments healed them, but they could have very well just maintained a professional relationship. Instead, many of us became friends. It could be because they trusted me. If they could freely share their health issues with me, surely they could discuss other matters. Also, like many in the film fraternity, I came from the north. We understood each other. Besides, I was fond of films and music and therefore we could chat on any subject, from medicine to movies.

Rakhee, Shatru's co-star in many of his films, including the 1979 hit *Kala Patthar*, was another film personality I became friends with. Not many know she was a good chess player. We would often play chess at my house. Rakhee was also a great cook, especially of non-vegetarian dishes. One day she got a huge, multi-tiered lunchbox for me from home. Each tin was filled with a delicacy she had made. I mixed it all up and ate it. That was my habit, perhaps because it saved time.

Rakhee was upset. She told me that such food had to be savoured. Each dish had to be sampled on its own. It was blasphemous to make a khichdi of everything on the plate. I held my ears and said 'mea culpa'. Never again would I not give each course its due attention.

It was thanks to Rakhee that I attended the first film premiere of my life, at Apsara Theatre. The movie was a multi-starrer and the police was having a hard time controlling the mobs, some of whom had climbed trees to get a glimpse of their idols. Nalini and I, however, needed no such stunts to be among the stars. As Rakhee's guests, we had some of the best seats in the house.

When Akshay was born, Rakhee gifted him a gold coin, which she had actually saved for her daughter Meghna's wedding. For her to part with something so special made my eyes well up. Eventually, we lost touch, but for a while she was a wonderful family friend.

21

They Came, They Saw, They Painted

My grandson Hriman and I enjoy silly humour. The Pee Wee Herman movies are among our favourites. Pee Wee has a mechanism in his house—an orange balloon that pulls him up through his roof every morning and he's on his way to work. I'd have loved to have such a fun mode of transport from my clinic in Chowpatty. But even if I had had the technology, I wouldn't have been able to create an opening in my ceiling—it has a Husain painting on it. The large black-and-white work depicts a graceful dancer and a little monkey—the latter being M.F. Husain's mischievous touch.

We knew each other a little as we both lived in Jolly Maker III. But in the two or three years he took my treatment, we became friends. Some of his chronic health issues were cured. So one day—it was 20 July—he came to my clinic and said in his deep voice, 'I want to do something special for you.'

I remember the date because it was my father's birthday. I also had a Rotary meeting to go to. But when a master shows up, you cancel everything else. In just about twenty minutes, with rapid strokes of a long brush, Husain painted my ceiling. 'There, now you can tell everyone you have Madhuri Dixit on your ceiling,' he said. As is well known, Madhuri was his muse.

Seeing him in action was mesmerizing, such was his speed, sureness of hand and the power and beauty of the finished work. It was like watching a time-lapse video of the making of a masterpiece.

Husain started out in Mumbai as a painter of cinema posters. Clearly, that gave him the ability to paint looking up. As he finished the painting, he mentioned that the best art was often on ceilings, such as Michelangelo's work in the Sistine Chapel. He believed the optimal way to appreciate art was from a flat, relaxed position. When my patients lay on the couch in my clinic, they had the best seat in the house to admire the Husain above them.

While there were colourful paintings by other artists hung on the walls of the clinic, Husain's black-and-white work contrasted beautifully against them. It taught me the importance of differential marketing, though he may not have intended to be different for the sake of it.

A lot of people use fashionable labels like rebel or wanderer for themselves. Few are truly so. Husain was a genuine free bird. He had painted his car in various colours. When he left home there was no telling when he'd come back. He'd carry his brushes and paints and his airline coupons in his jhola. At times he would take off on whatever flight was available. It could not have been easy for his family. But that's the way he was. Find me another celebrity who for years went everywhere barefoot.

When Husain came to my clinic, he patiently waited his turn. Yet he was restless. He never hung around in the waiting area, watching the minutes tick. He would sit on the floor near the main entrance, which looked out to Bharatiya Vidya Bhavan, observing the scene around him.

Whatever he did, he did it in an unconventional manner. When he turned seventy, he called a select few of us for a dinner of Bohri thaal. It wasn't at some big restaurant or venue but at the chawl where he first lived when he came to Mumbai. He had done up the place nicely, with soft white cloth wrapped all around, giving it the feel of a shamiana.

The two of us also shared a love for Indian mythology, since Husain was well read and grew up in Pandharpur, the town of Vithoba. One year, he couldn't make it for a free homeopathy treatment camp for about 2000 people at Wilson College that the Indian Express Group and I had organized. He had agreed to come but didn't. Though a bold artist, he was not comfortable among large crowds. Instead, he made a painting for me and sent it across. It portrayed me as a Hanuman type of figure carrying a mountain towards a family. 'Batra Sanjeevani Booti', he titled it. There was a short message at the bottom, 'Mukesh, you are doing great work to keep our people healthy.' It was a big tribute and I still have it in my office.

His fascination for Madhuri bordered on obsession. One evening at the clinic, he displayed a rare sense of hurry. 'I'm having dinner with Madhuri today,' he said. If I remember right, he saw her 1994 blockbuster *Hum Aapke Hain Kaun* only ninety times!

'You haven't seen the movie if you haven't seen it with me,' he said to me. 'I will explain to you every scene and then you will appreciate what a wonderful actress she is.'

Sadly, I never got the time to do that. Equally unfortunate was that Maqbool Fida Husain, who loved India and his own people, lived out his last years in exile. But his memories and art are all around me, including his creation on the ceiling. So far, it has withstood the test of time. The only thing is, when we have to repair or paint it, we have to be careful.

Badri Narayan, Samir Mondal and Akbar Padamsee were among the other painters I got to know well. Badri was the paan-chewing, multifaceted brother-in-law of the famous artist K.K. Hebbar.

Painting aside, Badri also wrote and narrated stories, and was therefore popular with children. We came in contact when he taught art at Bombay International School near my clinic. His wife and daughter needed treatment. I did not charge them. It was a policy I had for artists, as I felt most of them had a tough life.

A few months on, a grateful Badri walked into my clinic with a huge painting for me—a rare oil on canvas. Over the next few years he gave me lots of black-and-white paintings and a watercolour as well. As for Padamsee, he presented me with a beautiful mechanical pencil.

Samir Mondal's watercolours are famous, but I knew him from the time he was a relative newcomer. He presented me with two portraits. Around the time he made a painting of Darsheel Safary, who starred in *Taare Zameen Par* (2007), he made a similar one of my grandson Hriman. It made me very emotional.

Former Indian Prime Minister V.P. Singh also took up art in his final years. I met him at an exhibition of his paintings. He spoke about how homeopathy had cured his wife's migraine. I was happy that almost wherever I went I found some beneficiary of homeopathy. I bought one of Singh's works. It turned out that he took some lessons from Mondal.

As for Mondal, I commissioned him to do some paintings, as I no longer felt comfortable getting art from him for free. Today, I have four huge Samir Mondals at home. Later, when I became acquainted with Maneka Gandhi, she advised me on what art to buy, encouraging me to acquire works by Tagore and other leading artists. After that I built my own collection. I can say I have a nice range which includes almost all the Indian contemporary masters, such as Husain, Raza, Souza, Padamsee and Ram Kumar.

Also among my treasured associations was B. Vithal, the painter and sculptor who made the lamp that hangs off the ceiling at Y.B. Chavan Centre in Mumbai. His wife was B. Prabha, a well-known artist herself. Vithal was in poor health and severely anaemic when he met me. With homeopathy, we were able to help him live another six months. He was grateful. He made a charcoal portrait of mine and gave it to me as a present. He also gifted me a Ganesha he had sculpted. I have kept these in my office.

Husain would often quote to me the saying 'The science of medicine is the art of healing'. Now I see why. I may not have watched *Hum Aapke Hain Kaun* ninety times, but I can spend hours looking at art.

22

Dubai, Dior and a Naughty Kid

IN JANUARY 2019, THE DUBAI TOURISM AUTHORITY UNVEILED A NEW campaign to make the emirate the world's most visited city. The slogan of the mission was 'Only in Dubai'. I smiled as my mind travelled back to 1982. Not only was the Positive Health Clinic born that year, it was also when I made my first 'phoren trip', a milestone for Indians at that time. The destination was Dubai. An Arab friend of an Indian friend needed medicines for his little son, who was suffering from asthma. The boy's father was wealthy. He spared no expense on my journey and stay. I was booked on Air India first class.

At the age of thirty-one, the closest I had come to luxurious travelling was the Rajdhani Express. I had not been on a plane, let alone first class. My family was overjoyed. The day of the flight, Nalini took the kids to Juhu beach so that they could spot my plane. I later learnt that my son Akshay, in his excitement, ate sand.

When I entered the aircraft, an Airbus, I took in the new sights. After returning the greeting of stewardesses dressed in Indian finery, I walked to my seat, a plush red chair by the window. Like every first-time flyer, I was nervous about the buttons and seat belt, about appearing like a novice. Finding a place to keep my handbag was not a problem. There was plenty of legroom and I found a corner for it. But the innocuous seat belt did give me the heebie-jeebies. Still, I played it cool, whistling and pretending to play dandiya by tapping one end of the belt against the other, but having no idea how it fastened.

Luck was on my side. The thing with doctors and teachers is that they are always running into patients or ex-students who are ever ready to help them. My neighbour on the flight was a young boy whom I had treated once. He asked me if I needed help with the belt. I did the sensible thing and admitted I did. And I was set to be airborne for the first time in my life.

Three hours went by happily. First-class passengers were fed non-stop. I ate a bit, took a nap and watched some in-flight entertainment. And then it was almost time to land. As sitar music played in the cabin, beneath me I saw a sandy beige landscape dotted with cars, some buildings and palm trees. The construction was nothing like today. It was scattered and the buildings were not very tall.

However, before I could set foot in the kingdom, an adventure awaited. When we landed, there was a loud sound. A tyre on one of the wheels burst, causing the aircraft to skid, sway and make a whining sound that sounded like approaching death. Thankfully, the pilot got the plane under control. The shriek of the engines calmed and we got out, surrounded by fire engines and ambulances.

I was shaken when we got down on the tarmac. Walking in the blazing heat towards the small, two-storey terminal, I reflected on the events of the past few days. I had agreed to the trip for different reasons. It wasn't just a joyride for me. My sense of duty had driven me to help a boy whose childhood was being compromised by his condition. And yes, I also saw it as a chance to spread awareness about homeopathy and about my brand. But while I was excited about the trip, there also was a fear of the unknown.

My biggest worry was how airport officials might react to the medicines I was carrying. Homeopathy wasn't widely known in Dubai. My well-connected host had assured me that someone from his team would be at the airport to receive me, and there would be no problem. But what if something went wrong at this point of no return?

My anxiety worsened when I did not see anyone bearing a placard with my name. After a few minutes, I could no longer delay the arrival formalities. With no local around to receive you, you realize how vulnerable you can be in a foreign land. I learnt a lesson that morning. Sometimes your passion and desire to do something good can get you into trouble.

Sure enough, when my bag passed through the X-ray machine, the officers asked me questions about the pills. I started to explain things to them, when I caught sight of a man carrying a familiar-looking book on his hip. It was a book I had written. This was the man my host had sent, carrying one book on the basis of which we were supposed to identify each other. I can laugh about it today. But at that time I was not too pleased.

Anyway, the two of us met. He told the officials there was nothing wrong with the medicines and that I was the guest of a high-ranking individual. And we left the airport.

As we drove to the hotel I was relieved and back in the frame of mind to soak in new sights and experiences. I noted that the car was a Datsun and was thrilled about it. It was a budget Japanese car, but for an Indian of that era, who only saw Fiats and Ambassadors on the streets, it was a big deal. Datsuns were also known for their high quality air conditioning. That is why they were popular throughout the United Arab Emirates (UAE).

I was booked at the Hotel Ambassador, one of the few hotels in the city at that time. The spacious room overlooked the sea. Dubai was a fishing village to start with, and I could see dhows gliding on the glimmering water. After a few hours, my host came to see me. He was a short man with a big nose, a moustache and a habit of slapping his thigh every time he made a point.

'I'm so happy you are here, and your first meal in a foreign country has to be at my house,' he said.

'That's very nice of you, sir,' I replied, 'but you don't have to take the trouble. I can eat at the hotel.'

'You are here for the first time. So let me tell you, you do not refuse hospitality.'

I got the message.

The hospitality did not stop at dinner. My host reached into his pocket and handed me a wad of cash. 'This is for you. I want you to enjoy while you are here and buy things for your family.'

Somehow, I managed to decline the money. And then we left for his villa, on the outskirts of the city. We drove in the Datsun that had picked me up at the airport. But what was an improved automotive experience for me was a punishment for my rich host. 'Ah, Japanese car,' he complained more than once. And then, at one juncture, we stopped, got out of the Datsun and into a Mercedes. And off we went again. My host looked at me, as if to say, 'You didn't really think the Datsun is my real car, did you?'

My host was a very straightforward fellow—at one point, he told me, 'We are a tribal people. In the desert our faces are covered and we do our business through the eyes. If I quote you a price and your pupils dilate, then I think I have quoted too much.' Learning to do business through eye language gains significance worldwide in the Covid world, where reading people's masked faces is otherwise impossible.

After we reached his mansion we freshened up and were led to a palatial dining room with a large thaal in the centre. It groaned with rice, meat and spices. Several people ate from it at once, including the man's son. Just as I was getting accustomed to my new surroundings and its traditions, I realized that there were many Indians among my host's domestic staff. At one point, he berated them for some reason. I lost my appetite and my eyes moistened. I remembered the purpose of my visit and excused myself from the table, under the pretext of travel fatigue and wanting to examine the boy.

In the meantime, the boy, his hands stained with food, ran towards the window and pulled at the expensive curtains near the window. Noting my surprise, my host said, 'My son very naughty. No problem, tomorrow we go to Christian Dior and buy new curtains.'

'My son very naughty' was a phrase he used often, while pampering the child as well as punishing him. For every 'My-son-very-naughty-tomorrow-we-go-to-Dior' there was a 'My-son-very-naughty-I-lock-him-up-for-three-hours'.

I checked the boy and gave him medicines. In a couple of days his breathing showed signs of improvement. The father was ecstatic and spread the word. This was a boon and a curse for me. In the next few days, I had to see hundreds of people from my host's workforce and also the women of the house. And since I had turned down the man's money, I agreed to his offer of buying some toys for my kids, so that he wasn't offended.

Eight or ten days later, I felt my work was done and expressed my wish to go home. My host was reluctant to let me go. I got the feeling that leaving was not going to be easy. I spoke to my wife in Mumbai and told her what was going on. General O.P. Malhotra, former army chief who was the governor of Maharashtra at that time, needed my professional help. My wife called his aide-de-camp (ADC) and made him connect with my host in Dubai. My host got the message that I couldn't be pressured into staying.

He tried to sweet-talk me into it one last time, suggesting I go for a few days and return. Or that I bring my family over. I stood my ground, saying, 'My son very naughty. Tomorrow I go to Mumbai.'

23

Dodging Bullets in Nigeria

SOMETIME IN THE LATE 1980S, THE FOUR OF US WERE AT A MUGGY airport—my wife, our sons and I. An Amitabh Bachchan film was playing on TV. I had a few days' work in a city. After that we booked a holiday. Sounds like a perfect Indian family moment, *hain*?

It could have been. Except that we were in Lagos, Nigeria. The Amitabh movie apart, there was nothing else around that was Indian or familiar. It is true that we were to go on a holiday to the famous Masai Mara National Reserve, but before that I had an assignment in a village near the city of Aba. We had flown from London to Lagos. And we were waiting for a domestic flight to Port Harcourt. From there it was another five or six hours by road to the village.

There was no sign yet of the flight to Port Harcourt. Even when it arrived there were no guarantees that we would be on it, because you had to grab seats, like in a bus. Till now I had not seen a country that was at least twenty years behind India. Nigeria was that country. Chaos was order here. If you didn't get a seat, you waited for the next flight, which could arrive in three hours or five years. On the plus side, you could watch a lot of movies in five years. And memorize proverbs, a big part of Nigerian culture, written along the walls.

'Monkey no fine but I'm mama no like am (The monkey might be ugly, but his mother loves him).'

'After God, fear woman.'

'The man being carried does not realize how far away the town really is.'

No one was carrying us, but we knew the town was far. And my sons were getting hungry and restless. I walked up to the lone food stall and bought sandwiches. Before taking a bite, I took a cursory glance at the contents between the slices of white bread. There were snails, their eyes engorged from the cooking. Our stomachs turned, and we left the snack alone.

Why exactly were we in Nigeria?

While on a homeopathy lecture tour in London, I had a Nigerian student. She took medicine from me to treat her son. Her husband, she said, was Ava Kadu, a provincial king back home. After a few days we returned to our respective countries and that was that.

A few months on, she wrote to me saying her son was doing very well and that she now wanted to open a homeopathy hospital in Nigeria. 'Please come and help me lay the groundwork,' she said. Once again, I saw a chance to promote homeopathy and agreed to go. And since it was Africa, I thought I'd extend the trip at my expense and take the family to Masai Mara. We could also spend some time in London, as there was no direct flight to Lagos.

My student and her husband, the king, agreed to everything. In fact, they said they would send a trusted lieutenant to London so that he could escort us to his kingdom. My chest swelled as I felt like a royal guest. On the appointed day and hour at Heathrow, we reached the gate for our flight to Lagos. The enclosure had already become a mini Nigeria, just as any Heathrow gate before a flight to India quickly turns into Karol Bagh.

Everybody around at the Lagos flight gate was tall. A soft-spoken man then approached us and introduced himself. Towering over me, he said he was the emissary sent by the king. However, he made a strange request. He wanted us to carry his bag, which had shoehorns that looked like they were made from ivory. I refused and he got upset. That's right. He got upset because I did the right thing. Not wanting to take any chances, we left the man and returned home from the airport, the flight be damned. I called my student and expressed my displeasure at the behaviour of her acquaintance.

She pacified me and four days later sent someone else to fetch us. This time we took the flight to Nigeria. But in Lagos, our guide revealed that he too was not some paragon of virtue. He asked me for a couple of hundred dollars to bribe the airport officials so that my medicines could go through. I realized that bribing was rampant in the country.

The inconvenient flight to Port Harcourt was followed by a tiring, anxious six-hour drive to the village. It was late evening and we drove in pitch darkness, having no idea what to expect. Along the periphery of the road grew nothing but thick tall shrub. If we were killed and thrown into the grass no one would have known. Was this all a conspiracy, like the email scams of today which often originate from Nigeria?

We felt somewhat better when we saw some lights, and then the sign 'King Ava Kadu's Palace'. As we got out of the car, Nalini and I took out a box of chocolates that we had carried for my student's son. And then we learnt a few things that were common in Nigeria, but had not occurred to me.

My student was in a polygamous marriage with Ava Kadu, who was just about forty-five and younger than I expected. When we met, he was dressed in a kaftan of sorts and wore colourful headgear. My student was one of his twelve wives. In fact, he was about to acquire the thirteenth Mrs Ava Kadu, a sixteen-year-old girl who was being groomed for betrothal by the other ladies. We had thus reached on an auspicious occasion. Some of the ladies also took a fancy to me, especially my chest hair. They found it unusual and sexy, as Nigerian men mostly had smooth pectorals. Before I could get carried away by images of myself in an African robe and headdress, being fed snail sandwiches by local beauties, I remembered the chocolates.

How stupid we were. My student's son—the boy I had treated—was one of Ava Kadu's forty-odd children. And we had a grand total of one chocolate box. We had no option but to sheepishly offer it to our hosts.

The rules of the palace were such that a child did not know who his biological mother was. All the king's wives were the mothers to all his children. It was a peculiar culture, one which was feudal and progressive at the same time. The wives had daily duties and together functioned more like a sisterhood than a mean girls' club competing for the king's attention. It was understood that their husband would go to bed with anyone at any point.

On the other hand, women were allowed to not just study but also go abroad, like my student in London did. Children were sent to top universities around the world. And the brightest child—who might not be the eldest—ascended to the throne. However, wives and children on travels abroad were expected to ultimately return home.

The palace was beautiful and had all the comforts, a stark contrast to the poverty that we saw outside. But we could not adjust to the food. For some reason the dishes always had the eyes of a creature staring at us, and not the kind that would inspire anyone to besottedly sing '*In ankhon ki masti ke*'. Luckily, the garden had a tangerine tree. The fruit helped us survive. All we had to do when we got hungry was to give the tree a shake. It would bless us with a mini shower of tangerines. That apart, bread and some version of tea kept us going. My sons were still quite small and were in the habit of drinking milk. But even a quart of milk necessitated a long drive to the market. I cursed myself for putting them through this.

Nigeria did possess natural beauty, which we saw in snatches, when not overwhelmed by its other realities. At night, the sky looked like sequined black velvet. The scent of hibiscus and rose filled the air. Cicadas chirped among the trees. We would use the sights and sounds to try and forget our hunger and lull ourselves to sleep. I probably lost eight kilos on that trip, not to mention a lot of money.

The king understood our plight. The day I finished the work on his wife's project, he arranged for me and my family to be driven to the Concord Hotel in Aba for dinner. We drove in a Peugeot 504, which seemed to be everyone's favourite car in Nigeria. When we reached and our starved bodies picked up the scent of rotis and curry, we almost fainted. We ate to our heart's content and looked forward to a quiet ride back home, glancing at the stars, and then hitting the sack.

We started the drive back, and when we left the city and got on to the unpaved country road, it became pitch dark. The Peugeot's headlights, like the eyes of a nocturnal creature, saw through the darkness and we soldiered on. My boys clung closer to their mother. In the front row, the driver and I sat in silence, but I felt he was a bit concerned.

I tried to defuse the tension.

'Who's seen which star or planet today? Take a look at the sky, as we'll be reaching soon,' I said to my sons.

But my mouth went dry when I spotted another pair of headlights appearing in the rear-view mirror. Experienced drivers can sense intent in another car, even when it's dark. This car seemed to be moving towards us for a reason. And not because they wanted to gaze at planets with us.

'Who are these guys?' I asked the driver.

Barely had I asked the question, then our driver floored the accelerator and the Peugeot lurched ahead. 'Get low in your seats, crouch,' the driver said. Within moments, bullets pinged out from the car behind us. *Bada bingbada boom.* In the back seat, my younger son started whimpering and held on to his mother. The driver crouched too, but kept his eyes on the road, while his hands and feet expertly manoeuvred the car through this precarious situation. After what seemed like an eternity, the palace of the smooth-chested king came into view, and our assailants backed off.

We were relieved when our day of departure approached. But that wasn't without drama either. There was a long, traditional farewell for us from the king, and due to the delay in the arrival of a ceremonial cup filled with grains we missed one of our connections. A never-ending speech from one of the king's fathers-in-law, who also happened to be the Prime Minister, did not help either. Soon after, another flight was cancelled because the man standing in front of me in the queue was shot dead by someone. Back home, my father found out through his connections in Air India that I had missed a flight. He was getting worried.

When we at last got on the plane to Nairobi, we were wary of rejoicing too early. You simply never knew what would happen. But then the big bird took off, and we could breathe and smile again. In the in-flight magazine, I came across a quote by Winston Churchill: 'Nothing in life is so exhilarating as to be shot at without result.'

I now knew enough to say that he wasn't wrong. But for me, despite the challenges in Nigeria, the most exhilarating part was being able to set up a homeopathy hospital from scratch and provide healthcare to people deprived of it so far. Once again, I had triumphed over difficulties to accomplish my mission towards health and homeopathy.

24

Not So Batty After All

MOST PEOPLE WHO ARE NOT MY FAMILY MEMBERS CALL ME Dr Batra or Doc. My staff addresses me formally, senior colleagues included. I prefer it that way, as I'm conservative in these matters. Our company is not like an advertising agency or a newspaper office.

But she calls me Batty.

She is Simi Garewal, my friend for many decades. She has been with me through thick and thin. Perhaps she calls me Batty not because I'm crazy (or maybe I am and I don't know it), but because my out-of-the-box treatments have worked for her and her family. She has often said to me, 'Batty, you have to outlive me, because I can't live without your medicines.'

Simi's sister Amrita, or Gugi, was a student of mine at Sophia College, where I gave a class introducing lay people to homeopathy. Simi and I, and sometimes Amrita too, have chatted for hours about personal and professional matters, all of us dressed in white. (Okay, I made up that last bit.)

Once Simi wanted to take her show to a different channel and asked me what my thoughts were about it. I also remember conversations about a Rajiv Gandhi documentary many years ago. At times I'd ask her for suggestions for something on the work or personal front. A few years ago, I bought a weekend home in Aamby Valley, Lonavla. Simi wanted to get one too. 'I can retire then and be your neighbour,' she said. It didn't happen. But we remain friends and share a comfort level where we can be serious and silly.

There is hardly a film family that does not believe in homeopathy. Thanks to my profession, I got to interact closely with them. I miss those friendships now that I'm retired.

In fact, many actors or their kin were experts on homeopathy. As mentioned earlier, Manoj Kumar was one. So was Ashok Kumar, who'd studied homeopathy and would even prescribe medicines if someone on the set was unwell. In his popular '*Rail gaadi*' song, Dadamoni rattled off names of stations, 'Bangalore, Mangalore, Mandwa, Khandwa—'. It's possible he could recite the names of homeopathic medicines with the same zest, 'Belladonna, Calendula, Dulcamara, Drosera—'

When Kishore Kumar was sick once, Dadamoni asked if he could be taken to the homeopathic hospital in Irla. But it wasn't in good condition then. 'A person of Kishore Kumar's stature can't be admitted there,' he was told.

The actress Shaukat Kaifi, Shabana Azmi's mother, had several homeopathy medicines and books at home. When Shabana launched one of my books, she spoke about how her mother was practically the family physician. Shabana too swears by homeopathy. That is why she makes time for our events and speaks well of me.

Asha Bhosle and Lata Mangeshkar were also my patients for a while. Ashaji would always be chirpy and crooning a song during a consultation. And many years ago, I met Nargis at a film trial at Dimple, Rajendra Kumar's studio. She made my day when she complimented my work. Sridevi, another patient, once inaugurated a photography exhibition of mine.

When Salman Khan was just starting his career, he would cycle from Bandra to the clinic. He was lanky then. And it may surprise some to know that he was well behaved and would quietly read magazines in the clinic while he waited his turn. Meenakshi Seshadri would often have her food from her dabba while she waited. I would know immediately that she was around, as the aroma of sambar would waft through the clinic.

At times, I would be asked to cure an external ill. Krishna Shah, the Hollywood-trained director of the 1978 movie *Shalimar*, was fed up of his smoking habit and came to me for help. 'Doc, I believe there is a medicine in homeopathy to give up smoking. I really want to stop smoking now,' he said with a slight California twang. I could see that he was anguished. Here was a man who clearly had tried many times to kick the butt but had not been successful.

'Alright,' I said. 'What do you smoke?'

Expectedly, he took out a gold-coloured pack of '555' from his shirt pocket and placed it on the table. It was the rich Indian's brand at that time. The less fortunate killed themselves with 'Charminar', while Bollywood types elegantly held a '555' between their fingers. And in most cases their lighter was Cartier or Dunhill.

I looked at the cigarette pack and said, 'Great, I have just the right medicine for you.'

'Ya do?' Shah asked in his Mumbai-meets-US accent.

I crushed the packet and tossed it into the waste-paper basket.

'There, you're cured,' I said.

Shah was shocked and also got the message. The ultimate medicine to stop smoking was in your mind.

But by far one of my most delightful celebrity encounters was with the ghazal maestro Ghulam Ali. I adored the genre and had the opportunity of hosting Ali Saab for lunch at home. He was touring India and had developed some health niggle. Dilraj Kaur, the singer of hits like '*Mausam mastana*' from the 1982 film *Satte pe Satta*, referred him to me. When he came to the clinic, I asked him if he could come to my place for dinner one day.

'I'm sorry, all my dinners are booked,' he replied. 'But I'd be happy to come for lunch.'

When Ali Saab walked into our apartment in Maker Towers, wearing a grey silk kurta and a stole around his neck, he was his usual genial self, an almost permanent half-smile on his face. One of the first things he said was, 'Where is everybody else?'

'How do you mean? It's just my wife and I,' I said.

My guest was pleasantly surprised. 'From the time I have come to India, whenever I am invited for dinner, it's a big crowd and they ask me to sing for free. In your case I came because you treated me.'

Happy to at last meet someone who wasn't a freeloader, Ali Saab relaxed. He enjoyed the lunch and appreciated the opportunity to speak in Punjabi. '*Main Punjabi vich gal kar sakha twade naal.* I am so happy,' he said.

Meanwhile, his tabla player was waiting in the car. Ghulam Ali sent for him. I did not even have a carpet at that time. But all of us sat on the floor and just like that, the most famous ghazal singer in the world proceeded to give me and my wife a private concert of sorts. For a music addict like me, it was an absolute treat. It was like a Swiss chocolatier showing up at a chocoholic's door and preparing a personal treat for them.

Some years later, I ran into Ghulam Ali in the lift of the Taj Mahal Hotel. We exchanged pleasantries. '*Doctor Saab, ki haal hai twada? Changey ho?*'

I asked after his health too. He mentioned a minor bother. I said, 'Don't worry, I will send medicines to your hotel.' I was sure my unique formula would work for him, so I would live up to my name, 'Batty'.

25

Think Differently

When Steve Jobs gave the commencement speech to students at Stanford University on a sunny California day in 2005, he signed off with the advice, 'Stay hungry. Stay foolish.' Jobs did not coin the phrase. As he said in the speech, it was his favourite childhood magazine's goodbye message to its readers when it shut down.

But Jobs did live by those words. And for a while, so did I. In 1982, around the same time that Apple was building its landmark Macintosh, I spent Rs 1.5 lakh on a computer for my new clinic in Mehta House, Chowpatty. It was a clunky HCL machine which would occupy half the desk. A pale green screen was its distinctive feature. I would call it the Evil Eye. Alongside Evil Eye was Evil Laughter, a dot matrix printer which went tok-tok-tok-tok and shook the entire building.

Everybody told me I was crazy. They said I could have hired a team of doctors and a chartered accountant (CA) with the money I spent on the electronic rathimaharathis now occupying half of my small, 400-sq ft clinic. They had no idea that my foolishness would be vindicated soon.

Like an underground operative roping in young tech whizzes to save the world, I first got a nerdy young patient of mine on board. He then got two of his friends on the project. Together, we worked hard to design a software and feed it into the computer, so that it would work optimally and fast. We made the first manuscript of an electronic medical health programme in 1982.

In homeopathy there are catalogues called *Repertories*, which suggest medicines for different symptoms. The problem is each dose has thousands of permutations and combinations. Earlier, doctors would consult multiple books over two days before prescribing medicine. With the software, I could enter the symptoms and within seconds I would know what medicine to give. And then I would use my sense and experience before arriving at a final decision. Thanks to our tech-presence, we have digitalized reports of all our patients since 1982; while even a country as advanced as the UK can even today claim only 13 per cent digitized records by its GPs.

My clinic was the first computerized homeopathic centre in India, and it generated a buzz everywhere. Journalists wrote about me. More importantly, doctors from prestigious institutions like Bombay Hospital, Jaslok Hospital and Breach Candy Hospital would come to see the set-up. Years later, computerization helped me to set up the world's first cyber clinic as well. It was the director Shekhar Kapur who gave me this idea.

He happened to be sitting next to me on a flight—he was on his second honeymoon, with Suchitra—and he started talking about the internet. This was way before the first tech wave. As serendipity often has it, we happened to be in the same hotel, and we talked about it again over breakfast. 'Since you are already using technology, you could use the internet to spread the benefits of homeopathy to many more people,' Shekhar said. A few months later, he inaugurated our cyber clinic.

The clinic also broke new ground in different ways. Not only was it a pioneer in technology, it also was an example of branding. Till then, clinics did not have well-thought-out names. They would just be called Dr XYZ's dispensary. We, on the other hand, were Positive Health Clinic. Though the clinic was small, it was smart and modern, built in the style of a Swiss chalet. My architect friend Keshav Pansare designed it. I poured every drop of my energy into it because I wanted it just so. In fact, the nights before it opened in October 1982, I would be there till late. And on the day of completion, around five in the morning, as the first bells rang in the nearby Babulnath temple, a tea-shop owner offered me a cup of tea. I was grateful to him.

Make no mistake. I was doing well at Cuffe Parade and Matru Ashish, pulling in Rs 25,000 a month. It was much more than what MBBS doctors or accountants made at that time. But I was forced to start a new clinic because I had to vacate Matru Ashish. The owner's son had become a doctor and needed space for his practice. 'Fair enough,' I said, and just asked for a reasonable amount of time to pack up.

It is my policy to leave gracefully when I'm asked. I do not get into arguments or dilly-dallying. It is not my property and I really have no right to throw a tantrum even though, in those days, it was not easy for a doctor to relocate. It meant leaving behind your practice. There was no Google to direct your patients to your new address, and so leaving a place meant leaving behind a reputation and the goodwill that you had worked so hard to build. There was simply no way of continuing seamlessly elsewhere; one's practice at every location had to be built from scratch.

A complete contrast to me as a tenant was the owner's best friend, a dermatologist, who would come in after I left for a couple of hours. When the owner told him that he would have to leave, the man had the gall to sue him. The case dragged on for four years and the owner ended up paying his ungrateful friend Rs 4.5 lakh.

Life is not always fair, but I believe God does watch, and goodness and evil both come back to you in some form or the other.

Something else happened at Matru Ashish too and my ethics once again enabled me to find a solution to a prickly issue. I had been wanting some extra space for my practice, and had requested a pathologist if I could use his room when it was free. After a point, looking at my growing practice, he said I could use his room only if I made every patient of mine get tests done from him. This was unacceptable to me, but I needed the room. So I told the pathologist that I would pay him the charge of the tests without making my patients go through them.

Once Matru Ashish was a closed chapter, setting up a new clinic needed another act of foolishness from me. In those days, banks wouldn't court doctors with loan offers. Healthcare was not considered an industry and hence not funded. Doctors were respected as always but not seen as wealthy. Luckily, a patient of mine was a chairperson at the Bombay Mercantile Bank, and they loaned me some money. The rest I borrowed from individuals at the staggering interest rate of 36 per cent. This absurd figure was standard practice in the film industry, as there was never a guarantee if a movie would do well. I was in glamorous company, as my enterprise too was deemed high risk.

Jokes aside, the interest was stifling. I had two sons now and had to earn Rs 63,000 a month just to keep up with the loan instalments and provide for the family. But I was hungry. I had self-belief—very important for an entrepreneur. You need to put your money where your mouth is. I believed that with age and momentum on my side, the loan would be paid off sooner or later, and my company would be debt-free. As the founder of Positive Health Clinic, I could ill afford to be negative.

26

Differentiate Yourself

Every Christmas, thousands of people get off at Knightsbridge station in London and head to the festive sale at Harrods. There was one simple thing Harrods did that set the store apart and won over customers at very little cost. As people waited in the long queue, they were served tea, coffee and snacks by Harrods' butlers, impeccably dressed and wearing white gloves. On one occasion the butlers also performed a tap dance.

It was a smart move. Harrods could easily afford to give away tea and snacks. They could easily afford the butlers. Most likely, the gesture did not disturb their bottom line at all. And in return, they gained hundreds of pounds worth of goodwill.

In any line of work it is important for a person or an organization to differentiate themselves from the rest of the pack. It is also important that their customer has a good experience. That is how you will make an impact and become a brand. Branding is not just about the packaging (although the latter is a big part of it). Branding is also about intangible forces like quality and reputation.

As Jeff Bezos said, 'Your brand is what other people say about you when you are not in the room.'

There were two reasons I chose the name Positive Health Clinic for my new space, complete with a specially designed logo so that people did not confuse it with the category called PHC, which stood for primary health centre. One, I wanted to differentiate myself from other homeopaths. My charges were maybe 20 per cent more, but I was offering patients the latest methods of treatment, thanks to the computer and our database, and a better clinic experience, thanks to our little Swiss chalet in Mehta House. They were coming to a brand and there was a certain value to it, as the brand was offering them one-of-a-kind service in return.

The second reason was that I had about a decade's work experience by then, and I had begun to believe that ensuring absence of disease could not be the sole purpose of medicines. It could not be the sole definition of good health. Good health is a balance of physical, mental and spiritual health. And at Positive Health Clinic, we offered all of that. Along with our regular treatments, we gave counselling, diet and exercise plans, general health medicines and a lot else. We were ahead of the curve compared to other homeopaths.

Even our technological strides did not stop at the computer. As a doctor, I was particular about a couple of things—accurate dosage and patient compliance. And so I designed a packaging machine for blister-packed medicines. I believed that homeopathy had to be modernized and made acceptable in the medical world. Every entrepreneur needs to innovate regularly to stay relevant. Blister packaging made it easy for the patient to remember their dose and the medicine stayed in good condition. Also, this way, a part of the clinic was going home with the patient. His or her experience of us wasn't ending at the clinic.

It is possible that I had more energy to innovate and grow now as I had built my own ship, unlike Matru Ashish, which was a polyclinic, where I had to have one eye on the clock. Many times I had to refuse patients if my time slot was ending. At Mehta House, I did not have to turn anyone away. In fact, thanks to word-of-mouth publicity, the number of patients was increasing. I reached a practice of hundred-odd patients every day. The queue would stretch out of the clinic and on to the road. Unfortunately I did not have butlers to entertain them.

When Positive Health Clinic started doing well, it was time to close my Cuffe Parade practice. Once more, many friends and relatives told me that I was being stupid by pulling the plug on a good thing at Cuffe Parade. 'These years won't come again. You are on top of your career, why are you doing this?' This was the gist of their argument. But I put my foot down. It's not like I was shirking responsibility. I tirelessly saw every patient who came to me. My brand was now strongly connected to Positive Health Clinic. I did not want to dilute it by offering an alternative.

27

Build Your Image

'SANDESE AATE HAIN' (BORDER, 1997) IS ONE OF THE BEST SONGS of the modern era, in Indian cinema. It captures the emotion of the soldier and his simple but profound joy at receiving a letter from home. A letter goes beyond just pen and paper. It means someone remembered you.

There was a time when letters poured in by the hundreds for me too. I say this not out of vanity but gratitude. I was a health columnist for the influential magazine *Illustrated Weekly of India*, and readers wrote in with their problems from all over the country. To be a part of the media counted for something then. Only a few papers and magazines like the *Weekly* held clout, unlike now where anyone with the loudest voice or a Wi-Fi connection can put his two-penny worth on air.

Before I explain how I got all those letters, I will give you some background.

A social media presence is a must for any brand or individual these days. It builds image, connects the brand/individual with people and generates revenue. Look at the young New Jersey doctor and Instagram sensation Dr Mike Varshavski.

In earlier times, it was the print media and television that were all-important. I was active on both, thanks to my ambition and friendships. I did not want to be one among many doctors. I wanted to be at the top. If that meant burning the midnight oil to write a column after a full day at work, or changing nine outfits over a weekend to wrap up multiple episodes of a show, I did it. Of course, it helped that through my line of work I met leading media persons. And as my practice was doing well, they wanted to include me in their line-up of contributors, or front a show on health or homeopathy.

One of my patients happened to be none other than the top media personality of the time, Pritish Nandy. (Pritish will be pleased at this introduction.) He was the editor of *Illustrated Weekly of India*. As authors, both of us had the same publisher, Gulab Vazirani, who had published our titles under the Arnold-Heinemann label. Gulab's nephew Dinesh currently runs Saffronart, the art auction company.

I first met Pritish at the Old Lady of Boribunder, where he had moved after giving up a corporate job in Kolkata. There was art on the walls of his office, and a leather sofa. An antique typewriter adorned his side table. Sitting in a black swivel chair was the man himself, with several crumpled sheets of paper around his feet, even though there was a dustbin nearby.

Pritish offered me a regular column in the magazine where readers would write in their health problems and I would answer them. I agreed, and within months I became a household name. Letters came by the dozens first. Then they came in the hundreds. The column ran for about a decade. For many years after that I met people who told me that they still had the clippings. The pages had turned yellow but the fading words on them were still useful.

The column was a win-win situation for me. I could make a difference to lives. And I got paid Rs 2000 per piece, a huge amount at the time. The response to my column, however, was a bitter pill to swallow for Big Pharma. They did not want anything to threaten their position, least of all a homeopath who had the energy to work all day and night, and gradually bring about a change in the perception of the masses.

The dam burst when the *Weekly* carried a long piece on homeopathy by me. Members of the mainstream medicine industry, their credibility and bottom lines at stake, sent me and the magazine hate mail. This was trolling pre-Twitter, '*Sandese aate hain*' of a different kind.

Neither I, nor people who believed in homeopathy, were cowed down by the bullying tactics of the pharma industry. Homeopathy proponents wrote a rejoinder in the magazine, vouching for its benefits. Ghazal singers Rajendra and Neena Mehta penned a separate note in defence of homeopathy, which was published under the title 'Sing a Song for Homeopathy'. The Mehtas had suffered health problems that affected their voices and said that it was due to my treatment that they could sing again.

The popularity of the columns increased. Prominence in a national magazine meant that at some point TV came around asking as well. I became one of the hosts of '*Aap ka Swaasth*', a health show on Mumbai Doordarshan (DD). And then I came in contact with an old friend and patient, the writer Kamleshwar Prasad Saxena. At one time Shatrughan Sinha, Kamleshwar and I were a troika. We got along famously. All of us had a loud booming laugh which would punctuate our conversations. Kamleshwar rose to become the director general of DD in Delhi and offered me a thirteen-episode show on DD National called *Homeopathy and You*, in which DD anchors would interview me for half an hour every episode.

As the 1990s began, however, DD was falling behind the times. Cable TV had come to India. The production standards of the newer channels were far higher. No longer was it enough to just show up at the studio, comb hair and roll. Everything, from set to costumes to the coffee mugs on the desk, had to be slick. This also drove up production costs.

Zee TV quickly made a mark in this era. Mr P. Subrahmanyam, chief secretary of Maharashtra, was a patient of mine and he wished for me to be on Zee. 'You've done Doordarshan, you've treated me well and you speak well. I think you should be on Zee,' he said. One day he introduced me to Subhash Chandra, the channel's mercurial boss from Haryana who dropped his original surname (Goenka) as he was against the caste system in his culture.

Chandra was a grain trader who had come to Mumbai and set up a large aluminium tube packaging plant called Essel Packaging, before foraying into television, entertainment and news.

So far, I had gotten most of my media exposure quite easily. Often, media companies asked me to do something and not the other way around. But Chandra was not easily convinced. When we met at his Worli office done up with cane furniture, he told me bluntly, 'We are an entertainment channel. I don't see any place in it for health.'

'Subhashji, I will convince you that health is also a winning proposition,' I said. 'You must try it out.'

Chandra's mild Haryanvi accent came through in his words and was in direct contrast to his French beard and fashionable silver-streaked hair. He said he'd think about it. I did not have much hope. On the way out though, one of Chandra's senior colleagues suggested I make a pilot. And then we could take a final call. It would mean spending my own money. But it was worth a shot. At least I'd have the satisfaction of having tried.

Media mogul and entrepreneur Ronnie Screwvala lived in the same building as me. He had the studio space and manpower I could hire for the pilots. Ronnie advised me to shoot four episodes, as it was cost-effective compared to filming just one. The duration of each episode was to be twelve and a half minutes. It doesn't sound like much but it is hard work. So far I was used to single-camera set-ups at DD, where you looked at the camera and spoke.

Here there were many cameras moving all the time. There also were lights on cranes, which were moving too. The glare of the lights strained the eyes and their heat caused perspiration, despite the air conditioning. It took me about a dozen takes just for the first shot.

It was a show based on health and exercise. For guests, I dug into my contacts and called up possible candidates. Anup Jalota was happy to come. We both had a Lucknow connection and now he was my first guest on the programme. Then I invited Asha Bhosle and M.F. Husain. I remember that Husain did a huge painting during the show. But he did not sign it. I kept the painting carefully under my bed at home. A few days later, he asked me to destroy it. Even an unsigned Husain was worth a lot, but I honoured his wish.

Some of my other guests were Meenakshi Seshadri, Vivek Oberoi, Anu Malik and Sonu Nigam. Sonu had just bought his first car—a white Maruti van. He was so excited about it that after the show he took me to see it. 'Dr Batra, see my new car, I have just paid for it.'

At last, the pilots were ready. Subhash Chandra loved them, though he was not sure how he'd make money out of them. He offered me a deal. 'I'll air it free of cost on Sunday mornings, but you produce it. And whatever advertising revenue we get from the show, we will share it,' he said. It was tiring and expensive. But you need to believe in your ability and invest in yourself, else no one will. You put your money where your mouth is—every single last penny. I did that for a year. Everything I made from my practice went into producing this show.

The other adjustment I had to make was that the show was to be telecast via Hong Kong, which did not recognize homeopathy as a form of treatment. To make it work, we had to tweak our format and make it a general show about general health and fitness. Thank God I did not throw in the towel. The Positive Health Show, even in that format, worked out in favour of homeopathy and the brand anyway as 'Positive Health' was already associated with Dr Batra's®. It made 'Dr Batra' a household name. Sometimes, challenges come to us as opportunities to hone our ideas. It is worth practising dynamism and finding a way to stay the course.

And there we were, from 8.15 a.m. to 8.30 a.m. on Sundays—which later went on to become a full half-hour slot. I stopped only after three and a half years and over a hundred episodes, watched by Zee's national and international audiences. The production costs and time commitment was becoming too much to handle. In fact, at one point I had to get some funding from Reliance to pay my studio dues. I offered to run ads of Reliance on the show. Anil Ambani, who was part of the meeting, did not take up the ad offer. He just advised me to not give up the show's intellectual property (IP) rights, as 'content was king'.

Despite everything, it was worth doing the show. Along with writing, I now had hours of TV time under my belt. Through both media, I was able to popularize and propagate healing through homeopathy.

As an entrepreneur, you need to believe in yourself, be fiercely passionate about what you do and bet your bottom dollar or rupee in your belief to achieve success.

28

Book Your Experiences

MY FIRST BOOK, *EVERY MAN'S GUIDE TO HOMEOPATHY* WAS published by Arnold-Heinemann in 1982 and released by the governor of Maharashtra, General O.P. Malhotra. I have published eight books thereafter with different publishing houses like Jaico and Westland. Writing a book is testimony of your stature in your field. If somebody else is printing your book, they believe that your thoughts and your shared expertise will be useful for others to buy. Every entrepreneur, once he or she reaches a certain stature in their profession or business, must take time out to write a book. One of my most memorable book launches was of my book *Common Ailments* published by India Book Distributors (IBD) in 1991 and released at the governor's residence, Raj Bhavan.

I have met a lot of important people in my life. Some of them were absolute titans who made invaluable contributions to the nation. Bharat Ratna C. Subramaniam was one such man. 'CS' was the Father of the Green Revolution, during which India produced a record quantity of wheat due to special seeds sourced under his leadership. He held crucial portfolios like agriculture, defence and finance during the prime ministership of Lal Bahadur Shastri and later, Indira Gandhi. He was the governor of Maharashtra from 1990 to 1993. That was when our paths crossed.

Subramaniam was having some health problems. I was summoned to Raj Bhavan. He was in his eighties by then, but his faculties were razor sharp. He had thick grey hair and wore pristine white clothes. His appearance, coupled with his deeds, meant that he automatically commanded respect.

When I met him, we spoke about agriculture among other things. His nephew was in agriculture, and I had a small farm at the time, so I knew enough to hold a conversation. Subramaniam took a liking to me. He and his wife both exuded warmth. We spoke for quite a while over aromatic filter coffee, watching the sun go down over the Arabian Sea.

We met a few more times, and the treatment brought Subramaniam respite from his ailment. I was then officially made one of his personal physicians. He could go to any of the doctors on the panel for treatment, but all of us could mention the appointment on our letterheads or résumés—'Personal physician to His Excellency, the Governor of Maharashtra'.

Subramaniam was the rare politician who was not snobbish about his grand residence. In fact, his vision was to open its doors to people whenever possible. 'Raj Bhavan is meant for the public,' he once said to me. 'It should not be restricted to governors and officials.'

The estate had several treasures, including its own beach and helicopters. By and large, these lay unused and were beyond the common man. 'At least good people should be able to come here and experience these things. They are just lying here,' said Subramaniam, a man keen to share and give, not gain, in the final years of his life.

I ventured to ask him, 'Sir, how do you like the idea that I release my latest book in the Darbar Hall at Raj Bhavan?'

He loved the thought. 'Just tell me how many people and other details.'

I invited Pritish Nandy as the chief guest. And then Harkin Chatlani the owner of IBD, told me that his star author Dominique Lapierre was likely to be in Mumbai around the same time. Lapierre was one of the few Western writers who was a hit in India as well as internationally. India inspired two of his major hits—*Freedom at Midnight* and *The City of Joy*.[1]

What I didn't know was that Lapierre was a homeopathy follower, who contributed a blurb for the book *The Spirit of Homeopathic Medicines* by Didier Grandgeorge.[2]

'It just happens to be that Lapierre is coming from Paris,' Chatlani told me. 'He is going to Kolkata (then Calcutta) because he is a big fan of Mother Teresa. And he is giving all the royalties from *The City of Joy* to her trust. If you like, I can invite him and see whether he is in Mumbai on the day of your book release.'

This was a no-brainer. 'Of course,' I said. 'What could be better!'

A book launch that could easily have been a routine affair in some bookstore over bad coffee and half-hearted speeches, now took place in the chandeliered Darbar Hall at Raj Bhavan. It was a historic occasion, one of the first times that a lay person's event took place at Raj Bhavan.

A select audience of about 300 attended. The Darbar Hall was packed. Among those present was a colossus like Subramaniam, a literary heavyweight like Lapierre and a media personality like Pritish. It wouldn't have been possible had I shied away from requesting Subramaniam in the first place. My advice to young

---

1 Collins, Larry and Dominique Lapierre (1975), *Freedom at Midnight: How Britain Gave Away an Empire*, New York: Simon & Schuster; Lapierre, Dominique (1986), *The City of Joy*, translated by S.A. Pressinter, New York: Warner Books Inc.

2 Grandgeorge, Didier (1997), *The Spirit of Homeopathic Medicines: Essential Insights to 300 Remedies*, translated by Juliana Barnard, Berkeley CA: North Atlantic Books and Homeopathic Educational Services.

people is, if it's for a worthy cause, do not hesitate to ask. Manoj Kumar once told me: 'Always ask. At the most, the person will say no.'

Lapierre was included in the speaker's list at the last minute. I was pleasantly surprised when, at the start of his speech, he said, 'I love homeopathy. I believe in it.' He recounted how he had used it in his long battle with cancer. It was a big endorsement for the field from a world celebrity.

When it was Pritish's turn to speak, he said, 'I don't believe in homeopathy.' A dramatic pause followed. 'But I believe in Mukesh Batra.' And he took that theme forward. Finally, Governor Subramaniam spoke. From the Father of the Green Revolution, even a little push went a long way towards slowly setting in motion a medical revolution of sorts. Homeopathy was the winner that evening.

29

Medicine Is All-consuming

WHAT HAPPENS TO A DOCTOR DURING RIOTS? WHAT ARE HIS thoughts when treating criminals? What goes on in his mind when he receives a threatening letter written in blood?

All of this has happened to me and has taught me many lessons. First, that medicine has no religion and does not check anyone's criminal record. A doctor treats whoever comes to them as a patient. Second, doctors rarely get to take a break during crises, as was most recently seen during Covid. As for letters written in blood, you do the sensible thing and go to the cops. And then post a bottle of ink to the sender, so that the next time they use the right fluid for the fine art of correspondence.

I saw the Mumbai riots of 1992–93 up close. One evening, when the city was tense but not yet burning, a major general of the Indian Army called me for dinner to his house in South Mumbai. He and his wife were my patients. Since we lived not far from each other, and the situation was relatively calm, I went ahead with the dinner appointment. As I settled down and we chatted about this and that, an attaché came up to the general. Matters were worsening, he was told. Rioters had looted an armoury in the city and rampage was imminent.

Uh-oh.

The general excused himself and went inside for phone calls. When he returned after a while, I offered to leave. 'Sir, we can do this another time.'

He seemed in two minds, but decided to play both roles—a general managing a developing crisis, and a host who would not leave his guest high and dry. He insisted I stay. And thus I had the surreal experience of watching an army boss command the military to arrive in Mumbai at the earliest even as the dal simmered in the kitchen, in a manner of speaking. Once he had issued all orders, we had dinner.

It is difficult for doctors to see life destroyed by force because we work hard to preserve human health. We work hours just so a small bone in your body can heal. And then someone comes along and with one pull of the trigger ends it all. We value life. But there are some who think nothing of snuffing it out.

The riots were among the darkest hours in Mumbai's history. Neighbours and friends turned on each other due to communal fanaticism whipped up by politicians. Streets we roamed in without fear, became empty. All that remained was tension, rumour, destruction. Man distrusted man.

During this period one day I was at my clinic in Chowpatty when I heard a commotion outside. I looked outside the passage. A taxi driver was being dragged out of his car by a mob. They hit him and doused him in fuel. And then they set the man and his taxi on fire. Just like that, a life went up in smoke. Taxis were a symbol of Mumbai and of brotherhood. Drivers and passengers would talk about this and that but never ask each other about their caste or religion. The charred, twisted heap of metal and flesh in front of me, with its depressing smell of burning rubber and human tissue, left me traumatized. It made me value equality.

In our company we have holidays for all major festivals, and we do not have any prejudices when hiring.

Even with incidents like the slaying of the taxi driver taking place on a daily basis, I kept going to the clinic. It was something that was ingrained in me. If anyone stopped me, my doctor's ID card would help me get through.

Then there are times when you must understand that something is not in your control, and report the problem to the authorities. When Sikh militants gunned down Gen. A.S. Vaidya in Pune as revenge for Operation Blue Star, one political party in Maharashtra trained its anger on prominent Punjabis. I received their *pyaar ka izhaar* (love token) on a beige postcard, written in blood. A bit amused by the theatrics but also not wanting to take chances, I went to the police.

'So many people come to see me every day. If this threat is serious, it would be easy to harm me. What do I do?' I asked the police officer.

He said they would provide me with security, but that I shouldn't worry too much. Further on, there were no more threats to me, no more gory letters in the mail. But again, the experience saddened me. When I met Mrs Vaidya, we spoke about how doing my duty as a doctor and thus treating her and her husband had put me in harm's way, as if I had anything to do with Operation Blue Star itself.

As Punjabis, we were also at risk when Indira Gandhi was assassinated in 1984. We were in Bengaluru (then Bangalore) on a holiday. On that fateful day, my wife and I and our two young sons were having lunch at a north Indian restaurant. Angry mobs were attacking anything Punjabi. The restaurant had a glass façade, and people started throwing pots and stones at it. We were taken out from the back door. We ducked into our Ambassador car and drove off. Luckily, our driver turned out to be fast and skilled. He knew a parking lot in a quiet housing society and took the car there, and we waited it out in something resembling peace.

You have to sometimes trust a higher power. There was a phase when I took my grandson Hriman to the Sea Lounge at the Taj or to the Oberoi lobby every evening for a snack. I would have coffee and we would talk about his day. Hriman loved the red piano in the lobby of the Oberoi. In November 2008, we probably went there on 22, 23, 24 and 25. On 26 November, we didn't go. That evening, terrorists destroyed both hotels. Among the dead were many people I knew. And it could easily have been us. How does one explain that? Is it providence, good karma or just plain luck?

If there is a higher power, it is possible it will be kinder to you if you do your duty well. In my case, it means treating even those with a criminal background as humans. When I was on the medical board of Air India, I once got a message from Her Majesty's Prison in London. A patient who had benefitted from my treatment of a skin problem in the past was in their custody. His infection had recurred, so the prison asked me if I could send his medicine.

I was impressed by the kindness shown by the prison authorities. They had taken the trouble to find out who had treated the prisoner three years ago and had gotten in touch with me. I sent the medicine for free by courier, because I thought that if they can be so nice to him let me help him as well.

Another time, an elderly lady came to see me in Mumbai. I examined her and gave her medicine. Before leaving, she showed me a newspaper from the Middle East which had my picture and maybe an interview along with it. 'My son lives in Dubai and he asked me to see you. He said you are a good doctor.'

I thanked her for coming to see me and got on with my work. Later, somebody from the clinic told me that the lady had come in a fancy car. And her Dubai-based son was the most famous underworld don in India. Be that as it may, my job was to help my patient, and that is something I have always been clear about. Come bullets, fire, blood or a gangster's kin, I was oath-bound to do my duty.

30

Success Is Fleeting

On the morning of 11 September 2001, hundreds of people working in the World Trade Center in New York probably left their homes casually saying to their family members, 'See you in the evening.' Probably some of them did not even glance back at their homes. They were going to be back in a few hours anyway, right?

They never came back home. The hurried cup of coffee they had with their spouses in the morning turned out to be their last. Their casual tousling of their kids' hair as they walked out of the door was the last time they touched their angels. In just about two hours, these people were going to suffer a horrifying death.

Coronavirus has turned out to be just as catastrophic. Like 9/11, it has killed thousands of people for no fault of theirs. It has taken away jobs. It has taken away life as we knew it. Simple pleasures such as going to a restaurant or a movie have disappeared from our lives. The virus has been a leveller too. Rich or poor, you have to be indoors and do your own laundry.

The lesson from both tragedies is clear. Life is unpredictable. Don't take anything or anyone for granted. Value what you have. You may not have it tomorrow. Or you may not exist tomorrow.

I'm not saying anything new, but it baffles me that people still do not understand this fundamental truth. In my own career I have seen fortunes turn for better and worse. A dancing star, one of the highest-paid heroines of her time, whose songs get people tapping their feet even today, was my patient.

Our home was a hangout for her and her group of friends. Between me, Nalini and them, there would be silly jokes and banter over home-cooked Punjabi food. Producers who knew that she and other actors were my patients would plead with me, '*Mera set laga hua hai, sir. Madam ko please aane ko boliye. Aap bologe to maan jayengi.* (My set is already ready, sir. Please tell madam to come. If you tell her to, she will agree.)'

The industry was so star-centric at that time. It is so even today, but it is a far more collaborative and professional place. It was a time of excess in Bollywood. People wore shimmering clothes and drove big cars. If you were a movie star, you had to look the part. Today's actors earn much more than their predecessors, but they are guarded. Gloss is reserved for the red carpet.

Many stars during those days flaunted their power. On festivals they distributed goodies to poor people. Often, they held soirees which ended with an impromptu mehfil with performances from a maestro or two in attendance. I have enjoyed listening to Mehdi Hassan, Jagjit Singh and Reshma live in the homes of many stars. Some of these stars in the later years after losing their popularity and money now live a very simple life. Their homes were once a scene of boisterous merrymaking. But now the music has died.

Napolean is believed to have said, 'Do you know what is more hard to bear than the reverses of fortune? It is the baseness, the hideous ingratitude, of man.' I have seen both during my career. I have known people who, after just a little success, looked through me. I have known people whose lives turned, careening out of control due to bad luck, bad planning, arrogance or a combination of factors.

There was once a heartbreaking encounter with the family of K.L. Saigal. His daughter came to see me. While talking to her it came to light that the brood of the first superstar of Indian cinema was living in a one-room apartment in Thane. Saigal was the pillar of the movie business at one point. He was an actor and a pioneering vocalist. Legendary singers that followed him—including Mohammad Rafi, Mukesh and Kishore Kumar—learnt their ropes from Saigal's music. And now his family was reduced to living in a one room on the outskirts of Mumbai.

Equally sobering was a meeting with a descendant of Bahadur Shah Zafar, the last Mughal emperor of India. He came to me for treatment, but said he had no money. I treated him free of cost. But I was shaken. This was Bahadur Shah Zafar's family, just two generations removed from a man who technically ruled India.

It is true that the decline of the Mughal empire had started even when the Shah sat on the throne. He himself died in exile in Burma. His heart bled at not finding a final resting place in his homeland, leading him to reportedly write the famous couplet, '*Kitna hai badnaseeb Zafar, dafn keliye, do gaz zameen bhi na mili koo-e-yaar mein.*' It roughly translates as, 'How unfortunate is Zafar. For his burial, even two yards of ground was not to be had, in the land of the beloved.'

If destitution and loneliness could befall the emperor of India, and his descendants, nothing in life can be permanent.

31

'Achche Din' for Homeopathy

Few things are as heartwarming as collaborating formally or informally with an old friend. These are relationships soaked in the warm brandy of nostalgia and goodwill. And unless you are direct competitors, it's a pleasure to reconnect.

In the 2000s, we were setting up our second clinic in Gujarat, in Ahmedabad's Ellis Bridge neighbourhood. Two old friends of mine played a very important role in this chapter in our story. One was the architect Karan Grover, my Campion classmate, who lovingly designed the six-room clinic. Karan was based in Vadodara and would travel to Ahmedabad for the work. The other was the chirpy Mohini Bhullar, my patient and at that time the marketing director of *India Today*. Mohini helped me invite Narendra Modi for the launch. Modiji was then the Chief Minister of Gujarat.

Karan used fine yet responsible materials in the aesthetics of the clinic. Many things were shaped by hand. For example, local tiles were etched into door knobs. As a result, it took a while for the space to be ready. I didn't mind that. I wanted it to be a stunner, an experience to savour for staff and patients.

In the meantime, we were thinking about whom to invite as chief guest. One day, Mohini asked me, 'Do you want Narendra Modi to come?'

Mohini and I went back many years. In the 1980s, she was with *Bombay* magazine, which had featured me on their cover. She trusted me enough to ask me for investment advice. I'm also friends with her daughter-in-law, the food writer Rashmi Uday Singh. So when we were opening in Gujarat Mohini asked me, 'Is there anything I can do for you?'

I declined, saying, 'Thanks. But don't worry, it's all set.'

And then she asked about inviting Modiji as chief guest.

We were in the habit of pulling each other's leg. I thought she was joking when she suggested Modiji.

'I'm serious,' she said. 'No promises. But I will try.'

'Fair enough,' I said.

Even then, I knew it was a long shot. Modiji was the Chief Minister after all, with maybe no free days for months. So it's not like I was anxiously checking my phone. Nonetheless, I did not have to wait long for an update. Mohini called and passed on the number of a local journalist, who, she said, would coordinate with me.

'He will be in touch with you about possible dates,' Mohini said.

I still did not get my hopes up. Whenever something exciting seems likely but is not 100 per cent certain, and I am suspended in-between, I remind myself of the Gita's principle. Do your duty. Do not expect returns. As an entrepreneur always aim for the sky and try your best. Don't be disappointed if things don't go your way. Another example of this mindset can be found in the lines of Rudyard Kipling's, 'If': 'If you can meet with Triumph and Disaster/and treat those two impostors just the same'.

Then one day, the journalist called me. 'Saab (Modiji) wants to come on this particular day,' he said mentioning a date.

'That's fine by me,' I said.

Looking back, it seems incredible that a couple of phone calls and a few days was all it took to organize the visit of a man who, even then, was one of the nation's busiest and powerful leaders.

The day of the opening, the clinic looked spick and span. White-backed chairs were arranged in neat rows. Bright marigold garlands hung on door frames, imbuing the air-conditioned air with their scent. Modiji arrived on the dot, wearing a white kurta. His beard was more pepper than salt. He accepted the flowers we presented him and took his seat. The function was held in the reception of the clinic, and the receptionist's desk served as the table for the dignitaries. It was an informal event with more media than guests. Ahmedabad was a new city for us and we hardly knew anyone there. The presence of about forty journalists was due to the office Modiji held.

We showed Modiji around the clinic. Later, he made a speech. As usual it was extempore. He seemed to have an inherent belief in nature-based medicines. At one point, he took out homeopathic pills from his pocket. 'I take homeopathic medicine. I'm very happy that a good brand is coming to my state,' he said.

After the talk, Modiji patiently answered journalists' questions. He posed for pictures and shook hands with everybody. Unlike most politicians, he didn't make a cursory ten-minute appearance and leave. You may agree or disagree with his views, but there was a certain simplicity about him. His security detail was the only sign of his VVIP status. I still have a photograph with him in the clinic. I'm happy to see that since becoming the Prime Minister, Modiji has done a lot for homeopathy. The Ministry of Ayush is a boost for non-allopathic branches of medicine. It looks like for homeopathy, just as in the case of yoga, '*achche din aa gaye hain* (good days have arrived)'.

32

From One Doctor to Another

People call Dr Manmohan Singh an accidental Prime Minister. I think he prevented India from accidents—political and economic.

I first met Dr Singh, a man who embodies simple living and high thinking, some forty years ago. He was at that time governor of the Reserve Bank of India (RBI). Raghu Raj, the chairman of the Industrial Development Bank of India (IDBI) and later Air India, had suggested Dr Singh see me for treatment. I had a small one-room clinic in Maker Towers. It had a table, a fan and a bench with a rexine cover on which three people could sit. It was a far cry from the team of doctors with state-of-the-art equipment that would be at his service when he later became Prime Minister.

Dr Singh's office was then in Ballard Estate. He found it relatively convenient to see a doctor in Cuffe Parade. So he arrived one day and sat on the bench. There were two other patients there. They probably had no idea they were rubbing shoulders with a future Prime Minister. Even then he wore starched white clothes, a blue turban and black sandals.

Dr Singh was at the RBI from 1982 to 1985, after which he became deputy chairman of the Planning Commission. From there he moved to Geneva, where he was a part of an economic policy think tank.

At the start of the 1990s he returned to India and was made finance minister in the Narasimha Rao government. I sent Dr Singh my congratulations. One day, the governor of Maharashtra, C. Subramaniam, and I were talking about Dr Singh. 'You know, doc,' he said, 'when I was agriculture minister, he was agriculture secretary.' He added they had lost touch since, and seemed wistful about it.

I was to open a specialty clinic in the coming weeks, and thought it would be wonderful to have Subramaniam and Dr Singh, master and protégé, two titans of their fields, for the opening. Subramaniam was happy with the idea, and even offered me the use of Raj Bhavan's lawn and Darbar Hall for the launch. You don't see such magnanimity and absence of self-importance anymore. Today, people with a tenth of the ability of C. Subramaniam or Dr Singh are likely to say, 'Do you know who I am?'

Dr Singh agreed to come for the inauguration. He had just about taken over as finance minister and was the talk of the nation. Everyone wanted to felicitate him, not in the least his party cadres. So when he came to Mumbai for the inauguration of the clinic, his colleagues were upset. Politics is about egos and protocol. Party members felt slighted that he'd ignored their entreaties but had graced a private function.

The media wanted to know why he was flying all the way to see a doctor—was he sick? Any news of the health of the finance minister was bound to have an impact on the stock market. Dr Singh was above the pettiness and pretensions of political traditions. Instead, he was happy to meet his old boss, Subramaniam.

The ribbon cutting took place at the clinic in Chowpatty, and was telecast live to the guests assembled at Raj Bhavan. Then Dr Singh and Governor Subramaniam, along with some other dignitaries, and I headed to Raj Bhavan. There were some 1200 people there, spread across the resplendent Darbar Hall and the lawns that were bathed in the softening light of the tea hour. Deepak Parekh was among the guests. He was overjoyed to meet Dr Singh. Speaking warmly about homeopathy, Dr Singh said that he had been greatly helped by it.

A touching as well as amusing mini event then took place. Sculptor Vinay Wagh presented a bust of me in gratitude for saving his diabetic mother's leg from amputation. It was a surprise, hence it was not on the agenda for the evening. None of us knew exactly what to do. Out of politeness, the governor and Dr Singh jointly unveiled it. I ended up getting some flak. Apparently, living people in India are not supposed to have busts. Also, I used to have a moustache then, which, in a sculpture, can make a person look much older. So a lot of people thought the bust was my father's. I now carry it with me on dates. I'm kidding.

Through the years I have stayed in touch with Dr Singh, though he became extremely busy once he got caught up in the hurly-burly of Delhi politics—whether as finance minister, leader of the opposition, or as Prime Minister. He inaugurated my Delhi clinic in Panchsheel and agreed to be the chief guest at a workshop on stress and homeopathy. On that occasion, he spoke warmly about me and my treatment of him, and said, 'I had severe arthritis; I could barely move my fingers. With Dr Batra's treatment, I recovered. I'm grateful to him.'

On another occasion, Dr Singh cut a cake and launched our foundation—Dr Batra's® Foundation—at the Panchsheel clinic. Robert Vadra was also there. I remember him saying to me, 'He is a good man. We have given the country a good PM.'

Dr Singh's wife Gurcharan, who was called Lady PM at home, and their daughters and grandchildren have consulted me at the

Panchsheel clinic. Despite their status, Mrs Singh would drive herself in a simple red Maruti. If at all Dr Singh needed medicines during his days as Prime Minister, I'd go to his residence.

I could never give him any medication directly. I had to go discuss it with his team of doctors. Of course, I had to maintain patient confidentiality, an important aspect of a doctor's responsibilities. Whenever I met Dr Singh, I was very careful to not mention a word out of place to anyone else. Even slight worry about the premier's health had the capacity to impact the stability of the country. But once inside Dr Singh's book-lined drawing room, he was the same man, sans hubris, and keener to listen than talk. We'd have a cup of tea and he'd ask me, or I think any guest, what could be done to improve things in India. I did give him a couple of suggestions.

'Sir, if corruption has to be reduced, then face-to-face interactions with government people must be done away with,' I once told him. 'With computerization, there are less chances of corruption.' Another time, I told him that the 40 per cent import duty on raw materials for homeopathic medicines was too high. 'If quality medicines are needed in India, and homeopathy has to be promoted, the import duty needs to be reduced,' I said.

In the next budget, the duty was brought down to 25 per cent. I don't know whether he took my suggestion seriously or whether it was a policy decision by the government to lower our tariffs.

The last time I met Dr Singh was when I paid him a courtesy call at home, post prime ministership. We had tea. He asked after my wife and children.

I feel power keeps people young. But Dr Singh wasn't someone to derive a high from power. He seemed to have aged.

I asked him what he planned to do.

'I'm going to give lectures and I'm going back to academics,' he said.

I soon took Dr Singh's leave. He walked me to the door, said goodbye to me with a namaste and waited till I got into the car.

The vehicle started, and as it reached the end of the driveway, I craned my neck to look back towards the ex-PM's house. Dr Singh was there, looking in the direction of my car, his hands still folded.

33

With Values in Common, Partnerships Work

THERE IS A TERM CALLED 'NERVOUS NINETIES' IN CRICKET. IT describes a batsman who has crossed ninety runs, and is nervous because he is approaching the one-century milestone. In my case, the nineties, by which I mean the decade of the 1990s, were not nervous. Certainly not when they started. I was loan-free. The money I had borrowed for Positive Health Clinic at the anything-but-positive 36 per cent rate of interest, had been repaid. I could breathe easy. I was doing well and henceforth, I could simply enjoy my practice and my family, and provide all of us with a good lifestyle. No more adventures.

But when another opportunity for growth came along I took it, even though it meant plunging again into the stormy seas of finances, paperwork, hectic travelling and stress. I could not help it. The insults and patronizing attitude of people when they found out I was a homeopath still stung. I wanted to conquer. I was like a bull in an arnica shop.

Interestingly, this opportunity was in the form of a possible tie-up with Bioforce, the natural medicine giant from Switzerland, headed by the renowned Dr Alfred Vogel. From my Swiss chalet-style clinic in Chowpatty, I could now get a taste of actual Switzerland and its ways.

It all started when one of my patients, a businessman, asked me a pertinent question. 'Dr Batra, your practice is growing, but you get your medicines from elsewhere. Why don't you start making your own medicines?'

'It's not easy and I don't have the time to do it,' I replied. 'Do I see patients or do I spend hours making medicines?'

'Let's see if there are any options to collaborate with a respected manufacturer,' he said.

'That's a thought.'

We started our research. An international company with natural products, rather than just a homeopathy manufacturer, was what we were keen on. Bioforce came up on our radar. Vogel had earned fame with his book *The Nature Doctor*, and as a subject of several documentaries on the BBC and European channels.[3] He was over eighty then, but in robust health, skiing, trekking and maintaining a second wife who was younger than his daughter. Though diminutive and soft-spoken, Vogel had a forceful personality. He looked a bit like Einstein, though his hair was neatly combed. Swiss corporate culture decreed that the chairman meet very few people in person. Vogel adhered to this tradition. If he met you, it meant you were doing something right.

Strapping on our metaphorical skis, we embarked on the mission to woo Bioforce and started a correspondence with them. In the meantime, my patient formed a board of six or seven

---

3 Vogel, Alfred (1996), *The Nature Doctor: A Manual of Traditional and Complementary Medicine*, Edinburgh: Mainstream Publishing.

industrialists, including Jasjit Singh of Associated Capsules. And after a few weeks we were called for a meeting to Switzerland. I didn't have much knowledge of formal corporate negotiations, and we requested Singh to come along. He was experienced and in a position to advise us on all manner of things.

As the meeting approached, we flew economy class on Swissair to Zurich. Despite his status, Singh did not grumble about travelling coach class. In fact, as the flight wasn't full when it was time to sleep he lifted the armrests in his row and lay down across three seats. It was humbling to see a big industrialist make the best of the situation. He never complained or threw his weight around. I have seen this with most successful entrepreneurs. The higher they reach, the humbler they get.

The next morning, we met the Bioforce team in a conference room at their factory in Roggwil, near St Gallen. There was fruit and cheese on the table, a small Swiss flag, juices and tea and coffee. Broad beams of sunlight arrowed into the room from large glass windows. When we spoke I sensed a mutual trust and comfort level between us. Also, I had a gut feeling about this alliance. The one thing about deciding a partner, in life or in business, is to listen to your instincts. My gut told me that Bioforce was the right partner. Like Positive Health Clinic, it was family-owned and stood by the strong value systems of honesty and transparency. It is easy to work with partners where values are aligned.

On my first visit, I learnt an important lesson in Switzerland. Every document of consequence was countersigned by two people. Just one person did not have absolute authority. If the chairman signed, so did the managing director (MD) or joint MD. Two people took responsibility in the company.

Six months later their lawyer, who was also the lawyer to the Swiss Prime Minister, cleared the legal documents. The documents were now ready for signing by both companies. I was teaching in London and took a flight from London to Zurich. Both sides signed on the dotted line over a lunch of raclette, potatoes and salad.

The Bioforce delegates had arranged a dinner later with none other than the boss, Dr Vogel. But I had not been informed about the plan and so I said, 'I mean no disrespect, but you didn't tell me dinner with Dr Vogel was on the agenda. I have to go back because I have lectures to deliver to students.' My hosts were shocked.

'You are the first guy refusing to meet our chairman when you should be actually grabbing the chance,' one of them told me.

I also did not use the opportunity for sightseeing. This surprised the Swiss too, and also earned me their respect. 'You are the first international guy coming to Switzerland for a business meeting and going back without asking us to arrange a tour,' somebody said.

So without any champagne popping or show-sha, I did the boring but right thing of flying back to London. And then the sense of accomplishment really sank in. It wasn't just that we had a deal, but there was a good feeling between the two companies.

I felt happy and excited after the deal came through. We had shaped it with our own hands, starting from the first email sent to Bioforce. And now we were in business with one of the world's most respected names in medicine, a company that used only natural and quality ingredients.

As I slept that night, the images of the snow-capped Swiss mountains that had surrounded me just a few hours earlier appeared in my mind. And with it the song '*Yeh kahan aa gaye hum, yun hi saath saath chalte*' (Where have we reached, walking along together) from the 1981 film *Silsila*.

34

Overcoming Challenges

On a rare free day during a work trip to Switzerland, I boarded a large-windowed train at Zurich to go to Zermatt. I wanted to see Mount Matterhorn, and Zermatt presents some of the best vantages to do that. The conditions were blustery. After the train ride, I walked from Zermatt station, hands in my pockets, foggy, condensed breath blowing out of my mouth, to a small square. I found an outdoor café and took a seat. After a while, the clouds cleared and I spotted Matterhorn. It is not the tallest of peaks, but because of its hooked summit it is unique and one of the more challenging mountains to climb. According to a 2015 article in the *New York Times*, about a dozen mountaineers die on it every year.

Sipping hot chocolate, I contemplated Matterhorn's regal but ominous bearing. It seemed to say, 'I'm a pretty picture from afar, but come near me at your own risk.'

Starting a company is a bit like that. The idea of being at the summit as a boss, of making a difference, and of course the monetary possibilities, are all seductive. It is only when you strap on the boots and the air becomes thin that you realize the enormity of your task.

Christened Holistic Remedies Pvt. Ltd, our collaboration with Bioforce was technical and financial. Continuing with the mountaineering metaphor, both sides were on the climb together, helping each other with ropes and tents and supplies. However, we were the majority owners. Between me, our directors and the few shareholders we got on board, we owned 76 per cent of the company. Bioforce owned the remaining 24 per cent.

Holistic Remedies needed a lot of financial nourishment to grow and find its feet. It needed my attention and energy. For a long time, all the money that I earned in my practice went into the new project. The expenses kept increasing, as invariably happens in a new operation. One of the ironies of entrepreneurship is that growth is good but expensive, as it entails greater labour and infrastructure costs. Fortunately, we had a small place near Vicky Restaurant in Byculla, a world removed from Bioforce's headquarters in scenic Roggwil. We set up a manufacturing unit there along with a small office. During this period I would go to my clinic in the morning, visit the factory a couple of hours in the afternoon and come back to the clinic. I was a hamster running on two wheels.

And so, despite having worked close to two decades and making a name for myself, we lived frugally. Maybe better than earlier, but not to the point where our lifestyle was lavish. As I mentioned earlier, I followed the Raj Kapoor model. It was '*aar ya paar*', i.e., nothing half-hearted. If I took up something, I poured everything into it, even when at times the situation got to me.

If you are becoming an entrepreneur, be prepared for surprises and course corrections. It is the nature of the beast. Unexpected problems or new realizations will happen. You can never be 100 per cent prepared for all eventualities.

I set up my own manufacturing, despite having rejected the idea earlier, because the valuation of the rupee against the Swiss Franc kept changing, mostly for the worse. Our margins reduced. Secondly, the medicines were expensive for the Indian market. Thirdly, even if we had a letter of credit from Bioforce for six months, we didn't want to delay payments as then it would become a liability due to interest. All in all, if in six months you had not sold all the goods, then you were in trouble. That did happen quite a few times, forcing us to further spend out of our pockets, request Roggwil for time, or worse, borrow from friends.

Determined to stay the course, we invested in another property outside Mumbai where we could manufacture medicines. Again, it called for spending on land, labour and machinery. I personally started marketing and selling the medicines to doctors around the country, convincing them about their merits, briefcase in hand. I did not have enough money to hire sales representatives. I might have been the chairman but I was also the everything-else man.

The experience was a great learning experience and it helped me when I set up my personal care company many years later.

There is another important lesson when starting something of your own. Relationships can sour, as the lure of money is such that even those you trust may stab you in the back. At our new factory, a friend and investor I had appointed as the MD started treating the space as his personal fiefdom and neglected his duties. I had to have a frank, unpleasant chat with him. He had to leave. But he wouldn't budge so easily. In return, he demanded not just his initial investment but the equivalent of a percentage of the company. It took over a year of arguments and negotiations before he left. My wife then took over as the MD, having to go to the plant every afternoon after her morning practice. We had further spread ourselves too thin.

Luckily, dealing with the people at Bioforce was always pleasant. They were honest and professional. And they were great hosts. Every year, there would be conferences in Burgenstock, or some of the most beautiful places in Switzerland. I would present my clinical findings of their products, because they didn't have too many doctors of their own. They appreciated my inputs and showed their gratitude with thoughtful gestures and warm hospitality.

Our marriage to Bioforce was a three-part affair. We began with importing finished products in their original packing, but that turned out to be too expensive for a price-sensitive market like India, and we couldn't sustain it. We decided to bring products in bulk and repack in India. This reduced the price somewhat, but was still too high to be feasible. Finally, we decided upon a technical and financial collaboration which would allow us to manufacture in India. This reduced our dependency on our international partner and brought costs down.

The moral of the story? Marriages may be made in Switzerland, but you have to work on them if you want a happily ever after.

I had a wonderful relationship with Bioforce. After about a decade, though, I had to choose between my practice and Holistic Remedies. I couldn't run on two wheels any more. I handed over the control of the collaboration to my wife and younger son Pranav and stepped down from my roles. Despite the rough patches and the stress it caused, I cherish the experience. It took ten years to build that brand and by the time it was done, it felt wonderful to have made quality homeopathy medicines available in India.

35

Swiss Cow Bells to Beeping Heart Monitor

Bad news hits you in the unlikeliest of places. It's not like in poorly made movies, where ominous-sounding music and bleak visuals precede something terrible, giving the plot away. In real life, you could be in Disneyland eating ice cream when tragedy strikes.

In the 1990s, a topsy-turvy decade for me, I was in Switzerland, on one of my visits to Bioforce. It was a Sunday, and I was on a trek-cum-climb in Mürren, enjoying the pleasure that comes from exercise, clean air and beautiful sights all around. It was a clear day, and the sun felt hot and proximate due to Mürren's altitude (5374 feet). High altitude causes greater exposure to ultraviolet (UV) rays. I was fortified with sunscreen and sunglasses and was sipping water. Some members of the Bioforce unit were there with me.

I was forty-seven years old. When we had walked and climbed a fair amount, I started sweating. A lot. Breathing became harder. I knew this was not a good sign and turned right back. A couple of my companions came along with me. I was given preliminary care, enough to avert immediate danger and allow me to fly back to India. But while performing tasks like carrying luggage, my chest continued to pain.

After check-in at Zurich airport, I sat in the waiting area and looked around. The sight of brightly lit and buzzing shops lifted my mood a bit. I bought a few things for home from the duty-free shop and had coffee at a café. Whatever the future had in store, I thought I should live in the moment and make the most of these little pleasures of life. Who knows when I'd get the opportunity to have an authentic plumpricot cake again?

On the flight, I calmly analysed the situation, writing down points in my black diary, even as I told the stewardess without looking up, 'No dear, I don't want champagne.' I made a note of my family's history of heart trouble. Two of my uncles had died from heart attacks. One of them had been a pilot and had a Swiss wife, coincidentally. The other was Ram Batra, the builder and philanthropist. My father and mother both had cardiac issues. What's more, I was working round the clock, always on the move, managing clinics, treating patients and at the same time dealing with some challenging personal matters. I was ripe for a major health blow.

For the moment, thinking things through made me feel better. I felt in control. I would stay optimistic, I decided.

Once in Mumbai, I got things investigated thoroughly at Breach Candy Hospital. From the splendour of Switzerland and nature I was surrounded by tubes, beeping machines and nurses in sombre blue robes. The diagnosis was not good. I had angina, and my main artery was 99 per cent blocked. One per cent more and I would have died. The doctors did not want to take a risk and did an angioplasty. I felt better and gradually got back to my regular life.

Within a year, though, the symptoms returned. I would barely be able to walk half a kilometre without sweating a bucket. This time around, I was seriously worried, and sought counsel from the very best. I went to Dr Nitu Mandke, the eminent heart surgeon (who passed away in 2003). I chose him not just because of his fame, but also because he was known to be quick in the operation theatre, which reduced the patient's bleeding and the amount of time they spent on the heart–lung machine. Besides, he had operated on Balasaheb Thackeray. If his hands could stay steady under that kind of pressure, he was somebody you could trust your life with.

We did another angiography. It revealed a dire condition. The main artery was nearly blocked again and I now had five blockages compared to one just a year ago. My collaterals were blocked, along with arteries. Dr Mandke didn't sugarcoat his words. 'You have to get operated now. You can't wait,' he said.

I discussed matters with my family and we chose a date. Nalini was very supportive. It's not easy when your husband is going for a multiple bypass surgery at forty-seven. You don't expect it at that age. Suddenly you have to swing into action and shoulder extra responsibilities. You have to drop the grudges and connect to each other on a human level. I remember on one of those days we sat together listening to Mukesh and Hemant da songs, crying and laughing. Nalini and I are no longer together, we are divorced, but in one of the toughest moments of my life she stood by me not like a rock, but like a person.

With surgery only a few days away, I wanted to wrap up as much work as possible. I gave my patients medicines for one month. Even the day I was admitted to hospital I went to the clinic and then in the evening got into a cab and went to Breach Candy Hospital alone. My family joined me later. I stayed as strong as I could. In fact, I told myself, 'If God has given me the opportunity of knowing that my heart needs care, he must be wanting me to heal it and live.'

At 6.30 the next morning, they took me into the operation theatre (no popcorn allowed). The surgery lasted six and a half hours, almost the duration of a one-day international cricket match. Those days, surgeries were not microscopic as they are now. They literally sawed through my ribs, took my heart out and kept it in the heart–lung machine. Then they fixed it and stitched it back in. I have the scars on my chest even now.

I drifted in and out of consciousness after the one-day match. But I remember Dr Mandke coming at 3 a.m. to check on me. And just when I had fallen into a deep sleep a nurse would wake me, ask if I was sleeping well and leave. That's a type of an ironical nurse joke.

Some days later, I heard the magic word—'discharge'. It felt like liberation as well as a rebirth. The stitches hurt. It was painful to cough or talk. But I had come through the battle and was going home.

For a few weeks, I had a nurse through the day and night. After complete rest at home for about a month, I started going to the clinic for a few hours. Post-lunch, the nurse would take me to the clinic and help me along the stairs to my den on the mezzanine floor. She would settle me in my beloved black chair, and I would see patients for about three hours. The nurse would bring me back home. After some rest, we would walk a bit in the building. And then I would go home again and relax by watching TV.

Three months after my operation, I felt quite healthy and confident and asked Dr Mandke if I could start travelling. I wanted to open a clinic in London and have the actress Reena Roy inaugurate it. Dr Mandke gave me the go-ahead. After that, I did not look back.

I don't have an artery on my left arm. My pulse can only be checked on the right. One of my mammary arteries was removed and some of the veins in my legs are gone. I have scars from top to bottom. But I'm still standing. I cheated death when I was prevented from falling off a balcony as a baby, and a few years later I emerged unscathed in a stampede at the Kumbh Mela. Much later I cheated death in Ladakh during a photography expedition, when, due to high-altitude pulmonary oedema, I lay on the floor struggling for breath. And now I had cheated it with bypass surgery.

After this experience, I thought about what I wanted to leave behind, and decided to work intelligently and towards a legacy that would live on for several years. I set up a new company, and the rest is history.

I also changed my diet and lost 13 kilos. I turned vegetarian and started walking every day. But I don't give in to paranoia. Unlike many heart patients, I don't carry sorbitrate. You either live in fear or you live with confidence. There is nothing in between.

There was one last thing to do. Three or four years after my bypass, I went back to the same mountain in Mürren. I climbed it without much of a problem, and conquered more than a peak.

36

Branching Out

'IT'S A FATHER'S DUTY TO GIVE HIS SONS A FINE CHANCE,' SAID THE author Mary Ann Evans, a.k.a. George Eliot. In the Mahabharata, when a yaksha asks Yudhisthir what's higher than the sky, he replies, 'The father.'

Becoming a father is the final rung a man climbs on the ladder of adulthood. It is a rewarding experience, but brings with it complex responsibilities that are not always apparent to you. They go beyond obvious duties like providing for the children and nursing them. Fathers have such a strong influence on their progeny that almost everything they do affects their young ones directly or indirectly. They have to be very careful what they say or do in the presence of their kids.

How good I am as a father is not for me to say here. But I tried to do my best. In 1996, when Akshay was on the verge of becoming a homeopath, I did what Mary Ann Evans advised. Wanting my son to have the best possible start to his career, I built a state-of-the-art clinic with rare green marble and all the bells and whistles for him in Bengaluru. Our first clinic outside Mumbai evolved out of a need and was not part of a business plan.

We chose Bengaluru over Mumbai for a few reasons. I could not afford to buy a clinic for him in Mumbai. Meanwhile, my younger brother Rakesh had become a realtor in Bengaluru and I could trust him to give me the best suggestions and rates. I had my parents and other family members there too. In case there was a situation, Akshay would have someone to reach out to. Last, but not the least, I did not want him to sit with me in my clinics in Mumbai. I wanted him to learn the ropes himself and become independent. You may call it tough love. That said, I did not spare any effort on setting him up in Bengaluru. A part of me also wanted to make up for not being able to buy property for him in Mumbai.

Whenever you are entering a new city, make sure that your first outlet stands out. The clinic was originally a three-bedroom flat on the ground floor. It was huge. And a garden outside with a small waterfall provided a nice touch. As the place was coming up, I would fly to Bengaluru every weekend and look at every little detail, from the marble to the medical equipment to the coffee cups. And then it was ready to be unveiled.

I invited the right people for the launch so as to generate good word of mouth. Our launch was a gala evening, attended by Bengaluru's finest, thanks in part to my brother's connections. The governor of Karnataka, Khurshed Alam Khan, was there. He and his wife Saeeda are parents of the politician Salman Khurshid. Saeeda's father was Dr Zakir Husain, India's first Muslim president.

Khurshed Alam Khan and Shatrughan Sinha cut the red ribbon. The police commissioner was also present. There were lots of people from the builder community as well. White-gloved waiters from the Taj glided around guests, serving food and drinks (no alcohol). If you find this all a bit filmi, I can understand. But we were on a roll and we wanted to do things in a big way.

The people and media of Bengaluru had not seen this type of excitement around a homeopathy clinic. At that time, most homeopaths worked out of small rooms with barely one desk. Here was a spacious clinic, the opening of which had drawn out the A-listers from their bungalows and fancy cars. Along with style, the clinic had substance too. I had transferred one of our experienced Mumbai doctors there. In addition, we hired some young doctors. There were comfortable waiting areas for patients where they would be served tea and coffee. For VIP patients, there was a separate lounge.

Every room had a computer that had the data of all patients. And I could monitor it all in real time sitting in Mumbai, even though I was spending ten days a month in Bengaluru anyway. In spite of my physical presence and prominence, patients would ask, 'You may be famous in Mumbai but who have you treated in Bengaluru?' But I persevered and the efforts paid off. By 1998, we were seeing over 300 patients a day and had registered a monthly turnover of around Rs 50 lakh, which was higher than that of one of the top private hospital's at that time.

My presence for only ten days each month in Bengaluru led to a problem. Due to my television and print media presence, many patients only wanted to see me. I could not extricate myself from the clinic. Nor did I want to, I admit. The competitive juices and professional zeal kicked in. This was our first venture out of Mumbai. We had gotten it off to a good start. I wanted to build on it. Akshay stayed back in Mumbai. He was happy to be with family.

We were in for a surprise one day when a bald, elderly man with a prominent nose and wearing a simple white kurta and lungi walked into the clinic. I noticed him but continued to do my work. The local staff, however, could barely contain themselves. One of them passed me a note with the man's name written on it, 'Rajkumar sir, very big film star.' Of course I knew the name. He was, after all, the 'Nata Sarvabhouma', the emperor of actors, a versatile screen idol who was not just a lead actor but also a trained musician. But not being in regular touch with Kannada culture, I did not recognize him immediately.

I escorted Rajkumar and his companion to the VIP lounge. He did not speak Hindi or English. But with help from his assistant he told me that he had a film project coming up and he needed treatment for hair and his throat. I was delighted that he had come to me, and we discussed how we could help him.

By now a crowd had gathered outside the clinic. If Amitabh Bachchan comes to your home, you cannot hide it. The same held true for Rajkumar in southern India. When he left, it took a while before his white van could pass safely through the throngs. Over the course of his subsequent visits, we became friendly with each other, speaking in gestures, drinking coffee. I feel a man loosens up more if he has only non-verbal ways to communicate. The treatment was beginning to show results too. His voice returned and he presented me with his latest cassette. He even spent some time with us on his seventieth birthday at the clinic.

And then one day the news came. Dr Rajkumar had been abducted by Veerappan, the notorious sandalwood smuggler and dacoit. Gloom descended upon the clinic. Just a few hours earlier, he had been sitting with us. Ever since he became my patient, the kitchen staff would not use his coffee mug—white with gold trim—for anyone else. They treasured it even more now.

I felt for the man. At this stage in his life, and when he was working towards a return in front of the camera, he shouldn't have to go through such an ordeal. But it is a tribute to Dr Rajkumar's stature that even the ruthless Veerappan treated him with respect and ultimately released him.

Dr Rajkumar never returned to the clinic. But his many visits to one clinic helped us establish eighteen clinics in Bengaluru.

37

Unplanned Expansion

MARRIAGES MAY OR MAY NOT BE MADE IN HEAVEN, BUT SOMETIMES they take you to Vadodara.

An organization's expansion is not always planned. It can just happen. A casual conversation opens up an opportunity and you think, 'Why not?' There are also moments when a new branch comes up because a colleague you have spent time and effort on training has to relocate, but needs to keep the job.

A year after we launched in Bengaluru in 1996, Dr Nandita Desai, one of our doctors in Mumbai, was to get married and move to Vadodara. Her in-laws were a conservative Gujarati family. They were not comfortable with the idea of her working. But they had a good opinion of our company. One day Nandita said to me, 'Sir, my in-laws will never allow me to work unless it's at Dr Batra's®. You started a clinic in Bengaluru. Can you please open one in Vadodara?'

Her need was genuine and I wanted to help her. Moreover, I had spent nearly two years preparing her. Our initiation process was challenging and she had been through it. Almost every new employee, doctors included, had to spend a week or two doing various other tasks such as manning the phone or operating the blister-packing machine.

Doctors did not always like this. They came in with grand visions of jumping straight into their white coats, Superman costume style, and saving lives. But everyone had to go through the drill. The packing machine entailed pulling a hard lever again and again, and female staff found that difficult. But I made them do it. It was my goal for every doctor to at least have basic knowledge of the myriad functions that made the heart of this enterprise tick.

I considered Nandita's request. At the same time, I had no idea how Vadodara would be for us. Besides, Gujarat was a hub of the allopathic medicine industry. Could a homeopathy centre crack such a market? The challenge of it excited me. One thing was certain. If at all we were to take a shot at it, we needed a person in charge who would connect with locals. Nandita's husband was from Vadodara and was a trained manager. I asked him if he could help me run the clinic.

'Yes sir, I will,' he said. And just like that, we planted our flag in Vadodara. It happened almost entirely as a gesture. There was no elaborate planning or market research or surveys. It was almost on the spur of the moment, like a drive with friends to Goa.

We rented a bungalow in the city's Mamta Society. For the opening, we had cricketer Mohinder Amarnath and my lucky mascot, Shatrughan Sinha. Their arrival created a buzz among people and the media. Mohinder was a health freak, one of the fitness pioneers in Indian cricket. He had an informed opinion on the importance of good medicines. Shatru was Shatru, charming all with his distinctly Indian bluster and warmth.

Word spreads fast in a small town. An entrepreneurship located in a residential area and inaugurated by celebrities amidst fanfare and flashing cameras attracted all kinds of attention. One night, the Phase Pardhi tribe broke into the clinic and decamped with cash and valuables. Before leaving, they left us their traditional parting gift by defecating on the floor. Fleeing wasn't in our nature, though. We bought a new place and continued the clinic.

With the extra expenses, I had to cut costs. I had spent a lot on Bengaluru. Besides, my agreement with the doctors in my outstation clinics was that I would pay them not just salaries, but also a percentage of the clinic's turnover. As a result, they'd want me to spend maximum time in their clinic so that their turnover could go up. This may come across as immodest, but the impact of my television shows in smaller cities was even bigger. And if I was visiting a particular clinic, the patients would flock. And who'd take the pressure? Yours truly.

Vadodara was tailor-made for economical travel, which was invaluable to an entrepreneur-owned business. I would work through the day in Mumbai and take a comfortable overnight train from Mumbai Central which reached Vadodara at 5.30 in the morning. I'd go straight to my clinic, shave and shower and see patients the whole day.

In the evening, a Gujarati thali at Express Hotel for dinner was my small indulgence. From there I would go to the station and take the train back to Mumbai, saving the cost of an overnight stay. The train would reach its destination in the morning. I'd go home, shower and go to my clinic in Chowpatty. This is how I lived for some years, saving costs a rupee at a time and funnelling it all back into the business instead of spending on my comfort.

'*Itne hisson mein bat gaya hoon mai, mere hisse me kuch bacha hi nahin* (I have been split into so many parts that there is no part left for me).' These words capture the essence of what I was going through. While business was expanding, I began to feel pulled in all directions. Whether I ran a temperature of 104 or not, was of no concern to my patients as they expected me to be there. I, as a doctor with a conscience, could never let them down. Hence I was almost always working, in some city or the other, bag in hand. I was Willy Loman, but one who wrote out prescriptions.

We entered bigger cities than Vadodara in the years that followed. But Vadodara remains a special memory for me. It's not even the biggest city in Gujarat, yet it has been one of our top grossers in terms of turnover. And the space we bought back then is now a cosy three-storey building in a prime location. This was all unintended. A lot of good came out of our Vadodara foray, and I feel it is because there was an element of humanity in why we went there in the first place.

38

Planned Expansion

THERE WERE TIMES WHEN WE WERE ANALYSING THE EXPANSION OF our brand, I would feel like an army major pointing to a map with a baton and plotting our progress. 'Mumbai, Bengaluru, Vadodara captured. What next?'

New Delhi, of course.

So off we went to the capital in 1998. We bought a place in South Delhi and requested Dr Manmohan Singh to inaugurate it. It was a low-key affair as we did not know too many people in Delhi at that time. In a city that worked on knowing people, we were an anomaly. And in any case, Dr Singh would have been more comfortable at a quiet, personal event. Although years in public life had given him the ability to handle noisy affairs and put pesky guests in their place in his own polite but firm way.

After Delhi, we moved cautiously for the next two to three years, opening just a couple of clinics in new cities every year. We did not want to overinvest or spread ourselves too thin. It was more important to build a reasonable patient base and create good awareness via word of mouth before moving on to a new city. As it is, every new city I went to, people asked me, 'You may have treated hundreds of patients in Mumbai, but how many have you treated in my city?' That was a big learning for me and for anyone who wants to become an entrepreneur. People want to see results in their own city. They want to see their family and friends being cured before they come to you. Till that happens, you are an outsider, not to be trusted. But once the trust is established, word of mouth opens the floodgates. Patients flock to experience something they have not experienced before.

Expansion also necessitated a standardized business and clinic model that could be replicated with precision and speed. I quickly assembled a strong operations team to put together protocols. This comprised technology, the look and feel of the brand, standardization in medicine, training, treatment method and comprehensive localized marketing.

Initially, I would travel to every new clinic. Like a mother hen clucks over her chicks, my love for my work would make me hover around the site, making sure that every nail was in the right place. With the prototype tried and tested, no matter where we were based, our clinics would all look and feel the same, just like any McDonald's or Tim Hortons across the world.

The next challenge was to bring standardization to the quality of medicines that we prescribed for our patients across multiple locations. Through our collaboration with Bioforce (the Swiss company), we guaranteed the highest quality and effectiveness of the medicines. We also procured sealed glass bottles to ensure that the integrity of the medicinal properties remained intact, contamination-free and untouched by hand.

The front-desk staff was next on the list. These were the people that the customers met first. They provided the first impression of the brand. Then there were doctors, the most important pieces of the puzzle. To give our patients the best experience, we needed to first find the best fit when it came to people and then ensure that they were the personification of the brand, through training.

To create an aspirational brand, investing in people is vital. In the initial days of setting up the practice, we would have new doctors and staff flown in to Mumbai for a training course. Today, thanks to technology, we have an online induction and training module that every employee has to undertake. Additionally at Dr Batra's®, all new doctors undergo at least 500 hours of continued medical education (CME). Tenured doctors undergo at least 100 hours annually.

In India, while physicians had academic knowledge, clinical knowledge and consistency in practice varied from doctor to doctor. We therefore created a training model that consisted of real-life examples from my over forty-five years of medical practice. For each patient at any given time there are over 98,000 treatment permutations and combinations. To streamline our practice across varying geographies, we also built a computerized repository of these 98,000 treatments that helped all our doctors derive optimal solutions for their patients.

In addition to this, our state-of-the-art clinical management system (CMS) made sure that a doctor needed to complete a standardized format to be able to treat a patient. For example, if a female patient came for hair-loss treatment, the system would not allow the doctor to continue the consultation without the analysis of a ferritin (iron) test.

After standardizing our procurement, training and prototype, the most vital component of entering bigger cities became investing our capital correctly.

Our first clinic in each new metro was a one-of-a-kind clinic in the city. For example, one of our first clinics in Bengaluru was an independent three-storeyed structure, while another had a bungalow with a fountain and garden. One of our clinics is even situated on a high street in London.

We also learned through experience that in order to expand, taking risks is par for the course. And while investing in real estate is a huge risk, the learning that comes from it stays with you. For instance, when we opened our clinic opposite the Sahara Mall in Gurgaon, we thought that it would be highly profitable as the footfalls were extremely high. But we soon realized that many people were walking into the mall only to find respite from the heat of the sun as the mall was air-conditioned.

First impressions are also key, and brand recall plays an important part in ensuring success in market penetration. We therefore consciously sought locations that were in high-street areas while still being accessible and convenient.

Unlike retail endeavours—like restaurants, salons or shopping—that give people instant gratification, medicine, especially for chronic ailments, often takes time to yield benefits and therefore one might not see entrepreneurial success immediately. We learned that patience not only gets better patient outcomes, but also more consistent and tangible success.

After setting up base in the larger metros and having created the right marketing and procurement mix, penetration of the market was a natural progression. Having established the brand in a specific market, increasing our market size and share by penetrating the suburbs and peripheral locations helped us divide our overheads and marketing costs. Our strategy to increase our reach to people was based on a study that stated most patients will not travel more than 3–5 km for medical assistance. Therefore you will almost always find a Dr Batra's® clinic within walking distance of a major bus, train or metro line.

Delhi, Bengaluru and Mumbai went on to have sixteen to eighteen branches and the other metros six to eight over a period of time. This increased not only our presence but also our visibility in the city. If you drove around a bit you saw at least three to four signboards with our red and blue logo staring back at you.

Around this time, Axis Bank was on an expansion spree and opened one new branch every day for a year. We benchmarked their operations. The closest we came was to open one new clinic every week for six weeks. By then we had prototyped our interiors and had developed local teams to deliver them. Our turnaround time was the fastest in any industry. In four to five weeks from the time we took over the property, the clinic was ready to open. Over the next few years we inaugurated ten to fifteen clinics every year, mostly from internal accruals.

When opening new markets, it was also important to understand and know that each state had different regulations and compliance norms. For us at Dr Batra's® that meant different regulations and norms, both in terms of dispensation of medicines and also in the certification of doctors. That is to say if a doctor has to relocate to another state, they would need to re-register to practise in the new state.

We also learned the hard way what it was like to set up shop during a major state festival. Being ethnically north Indian and professionally a Mumbai boy, when we began to set up a clinic in Kolkata, we went about it as strategically and cerebrally as possible. Everything was planned, everything was in place. Ads had been put out and we were ready for a big bang press launch. What we hadn't factored in was how the city comes to a standstill at the time of Durga Puja.

Looking back on it now, I smile thinking of how we were able to overcome this hurdle. However, at the time it was almost touch and go. While we had almost everything ready for the launch, we didn't have a workforce. From carpenters to painters, to electricians and even the front-line employees, everyone in Kolkata goes on leave during this most religious of holiday weeks.

But as Durga Ma herself triumphed over evil, we too persevered and overcame our hurdles. With a bit of cajoling and a whole lot of teamwork from across other regions we were able to start our first clinic in Kolkata on 18 October 2000, ten days after the biggest festival in Kolkata—Durga Puja.

After we had successfully opened around ten clinics, mainly in the metros, our vision to take homeopathy to every home with Dr Batra's® brand, saw us penetrate tier-2 and tier-3 markets, starting with state capitals. These had their own set of learnings, in terms of both logistics and market intelligence. First on this list was Lucknow. I was keen to provide the city of my birth with good quality homeopathy care.

Our competitor here was not 'Big Pharma' but your local neighbourhood homeopath, who had not only grown up with his patients but was an integral part of the community. And while the local residents were definitely curious about the 'sheheri doctor', they were apprehensive to share their intimate details. Another key learning was that language and culture played an important role in patient experience and it was important for clinic staff to be well versed in both.

For example, one of our success stories was definitely the Chennai market. When we first set up there, we didn't know the language or the culture at all. The people of Chennai were wary of us as outsiders. In homeopathy, the first meeting is a detailed conversation between the doctor and the patient. Even though we faced initial language barriers, our treatment results built trust with the locals.

In smaller markets what also worked for us was our legacy of ensuring the best patient outcomes. State-of-the-art equipment, advanced technology coupled with local marketing in the form of pamphlets, coverage in local vernacular publications, radio channels, outdoor advertising in high footfall areas and, of course, on-ground activities in the local clubs proved to be the ideal marketing mix.

We not only provided our patients with the best treatment outcomes but the best patient experiences helped to create brand affinity and loyalty in these markets and also helped increase the patient base through referrals. A differential pricing strategy keeping the patient's pocket size in mind also helped increase the patient base.

In 2016, when the Brexit question was very much on top of everyone's mind, I told British parliamentarians in my address to the House of Commons that while they had a choice of whether or not to go with Brexit, patients did not have similar free will when it came to something as important as their health; they did not have the freedom to choose alternative forms of treatment.

Through our passion and a vision, we doggedly pursued our goal to take Dr Batra's® to every home and give patients a choice. And as the old adage goes—evolve or die. Our formula might not have always been right, but we were able to drive in the fast lane and take the Dr Batra's® brand from 1 to over 200 clinics in less than twenty years.

23-year-old Dr Batra watches
tently as Mr R.K. Talwar,
ıairman, State Bank of India,
augurates the young physician's
st clinic at Land's End, Malabar
ill, Mumbai, in 1974.

The Positive Health Clinic at Chowpatty, Mumbai, was the world's first computerized homeopathy clinic in 1982. To set it up Dr Batra had to borrow money at a stifling 36% p.a., though he looks cool as a cucumber here.

ominique Lapiere, renowned author of *The City of Joy*, at the release of Dr Batra's book, *Common
ments*, at Raj Bhavan, Mumbai. Lapiere said he was a strong believer of homeopathy as it had helped
eat his cancer.

Shekhar Kapur inaugurating Dr Batra's Cyber Clinic, the world's first homeopathic online consulting website, in 1996. Dr Batra was listed in the *Limca Book of World Records* for two consecutive years for having treated the highest number of patients online.

Dr Batra's® hits a boundary as it launches its e-commerce site at Cyber Clinic at the hands of Sunil Gavaskar in 1998.

. 1996, Dr Batra focused his practice on fourteen disease segments which gave proven results. Icons om different walks of life were present at the launch of the first Super Specialty Homeopathy Clinic Raj Bhavan. (From right): Dr Manmohan Singh, Finance Minister, Dr Batra, C. Subramaniam, overnor of Maharashtra, Shatrughan Sinha, film actor, and Sunil Gavaskar, cricketer. Partly seen . the picture is Dr B.K. Goyal, eminent cardiologist.

culptor Vinay Wagh made a bust of r Batra for saving his mother's leg om amputation with the help of omeopathic medicines.

As a tribute to Dr Batra for treating his medical problems, eminent painter M. F. Husain presented him this drawing. Husain likened Dr Batra to Hanuman possessing a mountain of 'Batra Sanjeevani Booti'. He wrote on the work, 'Mukesh, you are doing great work to keep our people healthy.'

Swiss chocolate? No, thanks. We'll take the medicines! Signing an MOU with Bioforce directors, Mr. Gieger and Mr. Ruf, to bring the esteemed Swiss brand to India (1998).

A group of international doctors attending an advanced homeopathy course by Dr Batra in Santa Monica, Los Angeles,US in the 1990s.

Dr Batra at Dean Martin's studio in LA where he shot short film on homeopathy a course material for student of British Institute of Homeopathy. People always thought Dr Batra would go to Hollywood some day.

Scissors for Shotgun: Shatrughan Sinha inaugurates Dr Batra's Vadodara clinic in 1996.

Few know the importance of fiscal and physical health as much as Dr Manmohan Singh, and few have his quiet dignity. Here he is seen opening Dr Batra's Panchsheel clinic in New Delhi in 1999.

Narendra Modi, Chief Minister of Gujarat, cuts the ribbon on Dr Batra's Ellis Bridge clinic in Ahmedabad. A few years later he would become the Prime Minister of India, and keep encouraging homeopathy.

After several ups and downs, Dr Batra's® first international clinic opened in Mauritius in 1997. Dr Batra helped to legalize homeopathy in the country. He is seen here with Sir Uteem Cassim, President of Mauritius, and the Healt Minister. It was a cloudy day but Dr Batra's shirt reflects his bright mood.

Maharashtra Chief Minister Vilasrao Deshmukh opens Dr Batra's Foundation a the Taj Hotel, Mumbai, on Dr Batra's fiftieth birthday. Deshmukh made a donation from the Chief Minister's Fund to kickstart the foundation, which is the CSR arm of Dr Batra's®

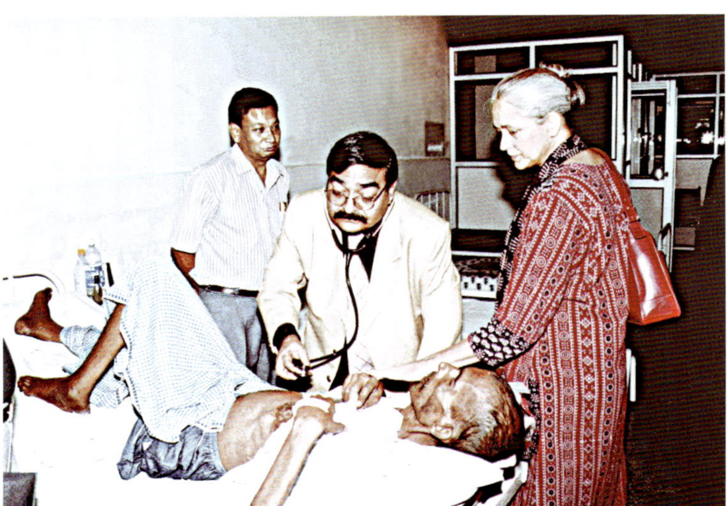

Examining an AIDS patient at Action India, an AIDS centre in New Delhi. The NGO was helped by Dr Batra's® Foundation with free homeopathic medicines Beside Dr Batra is his long-time patient, actre Nafisa Ali. In the 1970s just days before her acting debut, Dr Batra's medicines helped Nafis with her skin problem.

Dr Batra with the kids from Christel House India, Bengaluru. Christel House is a holistic model designed to transform the lives of impoverished children. His foundation treated 500 young patients with free homeopathic medicines. With a healthy body, these children would at least have a fighting chance at life.

The annual Positive Health Awards ceremony, which honours people who have overcome disability and contributed to society, have been an important part of Dr Batra's journey. Well-wishers from the film industry have always spared time for the event. Here we see Aishwarya and Abhishek Bachchan at the tenth edition of the awards function, which was sponsored by Bajaj Discover.

Hrithik Roshan with an awardee at another edition of the Positive Health Awards.

Yaadon ki Bahaar, an annual benefit where Dr Batra sings in aid of an old-age home, is another important event for the company. Here he is on stage crooning some tune while his young-at-heart guests jive to the music.

Photography is Dr Batra's passion, and he has used it to make a difference in the lives of those more deserving Dr Batra has held over fifty exhibitions of his photograph in India and Dubai in aid of the visually challenged and underprivileged children. Here, some school students are seen participating in a painting competition at one of Dr Batra's photography exhibitions. They are given free painting material and ca prizes for participation.

Dr Batra is India's homeopath in more ways than one. Meritorious and disadvantaged students from seven leading homeopathic colleges across India are awarded the Dr Mukesh Batr Scholarship. This moment is from an award ceremony at one of the colleges in Maharashtra.

r Batra's® products, launched in 2004, has a range of over 100 stock keeping units in over 20,000 ıtlets across India. During the Covid-19 outbreak these were reduced to 2,000 outlets, but the rand's online performance became stronger.

Former Indian cricket team captain Anil Kumble launches one of Dr Batra's books in Bengaluru. Dr Batra has written six books on homeopathy, the first being *Every Man's Guide to Homeopathy* (1982). All have been best sellers and as impactful as Kumble's googly.

From his grandfather's Agra *kothi* to Rashtrapati Bhavan. Dr Batra receiving the Padma Shri for Medicine (Homeopathy) from President Pratibha Patil (2012).

Dr Batra explains something to the Mayor of Brent, during the inauguration of Dr Batra's® clinic in London. The company also has a practice at the prestigious Harley Street in the British capital.

Bob Blackman (Conservative MP) and Virendra Sharma (Labour MP) felicitating Dr Batra after he had addressed the All Party Parliamentary Group at the House of Commons, London, in 2017.

Sunanda Pushkar and Dr Shashi Tharoor at the launch of *Homeopathy & You* magazine in Delhi (2013). It ran successfully for five years but had to be shut down.

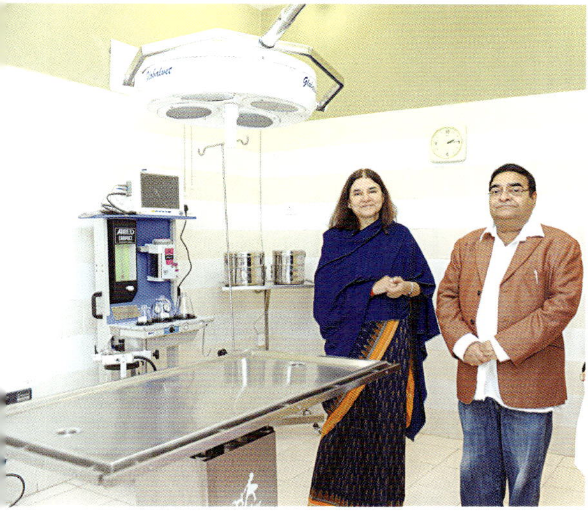

Maneka Gandhi inaugurates a state of the art Dr Batra's® Pet Care Hospital in Yusuf Sarai, New Delhi, in 2014. The centre had an OPD, operation theatre, grooming centre and offered homeopathic treatments and pet products for sale. Dr Batra's® also ran three day-care pet clinics in other parts of the country. After three years, the pet care vertical was closed.

ne luxurious Signature Clinic in Dubai's Al Wasl neighbourhood was an idea ahead of its time. It ıd the best doctors, facilities and décor, but could not be sustained.

r Batra's® Abu Dhabi clinic is the latest ternational clinic, and, as the picture shows, it is spick and span as the one in Al Wasl.

Dr Batra with HH Sheikh Nahyan Bin Mubarak Al Nahyan – Minister of State for Tolerance, UAE.

Signing an MOU with a large Chinese company to launch over 100 Dr Batra's® homeopathy clinics in their existing anti-tumour clinics across China. After the border skirmishes between India and China began, the project fell through.

Some cheer before the gloom. Dr Batra receives the Sheikh Zayed International Award for outstanding service in the field of Homeopathy in Abu Dhabi in 2020, just days before Covid-19 spread across the world.

Maldives president arrives in T'puram on private visit

TIMES NEWS NETWORK

Thiruvananthapuram: The president of Maldives has arrived here on a private visit to the capital. According to sources in the general administration department, Abdulla Yameen Abdul Gayoom, the Maldivian president, has arrived in the capital for medical reasons. He visited two private clinics in the city- Dr Batra's Homoeopathy Clinic at Karamana and Yogiraj Centre for Dermatology and Cosmetology at Pattom on Thursday. He arrived in the morning by an Air India flight from Male and after completing his scheduled appointments, retired for his hotel by late afternoon.

Though his programme was officially informed to the general administration (protocol) department, as is the practice when the head of a state or any other dignitary visits the state, there was no ceremonial welcoming since the election code of conduct is in force. But he has been provided with top security since he is a head of the state and is considered as a distinguished foreigner.

"There is a specific set of guidelines as per the ministry of external affairs which we have followed for the visiting dignitary," government sources said. He will return after his programme on Friday morning. It is learnt that he will be back in the state capital once again later this month for follow-up consultations.

Traffic regulation: In connection with his visit, vehicular traffic on certain city roads will be strictly regulated on Friday from 8.30am to 11am. Regulation will be effective on the roads near Xanadu, Bakery Junction, Underpass, Asan Square, General Hospital, Pattoor, Nalumukku, Pettah, Chackai, Airport and Eanchackal. There will also be a strict ban on parking of vehicles along these roads during the time. Strict action would be taken against those who violate the regulation, the city police authorities said.

Abdulla Yameen Abdul Gayoom on his arrival at the international airport in Thiruvananthapuram

You know the brand is well-known when the president of a country comes a-calling.

Music meets patriotism as Dr Batra sings at an emotional tribute to the heroes of the 26/11 terrorist attacks, organized by the Consular Corps, Mumbai, at the Gateway of India.

39

Challenges of International Entrepreneurship

In the television show *Ozark*, the principal character of Marty Byrde is seconds away from being executed by a drug lord. Death staring him in the face, Byrde, a financial whiz, makes a last-ditch attempt to save his life. He pleads to the don that if spared, he could help him launder millions of dollars. The criminal lets him off.

Marty Byrde thinks on his feet. It's how you need to be in any profession. There will be many occasions when you will have a few seconds to salvage a situation, not more. This ability to think fast, how do you develop it? Some are blessed with it. Others can build it too, through experience, a calm head and by closely watching the people in front of them.

Our first international clinic in Mauritius would not have come to be had I not noticed a skin eruption on the face of a man hollering at me. Not any man, but the vice president of Mauritius, Sir Rabindrah Ghurburrun.

This is how it all unfolded. In 1996, the husband of a beautician who had a nice salon in Quatre Bourne, near Port Louis, asked me if I could start a practice there. After a few months of email exchanges and phone conversations, I agreed to start a franchise, once again sensing an opportunity to spread homeopathy. There was no investment on my part. But I agreed to go to Mauritius for the opening ceremony of the centre. I had seen pictures of the place. It was a tidy flat converted into a clinic.

On the flight to Mauritius, I met an Indian journalist based there. He told me that he knew Vice President Ghurburrun, and that he could try inviting him for the inauguration.

'That would be wonderful,' I said. 'If I can get the vice president for the opening in a country where I don't know anybody, it would make a statement.'

After we reached Port Louis and picked up our luggage, the journalist took me aside and we stood leaning against a glass window. Outside the sky was blue like a swimming pool, and the Moka mountains formed a dark, jagged line on the horizon. To my surprise and awe, the reporter called Ghurburrun and handed me the phone.

Clearing my throat, I introduced myself and said, 'Sir, I would be very grateful if you could inaugurate my clinic.' I told him the day, time and venue. For added measure, I said, 'We could change it around a bit to a day when it is convenient for you to attend.'

From the other end, a booming voice said, 'Very good, very good. Yes, I'll be happy to come. You meet me tomorrow and let's talk about it more.'

Wow. Easy-peasy. Just minutes in a foreign land, my umbilical cord still attached to the plane, and I already had an appointment with the vice president. That does not happen every day. I thanked the journalist and walked out of the airport whistling. On work trips, it's a great feeling when the ball starts rolling right away.

The next day, after a hearty breakfast and fresh coffee, I went to meet Ghurburrun, like Tom Hagen goes to meet the movie producer Jack Woltz in *The Godfather* (1972), right before the famous horse head scene. The vice president had a beautiful house, with the flag of Mauritius fluttering on top. There was a swimming pool. The parking lot had a mix of luxury and security vehicles. Among them was a red Mercedes convertible that I later learnt belonged to his charming daughter.

In contrast to his voice, the man was short, and wore a hat. He welcomed me warmly. We sat on the sofas in his split level, wooden floor drawing room. An attendant brought me coconut water. And I once again explained the purpose of my visit and extended my invitation.

'What exactly is the clinic for?' he asked me with a smile.

'It's a homeopathy clinic.'

When I said those words, he got furious. Nearly a quarter century later, I remember his words.

'Dr Batra! You certainly don't expect the vice president of a country to inaugurate a ROOM.'

The penny dropped in my head. I had used the word 'clinic' when I spoke to him on the phone the previous day. In French Creole, the local language, clinic meant hospital. He was under the impression he would be launching a large healthcare facility befitting his status. And that is why he agreed. But now, Ghurburrun was blasting the life out of me.

'Homeopathy? I'm an eminent lawyer for God's sake,' he thundered. 'I have been a Queen's Counsel. I have practised in London. Homeopathy is not allowed in my country. How can you come here and practise something illegal? And how can you invite me for it?'

I sat there feeling headless, as if my neck had already been chopped off, like the horse in *The Godfather*. Maybe that's why I thought on my feet. And noticed something on the face and neck of the screaming man, who had gone from being vice president to 'voice' president.

With a real fear of spending the night behind bars welling up in me, I mustered up the courage to say to him, 'Sir, since how long have you had this thing, whatever it is?'

The enraged face under the hat looked at me, puzzled. One little question had left him speechless. 'What?' he demanded.

I pointed to the rash-like patches on his face.

'Oh! Forget it. I have had doctors all over the world look at it. Nobody can treat me.'

'May I have a closer look? I believe I can help you.'

Ghurburrun sensed I knew my stuff. And he said to me what very few people other than my wife have. 'Come to the bedroom.'

His guard down, the vice president and I spoke for nearly two hours, the sea sloshing outside the window. We went over his health and personal history. It helped me get to the root of his external problems, which are often a symptom and not the cause. It also helped me drive home my point. 'Sir, I'm not coming into this country to make money. I'm coming here because I want to help your people,' I said. 'I promise you I will not start the clinic till I get the licence, till homeopathy is legalized. But the launch is already set for tomorrow. The media is coming. Please give me a little note of your support.'

He got off the bed and paced around. 'Okay,' he said.

The next day, I met the media and showed them the clinic.

'This is where we are going to start. But only after the government legalizes homeopathy,' I said. 'In the meantime, these are the good wishes from the vice president of the country.'

It was challenging to set up an enterprise in a new country, especially when the vice president almost put you behind bars. Round one to homeopathy.

40

Use Contacts for Success

I HAD MANAGED TO MAKE SOME HEADWAY WITH VICE PRESIDENT Ghurburrun. To get the homeopathy vote passed, however, the Health Minister was the key. But his defences took longer to break. Every time I saw him he'd say, 'Let me think about it. Meet me in two weeks.'

I would fly back to India and return after a fortnight or so. And the scene would replay. Within me, a Sunny Deol was dying to erupt. '*Bas milti hai tareekh pe tareekh pe tareekh!* (All I get is a date upon date upon date!)'

In need of a break after one such meeting, I repaired to the Maritim Resort & Spa for a couple of days. As I sipped juice gazing at the cerulean waters of the Indian Ocean, with 'Macarena' playing on the audio system, one of the hotel managers, a sharp young man from Bangladesh, came up to me for something. We ended up having a conversation, at the end of which I made him a suggestion. If he gave me three rooms for a week free of cost, I would mention the hotel on my show on Zee, which was prime publicity in those years.

The next day, the hotel management agreed. One lesson I had learnt was that the appeal of the television camera could never be underestimated. What also worked to my advantage was that Zee was anyway looking to enter the African continent at that point, and would likely showcase the episode.

Within days I was back in Mauritius, ready to shoot, a three-member television crew in tow. It comprised the director, cameraman and my lady assistant. In Mumbai, she would carry snakes in her purse, probably to throw at perpetrators in the event of harassment on the streets. To our good fortune there were no reptiles in her cargo to Mauritius.

The hotel not only gave us the rooms but also laid on a buffet of aqua-sport activities for us to sample. I'm normally afraid of venturing into water. An astrologer had told my parents that it was dangerous for me, and it played on my mind a bit. I couldn't swim either. But here was a chance for me to look like David Hasselhoff on pristine blue waters. So I waded in. I even did scuba diving, which at one point had been unthinkable for me.

Next, I went to see the Health Minister with a different approach. I offered to organize a free health camp, to be inaugurated by the minister and covered by the media. He agreed.

We got another break when, one Sunday morning while shooting for Zee, we heard trumpets blowing and saw lots of people walking on the street. It was a parade. Camera still rolling, we joined the ambling masses. At the centre of the parade was none other than the president of Mauritius, Sir Cassam Uteem, a dignified-looking man with a white-flecked beard. The security around him was minimal. This is where quick thinking again came to my aid. If I could break the ice with the president, maybe the Health Minister would stop playing hardball with me. In that one moment I transformed from doctor to journalist, thrust the microphone towards the president's face and asked him a question. Nothing heavy, just a non-threatening lifestyle question.

'Mr President, I'd like to know how you keep yourself fit. Is walking one of your regular exercises?'

He answered the question, and then a couple of other ones. While leaving, I introduced myself and slipped him my card.

'You come and meet me at the palace,' he said.

President Uteem and I ended up having a lot of things in common. More than half the population of Mauritius is Indian. So was President Uteem. Bihar was his native place, and he longed to visit it. He and his brother were table tennis players, a game which I also was good at. Over tea at the State House, his residence, I urged him to come to India. When he finally made a trip, he skipped a small official function but came to a dinner I organized for him at Radio Club. Rajendra and Nina Mehta sang ghazals. We became friends.

In the course of the next few weeks I built relations with several important people in Mauritian politics, meeting them in Mauritius or hosting them in India. Mango diplomacy took place between the two nations much before India and Pakistan. Sir Ghurburrun, who had given me a note of support, was further won over when I gifted him Alphonso mangoes, which he loved. When he visited India, I organized a dinner for him on my terrace. White mattresses were laid out and once again my dependable friends, the Mehtas, regaled us with their singing.

India's high commissioner to Mauritius was Shyam Saran, whose home I visited on 15 August on the occasion of flag-hoisting. Ripples of emotion ran through me as I saw the tricolour flying high in a foreign land. Subsequently, I met him and his wife Anita over tea and he was very helpful.

I also got a chance to visit Anerood Jugnauth, the former Prime Minister and father of the present Prime Minister, Pravind Jugnauth. When I arrived, a durbar of sorts was on, where people consulted the leader for their problems. I was amused to note that many of the issues were trivial. One gem was, 'Sir, today I had a fight with my wife.'

I explained my mission to the former Prime Minister. The health benefits of homeopathy and its reasonable costs were among the points I made. I also highlighted to him the model of the business, which clearly showed there was no commercial gain for me. On the other hand, the clinic would help contribute to the local economy in Mauritius and create some jobs. I closed my piece with a simple, 'Please sir, give this a shot.'

There was a pause during which Anerood Jugnauth maintained a poker face and looked beyond me at the lawn.

'I hear you have many Bollywood friends,' he said.

I got the hint. Like President Uteem, Jugnauth was from Bihar. Secondly, the Mauritian government hosted a very big Diwali bash every year. And so I played my trump card. 'Sir, if you like I can bring Shatrughan Sinha as a guest at your Diwali party. I can try.'

The poker face cracked ever so slightly into a smile. I could see the finish line. Once again, I understood the importance of studying body language. I also sent medicines to Jugnauth for a medical problem he had. Earlier, some people had promised to treat him and send him medicines but they never did. He saw that I was genuine, and a man of my word.

That Diwali, Shatru, his wife, little Sonakshi and the Mehtas, along with me and my family, flew to Mauritius at my expense. As state guests, we breezed through the formalities on arrival. Outside, beaconed BMW cars were waiting for us. We were put up in sea-facing bungalows very close to the Prime Minister's estate.

The Diwali night was a spectacular success. The nearly 20,000 people present at the venue and several others who had climbed atop trees and parapets went wild when Shatru, their Bihari Babu, appeared on stage. Rajendra and Nina Mehta's songs lent a melodious dimension to the event.

Later during our stay, as the kids played on the beach, I sought an appointment with Prime Minister Jugnauth. When we met at his office, I told him, 'Sir, can we please have homeopathy legalized?' I also told him what degree has to be made mandatory for homeopathy doctors and waited for his answer.

He smiled and signed on the dotted line.

Relief and joy washed over me. Six months of waiting in offices, travelling between the two countries and cultivating people, six months of hopes rising and dipping, had culminated in success. The Mauritius Broadcasting Corporation sent a crew to India to make a two-part biopic on me which was telecast on prime time.

However, there was heartbreak further down the road, when my partners sold the business at a premium without telling me and moved to Australia. It was an important lesson learnt that the reselling of shares should only be done with your permission.

The new partner was a politician and was not hands-on. The local management suffered even though we opened another branch. After putting in so much effort in building the brand, and bringing homeopathy to the country, we moved out in a few years. While we are no longer in Mauritius as a brand, homeopathy is now a popular and flourishing system of medicine in Mauritius. I will always have the satisfaction that I started homeopathy in a new country, and took Brand India to foreign shores.

41

Bridging the Gulf

TO THE TUNE OF ARABIC MUSIC, A DOCTOR ON A CAMEL EMERGES on the sandy horizon of Dubai. He comes into the city. He opens a clinic at the Dubai Healthcare City (DHCC) first, and then at other locations, including a swanky super specialty offering in Al Wasl. He has a falcon on his arm which also marks out territories in Bahrain and Abu Dhabi. There is a maze of strict rules to follow. There are ups and downs. Money is lost and earned. But the doctor stays the course. He knows that perseverance is the key to growth.

If someone is crazy enough to make a film on my life, this could be a scene. I knew there was a Steven Spielberg within me somewhere.

Foraying into Dubai was a wonderful experience, but also a challenge. The laws were stringent. For example, you needed the health department's permission for every advertisement and communication you made. Why did we bother, then? We had ambitions. Dubai was an obvious stop in our international expansion—it was a fabulous place just a short flight away from

India, had a growing economy and had many Indians living there. And we chose DHCC for our first centre as it allowed us to run an operation without an Arab partner, which was otherwise mandatory in most other parts of Dubai.

But here's a lesson to entrepreneurs. Always read the fine print and the rules of the city you are attempting to serenade with your skills and charm. People talk about 'first-mover advantage'. I think there are actually disadvantages in being a first mover. You have no reference points. You have no footsteps to follow.

Fine as DHCC was, there were restrictions on signage. It was allowed inside the building, and you did feel proud seeing your name among international heavy-hitters at the main entrance, but it was not permitted outside. So it took time and effort to popularize our clinic. I had to make several visits to Dubai, do radio and television shows and spend money on advertising to get it going. We wooed customers in phases—first the NRIs, and then the Arabs and expats. There was a heavy cash burn in the first five years. The overheads were high and the footfalls low as DHCC was a little away from the city centre.

Some other rules further tested us. Clinics could write prescriptions but not dispense medicines. This meant that many patients, once they got a doctor's note, did not return for a follow-up. It was also an expensive proposition for patients, as most of the medicines were imported from Europe and were costly.

A doctor had a licence to practise only in one clinic at a time. This was another law. To put this in perspective, it meant a doctor in a Bandra clinic could not work in the Andheri branch of the same establishment. For an employer, this meant staff could not be rotated. Moreover, you couldn't get an extra hand for a few months; you had to pay that person a full year's salary.

The authorities would often rap on the door for surprise checks and audits. Even a minor oversight had stiff penalties. And then, as per the law again, you had to give employees a month's holiday. Not just that, you also had to pay for their ticket to their home town, even if that was overseas. In addition there was one month of Ramadan, when work would be lax. And there would be two months of extreme heat. Effectively, four months of a year were nearly lost. You only had eight months to meet your goals.

As an entrepreneur, always expect the unexpected—especially when working in a foreign country. A freak accident in one of our clinics (a shutter fell and hurt one of our staff) led to a prolonged case in the labour courts, which we ultimately won. Another time, one of our doctors, who had applied for professional indemnity, started practice a day before it came through. It led to a hefty fine and the closure of a new clinic for two months, just when it was launched. Lots of money and some reputation was lost even before the first patient walked in.

However, we persevered, even though I could have easily thought, 'I am hemorrhaging money here. I will wrap things up and enjoy my little kingdom in India.' Friends and family advised me to do the same. But it is not my nature to cave in at the first sign of trouble. It was not yet time to quit. The clinics in India were stable and I could use some of that money to keep Dubai afloat. The tax breaks in Dubai helped. What we earned stayed with us. Also, homeopathy started being recognized by insurance companies, in part due to our efforts and visibility. That opened the floodgates in terms of footfalls. When the company is paying, people visit you for every little problem. And thus, much of the money we lost in the first five years, we made up in the next five.

We also were honoured when some members of the royal family sought our treatment. Buoyed by the turnaround, we decided to open more branches in the UAE. Our next clinic was in Jumeirah Lake Towers (JLT). Once again it was a designated space where we could function without a local partner. There were lots of NRIs and people of other nationalities living there. We were right above a noisy Carrefour supermarket, where children wheeled themselves around on trolleys. Signage was allowed too. And then we opened a third clinic in Al Nahda, near the Sharjah border. But here it was mandatory to have an Arab partner.

Success gave us the energy to accept the rules and work within them. We were the first branded homeopathic clinic in the UAE, with a chief executive officer (CEO) and a management team. I doubt any other homeopathy brand had professionalized their functioning to this extent. In about a decade, our clientele evolved from being almost 100 per cent NRIs, to including about 30 per cent locals and other nationalities.

Around this time we got an offer that allowed us to grow in the Gulf, at no great cost to us. The KIMS Group, which had an allopathic hospital in Bahrain, approached us to start a clinic in their building. We didn't have to pay for the use of the facility. If we agreed, they offered to organize an inauguration at my hands. Bahrain is close to Saudi Arabia, by distance and also in terms of relations. For the longest time, homeopathy was banned in this part of the world due to the alcohol content in the medicines. Gradually though, it came to be allowed.

We accepted their offer and I flew to Bahrain for the opening. They made me feel like Elvis. Amidst applause, a giant banner bearing the words 'Dr Batra's® Homeopathy' was unfurled from the top of their building. It was fabulous branding for us, and also reminded us of the benefits of the clinic-in-clinic model. Apart from the logistical convenience for both parties, we also stood a chance of getting crossover patients. We were the only company in Bahrain allowed to import our own medicines from India.

With this tie-up and similar ventures later in Mumbai, including one with an eminent bariatric surgeon, we were able to start a new kind of model for integrated medicine. It helped us to spread homeopathy even to allopathy's doors.

42

Lose to Win

A GOOD ENTREPRENEUR NOT JUST KNOWS HOW TO MAKE PROFITS, HE also knows how to stanch losses. You may have created something very dear to you, but if it's failing and has become gangrenous, cut it off. Otherwise you will lose the battle.

I learnt this the expensive way.

It was a phase in my life when I wanted all my clinics to be grand, and homeopathy to be larger than life. So once we did the grunt work of making an impact in Dubai, I wanted to create a jewel for our crown. My ambition was to build a spectacular super-specialty clinic that would be owner's pride, neighbour's envy. It would be a Taj Mahal of sorts, even though there was no Mumtaz in my life then. It would have the best doctors treating eight or ten specific disorders, plush décor and star service.

We rented a villa in Al Wasl, an upscale area where the best doctors practised. It was the Harley Street of Dubai. The limestone-white villa had gardens in the front and the back, plenty of parking space and a nice terrace from where you could see the Burj Khalifa coming up block by block. I hired a designer to do up the place. Italian marble and the best furnishings were used.

As usual, technology was a priority. Once patients walked in through the automatic glass doors, they could enter their information on touch screens, and it would transfer to the doctor's computer. While people waited on sofas, a white-gloved waiter handed them a menu of health drinks to choose from. Only the best candidates were chosen for the various positions in the clinic—from front desk to doctors. Most of them could speak English and Arabic, and sometimes Hindi as well.

My palace was ready, like a gold-wrapped Diwali present waiting to be opened.

We unveiled it in style, like our Bengaluru property. Guests in fine clothes exchanged chit-chat and air kisses. There was lunch and mocktails. As afternoon turned to evening, I imagined fireworks going up in the sky. It was like being in the film *The Great Gatsby* (2013).

But, like Gatsby, the clinic too had a short life. I left it in the hands of an overconfident CEO who priced it ridiculously high. We'd barely get two or three patients in a month, at that price. The maintenance costs and overheads of this ivory tower were exorbitant. High rent, high salaries and little income was our lament those days. The financial strength we had built up over five years was at risk.

In a few months, the writing was on the wall. And after just about a year of operation, we brought the curtains down on my Taj Mahal. The law of the land was that you had to return a rented property to the owner in its original state. We gave it back in a much better condition. In any case, we wouldn't have been able to take the marble anywhere. It broke my heart to walk away. But it was done and now the only thing in our hands was to cut our losses. Just about an hour and a half away from Al Wasl lay Abu Dhabi, the site of our most recent clinic. If Dubai is the snazzy commercial capital of the UAE, Abu Dhabi is its calmer, statelier cousin. The bull that I was, it looked like a tempting red cloth to me. In fact, I was open to having multiple clinics in Abu Dhabi alone, since it had a lot of wealthy residents.

We found a nice two-storey place to rent right on the main road. We furnished it well. But then the first-mover disadvantage once again became apparent to us. Abu Dhabi had different rules from Dubai. Neither us, nor the administration quite knew what the guidelines were for the setting up of a homeopathy clinic.

Meanwhile, we hired the lone registered homeopath in Abu Dhabi. The process of getting her on board was a task. And so was getting a licence for us to practise. It took us four years, even with a local partner. We also had to change the office structure once and were told to hire an allopathic doctor if we were to provide dermatology treatments. Once, after we got a licence for a spa, we were told to reapply for a homeopathy permit.

One day we were even asked to pay a year's fee for eight parking slots, just because our clinic had eight rooms. The amount was in the range of about Rs 10 million. We promptly reduced the number of functional rooms to three. The Abu Dhabi clinic has now been functional for more than a year. Before the coronavirus pandemic started, the clinic was pulling in decent numbers and patients were happy with the treatments. Recently, however, we decided to move to another location nearby at one-third the cost. This time around we managed to set up the clinic from scratch within four months.

We now have five clinics in the UAE. Most of them are doing alright. We saved more money further on when we let go of a highly paid CEO we had appointed in Dubai. We had hired him because Dubai was our international headquarters, and we felt it needed a blue-chip CEO. This is again a lesson to learn in management. You need not have expensive people at your newer centres. They may be qualified and deserving, but they don't always justify their salaries.

Since then, my son Akshay has been in charge of international operations. In just about a year, he has again made our company profitable. More importantly, homeopathy has gained acceptance and popularity in the Gulf due to our commitment and staying power, our ability to ride the ups and downs.

Life keeps pulling us in different directions, sometimes to distant lands in the interest of expansion, sometimes back home for the sake of self-preservation. We are tethered to some things but are never idle. I'm tempted to take some creative liberty and reference Gatsby again, and quote F. Scott Fitzgerald's stunning last line in his book: 'So we beat on, boats against the current, borne back ceaselessly into the past.'[4]

---

[4] Fitzgerald, F. Scott (1925), *The Great Gatsby*, New York: Charles Scribner's Sons.

43

Other International Forays

BEFORE 9/11 CHANGED THE WORLD IN 2001 AND MADE PEOPLE resentful of other nationalities, London in the 1990s was a home away from home for many Indians. It still is. But there was a degree of comfort and acceptance then that has all but vanished now.

I was forty-seven and had just recovered from the ravages of my heart surgery. I had a new outlook on life, a new appreciation for time. There were things I wanted to do. For one, I wanted to expand our overseas footprint. Our obvious choice was London. I had taught there for many years and was familiar with the place and the people.

We opened our first clinic in Southall, in London, at the hands of Reena Roy, amidst the colours and contrasts of the area—one street corner would smell of jalebi and the next of fish and chips. You would hear strains of bhangra along with rap and jazz.

Dr Bindu Sharma, currently our director of medical services, was given the reins of the clinic. At that time she was a young doctor who was personally trained by me. She ran the clinic for three years while earning a local MD degree, that too with a gold medal.

We had a local partner in Southall. Sadly, the relationship soured and we had to shut the clinic down after some years. It broke my heart, but that's entrepreneurship. Besides, it taught us a lesson. So when we returned to London in the 2000s, we did so entirely with our money.

I wanted to bring for homeopathy the status it deserved. We therefore went to great lengths to get a spot on Harley Street, which is to the medical profession what Savile Row is to tailoring. The best doctors in the world work there, commanding fees of hundreds of pounds per consultation. Florence Nightingale worked there. So did the personal physician of Winston Churchill.

The trustees of the Howard de Walden Estate took some convincing, since they felt an alternative medicine brand might compromise their lofty reputation.

In response, I listed out the benefits of homeopathy, briefed the trustees on the performance of our brand in India and abroad, including the UK. I also mentioned the use of homeopathy by members of a certain family that lived in Buckingham Palace. They came around.

As pleased as we were to be on Harley Street, we did not sit on laurels. We opened another clinic in Wembley, a blue-collar area with a large Indian population. The mayor of Brent County and a senior official from the Indian High Commission came for the launch. Our tea menu was symbolic, with cucumber sandwiches as well as samosas.

And about three years ago, we opened once again in Southall, this time with our own funding.

Coronavirus, however, forced us to offload some of our properties. Currently, we just have a clinic in Wembley, smaller than the one the mayor had launched. On Harley Street, we use a rental polyclinic type of place. The important thing is we are financially stable in the UK.

Regardless of that, what readers could learn from my experiences are the endless challenges in launching something abroad.

For one, the reputation of Indian companies in international markets wasn't flattering for the longest time. Second, the pound is a formidable currency. Against the rupee, which is almost always falling, it acquires Ravan-like ten-headed proportions. Yes, you earn in pounds. But you also spend in them. Besides, few really knew our brand other than NRIs. So we had to advertise and that meant more battles with Ravan. And even then, the advertising controls were very strict.

Luckily, we were making some money in the Middle East and could fund our UK operations for a while at least. After all, once you enter a market you do not give up without a fight, and without trying different approaches.

Persistence, ambition and adjustment aside, there is another big lesson from our London story. It is important to invest in deserving members in your staff, as we did with Dr Bindu. Due to that, we had someone in the UK who understood our brand and who also earned a qualification to train other doctors.

Being open to the needs of others also brings about opportunities. One of our patients in London had a father who had heart trouble but was stuck on a three-year-long waiting list in the National Health Service (NHS) system. So I treated him instead. His son was pleased. The boy eventually became an osteopath. We tied up with him for one year and ran a homeopathy and back clinic in the lovely area of Harrow on the Hill.

After London, we, the zealous missionaries of homeopathy, went to Estonia, Dhaka and Muscat. Everywhere, there were hurdles to face. In Muscat, a doctor we sent to work from India got married to our partner there. So, technically, my subordinate now became my partner. If that wasn't awkward enough, the original partner committed suicide for some reason. It was all a bit too much. We had to bid goodbye to Muscat.

In Dhaka, we partnered with an Indian man who had businesses in Bangladesh. But it did not work out and we moved out of the arrangement. Now we have a local partner and have recently added a second clinic. But an entrepreneur's life is full of challenges and we keep facing some challenge or the other.

And Estonia? How did that happen, you might wonder. Around six years ago, a young Estonian lady attended Akshay's book launch in Delhi. Afterwards, she met us and exchanged cards. She wanted to start a clinic with us back home. But after that meeting, neither side pursued the matter. About a year ago, we felt we should explore the idea of starting in Estonia. But when we got in touch with the lady, she was not so keen any more. Fate conspires to make things happen. Sometime later, on a cruise with my grandson, I found out the ship was going to dock for a day in Estonia. Always looking for opportunities to push homeopathy's cause, I wrote to the lady and she agreed to meet. In fact, she came to the ship to receive us. Then, over lunch and a stroll through the capital city of Tallinn, I answered all her questions and laid her fears to rest. And in December that year, we opened in Tallinn. This was after Brexit, which made it our first clinic in Europe, as London was now no longer a part of continental business, in a way.

So far, so good. Locals were happy to have the clinic too. But the challenge was in getting medicines. Estonia didn't have them. We had to get them by courier from Latvia. It was hard to do it on a regular basis, as the requirement of medicines differed from person to person. And then the coronavirus wiggled and wormed its way through the world, including the cobbled streets of Tallinn.

The clinic has been shut for a while now. In fact, we had sent a promising doctor from Delhi there. After Covid, we had to bring him back. But given our ability to meet challenges, and the burgeoning popularity of homeopathy, don't be surprised if our flag flies again in Estonia, and in more parts of the world.

44

Think Outside the Box

'Research is creating new knowledge,' Neil Armstrong, the first man to set foot on the moon, reportedly said. My advice to professionals is that while surveys are not cheap, and at times seem superficial, they are worth it. They will show you what is working and what is not. And you can then proceed on your journey with greater clarity.

In 1996, I reached a point where I wasn't getting job satisfaction, even though we were growing. I saw more than a 100 patients a day. Even if I had fever I would go to work. The temptation to call my clinic and say, 'The doctor is sick today', excuse the pun, was strong. It would be so nice to plop down on the sofa at home, watch TV and just vegetate. But then I would get word that someone's young son was unwell. And I'd think of the boy and drag myself out of home, duty prevailing over desire.

The fundamental problem was that I was functioning as a GP and in an unstructured, flying-blind kind of way. Some of the patients would come back for a follow-up. Others wouldn't. That was frustrating. I was prepared to get any feedback, good and bad. I wouldn't have minded if they told me they were seeing another doctor. But I wanted to know.

Out of the blue, at a party or event, someone would tap me on the shoulder and say, 'Oh! Dr Batra, you know, I'm completely cured after your treatment.' Or someone would say, after grabbing a fistful of peanuts at a party, 'Dr Batra, you gave me medicine for stomach ache but then I found another doctor closer to home, you know.' And I'd think, 'No, I don't know. But thanks for telling me belatedly. And go easy on the peanuts.'

I was also burning myself out with the extra work I was doing, mainly writing and television. I had to take a break. I had years of experience and had treated nearly 50,000 patients. Thanks to my investment in technology since the early 1980s—for which everyone laughed at me initially—I had the records of nearly all those people. Now I needed to organize all this information, step back and find patterns and a direction for the future.

One of my patients was the branding and advertising specialist Kiran Khalap. He had designed my first ever patient survey. It was a folder with the headline, 'Can you pass this IQ test?' It had four questions aimed at educating people about homeopathy and addressing their misgivings about it, if any. It was a good exercise.

Now that I had all these existential questions about my practice, I once again engaged Kiran, who was with Lintas at this point. I wanted to do a brand tuning exercise for Dr Batra's®. So far, we had rarely advertised. My practice had grown on the basis of word of mouth. When your brain is fried, it helps to let a qualified person with fresh eyes to take a look.

'Why don't you try direct mailing?' Kiran suggested. 'I think that will help you.'

The thing is, direct mailing has a very poor conversion rate. If you send a mailer to 100 people, one of them will become a customer. But sometimes the benefits of such exercises go beyond the conversion rate. It's like a bowler who only takes one wicket but has some other intangible impact on a game. So I kept an open mind.

'Okay, what exactly do we do?' I asked Kiran.

'What type of data do you have?'

'I have got 50,000 patients and their histories,' I said.

'Let's analyse their information and see which diseases you had the best results on. And we will make a mailer.'

Over the next few months we dove deep into our files. And we found that diabetes, hypertension, asthma, allergies, skin and hair problems with women and children were among the dozen or so conditions we had had success in treating. We sent out mailers on our capabilities to deal with specific disorders. At that time there was no digital marketing where you could segment your audience, say, zip-code-wise. So the mailers were sent in all directions.

The entire exercise took six months to a year and cost me Rs 10 lakh. This was 1996, mind you.

Guess how many new patients I got. Two.

Commercially, the exercise was a failure. There are no two ways about that. But as I said, I went into it with eyes open. It had a silver lining, though. It gave my brand a new, clear direction. And in 1996, I started a specialty clinic and narrowed down my practice to only eighteen segments of healthcare. If anyone asked, I had the survey findings on my fingertips. This exercise allowed me to differentiate my services from other homeopaths. Differentiation of your product or services plays an important part in entrepreneurship.

For my new offering, I charged a one-time fee of Rs 6000 a year, to be paid at the outset. It may seem like a lot. But it covered medicines and allowed a patient any number of consultations, like a good, unlimited talktime plan.

I was happy with the entrepreneurial model for two reasons. First, it ensured commitment from the patient, unlike earlier when I had no way of keeping track of them. Second, it helped me give them time, and provide them holistic treatment with long-term benefits. In this model, I held their hand till they got well. Due to the pricing, I initially got only two patients a week. But I got a lot of satisfaction treating them. And the results were amazing. It was not uncommon for beaming patients to say to me, 'Doctor, my back pain was so severe. Now I can play tennis. Thank you.'

Word got around. Dr Batra's® 2.0 was delivering on its promise. The number of patients increased to about forty a day. Appointments were full for months. Walk-ins were not possible unless it was an emergency. From a financial point of view, I could scale up from internal accruals and with virtually no funding from outside, save for the annual fee patients paid. We were self-driven and self-funded. And we put the money back in our mission, offering better treatment options for patients and growing our geographies. We also improved the patient outcome results from 70 per cent to 90 per cent. I may not have been to the moon, but with the specialty clinic, I had taken a giant step for homeopathy.

45

Companies Outlive Individuals

The colloquial term 'ticker' is an apt descriptor for the heart. Ticking stands for time and movement. The day the ticking is impaired, the clock malfunctions. The same is true of the heart. And when that happens, you truly appreciate the importance of the time that you have on this planet.

When I was forty-seven my ticker all but crashed on me. Years of working non-stop had taken their toll. I had to undergo multiple bypass surgeries. It was a wake-up call, but except for a few initial months of recovery, it did not slow me down. On the contrary, it motivated me even more. My passion for homeopathy now had an added layer of urgency and a desire to build a legacy. When you see death staring at you and then life gives you a second chance, you feel you better do something good with it. For me, what could have been better than setting up an institution that would outlive me and take homeopathy to millions of homes around the world?

That is why I started the company. I had seen many doctors whose know-how and skill ended with their passing. But with a company, my work would live on. The life of an entrepreneur, though, is challenging, and there's a lot to learn from the challenges that I faced.

For one, I was an accidental entrepreneur. My parents were doctors, and I had no business school training. We also faced the risk of being the first mover, like Charles Lindbergh when he became the first human to fly solo across the Atlantic. As I mentioned earlier, marketing gurus speak of a first-mover advantage, but that can also be a disadvantage when there is no path to follow and you have to create your own road map. The cost of experimentation is sometimes high and we too learnt the ropes the hard way. Secondly, while we grow the market at our cost, others copy us and just muscle in.

The third challenge was the time it took for us just to build our base and gain some traction. Almost ten years were spent putting the right systems and people in place. But it was fun too, a bit like playing Monopoly, as we were so passionate about the whole thing. First, we rented an office near Dadar station, amidst the clamour of vegetable and flower vendors. It was an old building, but we had three floors of space.

Next, we had to hire people. A marketing head was our first priority. It was difficult to attract talent, as we were sort of known but not so much. This was also a time of the dotcom boom and bust. At a time when the potential of the internet was first registering on the world, top graduates weren't exactly lining up at our door. If they did join, we did not know how to handle them, so they'd leave. They were corporate professionals, we were doctors. It took a few years to actually get the right kind of people on board.

With the setting up of the company, my own job profile changed. That is another lesson from this chapter of my life. At times you have to shift your focus from your original passion to something that needs your attention. No longer could I spend as much time in my clinic attending to patients. Increasingly, I was at the corporate office in Dadar. Also, by this time, Akshay had graduated, so he could work with patients at our suburban clinic in Santacruz.

But as the company grew and we started hiring more people, I could no longer manage being here, there and everywhere. We had also opened in Bengaluru at that time, so I withdrew from active practice. This was a setback for long-standing patients, with whom I had a personal rapport dating back thirty to forty years. There was excitement that there was a Dr Batra's® brand, but they missed their personal interaction with me. I had to spread word in the market that I was researching new treatments and cures, while I was building the company.

Even as we chased growth, there were some things I never compromised on. Values were one of them. Our company's values of safety, innovation, passion for excellence and care with compassion have stood the test of time. It has helped us to build a value-based organization. Value-based organizations succeed in trying times when others fail. As Mark Twain said, 'Always do right. This will gratify some people and astonish the rest.'[5]

People in the company had to be honest and above board. It was non-negotiable. I didn't mind it if people made mistakes, but they had to be truthful about them. I also did not allow partial or selective honesty, where you were truthful about some things but not all. I always say you cannot be slightly pregnant, you are either pregnant or not. The same applied to integrity.

Many years ago, one of our marketing bosses was about to close a big contract for us. But one day he knowingly misrepresented figures. In my book, it was an automatic red card. Some people told me to let it go, that he was bringing big money to the company. But my decision was final. He had to go. Again, the problem was

[5] A handwritten note by Mark Twain, dated 16 February 1901, and addressed to the Young People's Society, Greenpoint Presbyterian Church, New York. Available at: http://www.twainquotes.com/Right.html

not that he didn't deliver the numbers but that he fudged the figures. At such times a lot of factors go into the decision you make. For one, you have to think about the message sent to the rest of the company. Office grapevines are very strong. When word goes out that the chairman ejected a star performer for lying, everyone takes it seriously.

Our values also applied to the way we handled payments. There is no cash payment to any employee in the company. We pay all our taxes and ensure our employees do so as well. We have also refused to buy properties which had a cash component and rented them instead. Honesty is truly the best policy. What you lose in taxes, you more than gain in growing your business.

Another challenge was setting up the company's IT infrastructure. We had already done a wise thing by investing heavily in IT for my first clinic in Chowpatty. So we had been on the tech ball since 1982. Thereon, we designed our own CMS and have kept upgrading and changing it every few years. Our CMS also helped us to treat patients during the Covid pandemic, as our doctors could use the systems and databases while working from home.

All our clinics are networked live and Management Information System (MIS) data on the mobile phones of members of the top management has a record of every patient who has entered any clinic in India or abroad. It also documents every rupee, dirham or pound that is earned. Our balance sheets are therefore closed in real time at the end of each financial year. Our new intelligent software helps our doctors in diagnosing and prescribing. In today's world, investing in technology is a must. Remember, it is not a capital expense but a recurring expense as technology gets outdated very fast. And then, you also need to hire software and hardware engineers.

My entrepreneurial spirit makes me a better doctor. It made me strive to formalize the practice of homeopathy. Contrary to perception, homeopathy is not an obscure art that works on instinct alone. Quite the opposite, there are systems and processes that ensure a predictable result, just like any other science. The innovator in me is always restless to aim higher, streamline further, modernize not just technology but also processes and treatments.

Today, through our company, I'm happy to say that we *do* provide a viable and formal system for many patients across the globe. And when there is a system, the ticker will never stop ticking.

46

Brands—Bigger than Individuals

In 2018, the coffee and food chain Dunkin' Donuts decided to rebrand itself as just: Dunkin'. The rationale was that the company had grown beyond donuts. More recently, but in rebranding of a smaller scope than Dunkin', Cadbury reportedly paid around half a million pounds to redesign its logo for the first time in over half a century. The familiar 'Cadbury' signature in chubby, cursive letters is now slimmer.

To a layperson, the difference may seem negligible. But the company feels its new logo is modern.

I can relate to such stories. Nearly two decades before Dunkin' and Cadbury, we had tweaked our branding. Between 1982, when I opened my first clinic, and the mid-1990s, India changed enormously. Economic liberalization and cable TV brought about financial and cultural transformations. People were better paid and had more exposure than earlier generations of Indians. They wanted to stay healthy and look good. What worked in 1982 was no longer relevant. So, every few quarters, we started re-evaluating our branding.

This is how Dr Batra's® as we know it today evolved. It started with a 'know your customer' (KYC) type of exercise, one that went deeper than just basic questions. We wanted to understand the customer's perception of us, and we did qualitative and quantitative analysis through a well-known marketing agency. The firm was Ormax Consultants, run by Vispy Doctor, or Dr Doctor, as he has a PhD in physics. Nowadays, you have online platforms like Practo where you can give feedback following a visit to a clinic or a physician. But at that time, we were one of the few healthcare companies to use scientific methods to better understand our customers and what we should be doing in future.

Someone told me there's an English song with the lyrics 'Doctor, doctor, gimme the news'. When we went to Dr Vispy Doctor, my brief to him was somewhat similar. Dr Doctor was a smart man with a shock of grey hair and a bushy moustache. After he had done his surveys, he gave me the news. Positive Health Clinic, he said, was a vague name. To some respondents it sounded like a massage parlour in a basement somewhere, or as if we were practising hocus-pocus with twigs, garlands and incense while chanting 'Jingalala hu hu'.

News No. 2 from Dr Doctor was that homeopathy was growing. It was gaining acceptance. He suggested we mention homeopathy in our signage. The reason I had not done it earlier was to differentiate myself from other homeopaths. But times had changed.

Then came another key insight. When the agency asked patients about our clinic, they would refer to it as Dr Batra's® clinic. They never said Positive Health Clinic. We couldn't completely eliminate the earlier name. So we started calling it 'Dr Batra's® Positive Health Clinic'. This way we had the best of both worlds for a while. Gradually, we changed it to Dr Batra's®.

Next, we needed new clothes, meaning a new logo. And that led us to our current red-and-blue branding. Much thought went into it. It wasn't like childhood holi by the water tank in my grandfather's Agra home, where we sprayed random colours on anything and anyone. This was a precise affair. The word 'Dr' is white on red, and 'Batra's' is white on blue. And between the two is a figure in white I call the Pill Man, or the PM. I feel the PM maintains the yin and yang of the logo, and represents the balance of the human body.

Red, white and blue denote three essential constituents of a balanced life. Red is for blood, and blue is for water and oxygen. Red and blue are also eye-catching colours. Many big brands use them for their signage, such as Coca-Cola, Levi's, Samsung, Facebook and even Superman. As far as white goes, it stands for purity and so much else, including pills.

Then came small yet important touches that made our brand stronger and stayed on people's minds even after they had left the clinic. We started giving medicines in environmentally friendly jute bags (we now use paper bags), so the brand experience continued even when the patients went home. Today, the bags would win the approval of the young-generation hipsters who support organic eating. People loved the little gunny and flaunted it, as if it were a shopping bag from a luxury store. So what if we were not LV, we were DB (Dr Batra's®). Many of our patients were in the age group of twenty-five to thirty-five. It was common for them to sling the bags around the handle of their motorbikes.

I'm almost retired now and not as visible across media as I used to be. Not everybody may recognize me by face. Mention Dr Batra's® though, or show them our trademark, and they immediately recognize the brand. They look at the card and the logo and say, 'Oh wow! Is this your company?'

Commercial success is important. At this stage in my life, however, it is brand recognition and happy brand experiences that provide me deep fulfilment. What also satisfies me is this—when we started building the brand, the individual behind it was bigger than the company; now, for the most part, it's the other way around.

47

Building the Hair Brand

When Vin Diesel visited India a few years ago, there was a flood of memes about us on the internet. Comedians joked that the actor had come for treatment at Dr Batra's®. Similar memes went around after the release of the Hindi movie *Bala* (2019), which dealt with male baldness. These days you pay up to Rs 2 lakh to meme creators for an ad. But we got it for free as our brand was strongly associated with hair treatment. It also had a lesson in it for entrepreneurs—do not look down upon online humour, especially in the era of social media. It can bring a company publicity worth crores, and score points with the youth segment.

Almost 45 per cent of our clients are hair patients and at our peak, we were seeing nearly 50,000 follically challenged people every month. Of all our products, shampoos and hair tonics sell the best. We have a wide range of invasive and non-invasive options so that your top does not look like Vin Diesel's.

How did this happen? I'd say by chance and then by design. That's been the story of my professional life, bar a few exceptions.

Opportunity is like a biscuit dunked in tea—a little delay and it melts away. Opportunity often comes out of nowhere, or a set of circumstances creates the opportunity. Then we pursue it. Sometimes this results in a winning horse.

Our hair identity grew due to advertising restrictions on other ailments. For example, we couldn't advertise 'asthma' treatment. You had to say 'breathing problems'. We couldn't use the word 'obesity'. You had to say 'weight management'. We couldn't say 'catalepsy' either. It narrowed down our advertising to hair and skin, where there weren't so many dos and don'ts.

In spite of all this, the Advertising Standards Council of India (ASCI) pulled us up many times. We were always a compliant company and when they made genuine and reasonable suggestions, which they often did, we heeded them. But many times they would be unreasonable. Once, they asked us to bring all our computers to them for verification of data. That was excessive. Even the courts wouldn't do that, certainly not for an advertising-related matter. Besides, the ASCI was not a scientific body to give us technical advice. Nor did it have the legal right to stop anyone from carrying our advertisements.

In the meantime, our hair adverts were connecting with people and generating the most queries. Baldness was setting in for men earlier than before. Previous generations would start having hair problems in their thirties or forties. Now it was happening any time, even in the twenties. By the way, we considered several visuals for our hair advertisements, including pretty landscapes and smiling faces and happy families with cuddly Labradors. What worked was the good old 'before and after' format. Simple and to the point. 'No bakwaas', as the Sprite ads say.

Around the same time, I made an important medicinal discovery, which gave more impetus to our hair practice. Years ago, my father would wake up at the crack of dawn and write notes on different drugs and ingredients in a journal. At the bottom of the page there would be footnotes, and at times they'd be underlined. When I read his books, I realized that the main text was not always the right place to find precious nuggets of knowledge, or clues to a breakthrough product. Often, they lay buried in the ink-smudged footnotes.

Therefore, I made it a habit to read the fine print in books and medical literature. One day I stumbled upon information about a hair medicine made from minerals found in a lake in Europe. The natural minerals helped reduce and control hair loss. Increased dihydrotestosterone (DHT) levels lead to hair loss. I researched and discovered a plant-based medicine that attacked the DHT and brought it down. When combined with the minerals, it made for a potent combo. I started using it and the results were encouraging.

Among hair problems, alopecia areata is one of the most complicated, where you lose hair in patches. The absolute worst-case scenario is a condition called alopecia totalis, in which a person loses all their hair. I had a patient who had it—a boy with his youth still ahead of him. When you are forty, you can deal with baldness and say I will just shave everything off and look like a wrestler. When you are young, it's traumatic. I wanted to help the boy. So I discovered the use of a new drug and it worked wonders. Within a year and a half, the boy had hair. He and his father were thrilled. It became a popular case, triggering a wave of positive word-of-mouth reviews for us. And this was another reason why, in the eyes of the public, Dr Batra's® meant hair.

My son Akshay was the other factor in the strides we made in hair. After he became a doctor, he wanted to make a name for himself and not stay in my shadow. He wanted to have his own specialization. Hair was his interest and also what the market wanted. So he went to London and over two years studied trichology. His mentor was Prof. Barry Stevens, a leading name in the field. Akshay did very well in the course and received the Robert Olding Award for best student.

When Akshay finished his course, he was armed with the knowledge of new research and techniques. He started training our doctors on what was happening around the world. At international trichology conferences, which he'd unfailingly attend, he'd convince leading figures to come to India and conduct workshops for our doctors. It made our hair clinics stronger and up to date in terms of protocols and treatments. We introduced hair extensions and a South Korean serum in our range of non-invasive options. For people who did not have the time or patience for sittings, who wanted to walk in as Vin Diesel and walk out with a head full of hair like Shah Rukh Khan, we started wigs.

So now we had homeopathic solutions for hair, as well as medical and some other non-surgical ones. We wanted to see if we could move from being a medical solution company to a wellness one which had a larger market. What we didn't have was surgical options. Generating hair growth is not easy. If you try to grow grass in the Sahara, the odds are against you. We couldn't satisfy every customer, which explains some of the criticism that came our way. You are fighting nature, after all. Besides, in hair and weight loss treatments, people are rarely happy. 'I lost 10 kilos, but I should've lost 25.' Or, 'I have grown some hair, but I want it to be like Tarzan's.' That's the attitude, even when they are cheating on their diet or slipping up on their hair routine.

That is why we needed to get into the hair transplant game. Results were almost always guaranteed with it and potentially permanent too. To keep our core intact we ensured that all patients who underwent surgery also were given homeopathy pre- and post-operatively and as part of a sustenance plan.

On one of his trips, Akshay met a representative of an American hair transplant company. They started talking and realized both sides could do some good work together. A few discussions later, we met in Hong Kong and signed a deal, under which we launched a chain of aesthetic studios called Dr Batra's® NuHart. They were operation theatres, really. Our first centre was in Mumbai, followed by seven more across other major cities in India, including Delhi, Bengaluru and Kolkata.

About a year and a half later, we had an amicable parting with our American partners. After buying their shares, Dr Batra's® NuHart became Dr Batra's® B Perfect and we owned the company entirely. We staffed the studios with the best plastic surgeons, unlike other hair clinics where the procedures would be conducted by dermatologists or MBBS doctors. B Perfect was gaining momentum.

Word got around quickly and we were soon doing at least one surgery a day at our metro city centres and sometimes even two over a weekend. Good surgeons, operation theatre nurses, anaesthetics and emergency backup ensured that all surgeries were successful. It was great to see patients come back after a few months with a head full of their own hair, including an eighty-year-old Rajya Sabha member and a seventy-five-year-old media baron! I remember a grateful transgender patient who went back with a moustache.

Around this time, since we had a new label in B Perfect, we again consulted the branding guru Kiran Khalap. We got his dates after several months of waiting as he was under a non-compete contract with a competitive hair company. And nothing less than a five-star hotel room would do for Khalap when he was ready to share his analysis with us. Essentially, he told us the same thing that Vispy Doctor did. Dr Batra's® should remain the mother brand. It was already established. On the other hand, a different name would need ten or fifteen years and crores of rupees to gain the same recognition, so B Perfect became Dr Batra's® aesthetics.

Sadly for us, the better the surgeons, the more ambitious they were. After spending some time with us and gaining experience, they felt they could make more ka-ching if they struck out on their own, or attached themselves to private hospitals. The rate of attrition increased. And we had to spend time and energy on training their replacements. It became unsustainable.

But almost always there is a middle path that keeps everyone happy. We closed the surgical division of Dr Batra's® aesthetics but retained the best surgeons as consultants. If a patient wanted a transplant, we referred him to our team of free-agent surgeons. We no longer do many transplants anymore. But our dream of becoming a provider of end-to-end hair solutions was fulfilled. So much so that one of our leading competitors wanted to sell his company to us. When even your top rival believes you are the best person to run their company, what more do you need?

48

'Dr Batra's®—Har Ghar Mein'

GROWING AS A PROFESSIONAL OR AS A COMPANY NEVER STOPS. AT various points of time, new realizations dawn upon you. You see certain gaps or needs in the market, and you aspire to fill them. In the early 2000s, I began to feel that while we were treating our hair and skin patients with homeopathy, they would ultimately lapse into using harmful, mass-market shampoos and creams. It limited the success of our treatment.

Complementary to this was my ambition for Dr Batra's® to have the numbers in mass-market products, without compromising quality of course. I wanted homes all across India to benefit from our experience, know-how, and our sparing use of chemicals. We were already making hair and skin products in small numbers and selling them at our clinics. The patients swore by them. We knew what suited Indian scalps and complexion, unlike multinational products, which perhaps were better suited for international use. Nirma was a good example of an Indian product challenging multinationals and succeeding. We wanted to do it too. This way, the brand and the customer could both have a mutually beneficial relationship even outside our homeopathic clinics.

It wasn't easy to get into the open market. The forces that lined up against us were not unlike those in Bollywood's insider–outsider divide.

I remember around ten years ago a chairperson from a fast-moving consumer goods (FMCG) behemoth had come to visit me in my clinic. He was a patient of mine. When I told him I wanted to get into the FMCG space, he smirked.

'We will kill your brand,' he said. 'It's a competitive market and multinational companies will throw you out. You are going to burn your fingers.'

'It is my dream. I want to do it,' I said.

I soon took the plunge in the shark-infested FMCG waters. We were among the first companies to cross over from services to products. Atul Kasbekar photographed a young, long-haired model named Sheetal Menon for our packaging and advertising. Sheetal's face adorned our shampoo bottles and gazed down from hoardings. Thousands of people passing by noticed her lustrous hair and our brand every day.

'*Jo dikhta hai, woh bikta hai* (What is seen, sells).' So we spent a lot of time on packaging, conducting surveys about details such as the label colour and bottle shape. We sent people to the markets, took photos of the shelves and then we photoshopped our products on the shelves to see how it'd look. If everybody else on the shelf was yellow we did not want to be yellow.

But while our effort was commendable, we were wrong about the colours. A key learning was that a gold label we tried for a while, thinking it would look premium, did not sell at all (all that glitters ...). When we went back to our signature red and blue, the product sold itself. Brand recognition of a known brand helps.

Another fascinating thing we learnt was that the original bottle had a large base, and took too much space on shelves of shops. We changed our bottles to a narrower base. We also ensured that our product was placed at the eye level of customers.

The shampoo had an active natural ingredient commonly used in homeopathy. Had we classified the product as a homeopathic one, we could have saved 14 per cent excise duty. But we did not. And here's a lesson for entrepreneurs. Sometimes you have to forego immediate financial reward and think in the long term. While we would have saved on some tax, we would have been able to sell the product only at a handful of homeopathic outlets. But by calling it an FMCG product and by paying extra duty, we could sell it in hundreds of medical and grocery shops.

We started with the smaller markets. Pune was our first fort. We bought ten or fifteen hoardings in the city, so that the Dr Batra's® brand and Sheetal's face registered on the population. At one particular distributor's, in the Deccan Gymkhana area, our shampoo was No. 1. Similarly, we tied up with 'Health and Glow' in Bengaluru. We were aware these were small markets, but it was a start. In Mumbai, however, we went flat out. Sheetal's Rapunzel tresses flowed out of about 1,000 outlets.

Better PH levels differentiated our shampoo from the rest. The PH balance of the human scalp is 6.5 according to the New Zealand Dermatology Society, which is known to maintain high standards of quality control. Our hair products are among the few in the world that have a PH of 6.5, closest to nature. They lather less but are safer than those with high PH and lots of lather. Therefore, our pricing was about 20 per cent more than mass-produced brands. This, combined with the volumes we were selling, made for some good numbers.

But we were running a long-distance race, to be determined not just by product quality but also cash reserves. We had gotten off the blocks well, but we needed money to keep going, to keep feeding the new baby we had created. Distributors told us to advertise more, as we needed to stay visible. Seasoned multinational companies (MNCs), that were running in the race too, probably smiled as they jogged behind us, thinking, 'Let us see how long they last.'

On our part, we poured almost all the profits of our clinic vertical to support the product vertical. There is an entrepreneurial lesson here. You have to be ready to lose your profits in one vertical, and increase promoters' capital or seek external funding in order to survive in a highly competitive, cut-throat marketplace.

Around that time, a rumour went around the market that LG, the Korean electronics company, was coming up with FMCG products. That really woke up the incumbent giants. Their response was the classic 'go for the jugular and hoard power'. They slashed the prices of their products by more than half, in some cases up to 67 per cent. With pockets as deep and full as the ocean, they could easily afford to reduce prices and chase the new entrants out of town. For example, in a market like this, our products, anyway costlier by about 20 per cent, were now 100 or 200 per cent more expensive. Who'd buy them? India is a price-sensitive market. Between a Rs 175 shampoo with good ingredients, and a Rs 35 chemical hellbroth, most will choose the latter, even if that turns their hair into bristles and they start polishing their shoes with their head.

The big guns were also winning the street wars of distribution. Every time we paid for product placement in a shop, the keeper would say, 'Sir, we displayed your product. But so and so company said, we'll stop sending you stock if you keep Dr Batra's® products.'

The price drop wiped us out. Again, despite showing results in just a year, we had to withdraw our products. Having to burn the stock—as the laws dictated—was painful. What happened in telecom recently, a wealthy owner bringing down prices to squeeze out his competition, happened to us too.

We retreated from the battlefield. We continued to make the products, though, and sell them in our clinics. I still wasn't done with my dream, however. 'Once bitten, twice try' is my motto.

After some time had elapsed, I wanted to enter the ring again. And this time with an able ally.

At that time Akshay was at the Indian School of Business (ISB), Hyderabad, for a training programme. There he met Hari Nair, an even-keeled, boy-next-door type of young man who worked for Marico in Gurgaon. He was looking after a couple of their factories. Nair had an impressive track record. If he was a key person at a brand as major as Marico's, he would be an asset for us, we thought. Akshay also had a positive all-round impression of him.

In the next few months, we reached out to Nair and asked him to join us as chief operating officer (COO), a higher post than he occupied at Marico. Despite the impressive title and the scope to go even higher, he took his time. Nair was well settled at Marico, a much bigger company than us. Also, Gurgaon to Mumbai is a big shift for a man with two schoolgoing kids. Eventually, after about two years of wooing, and once his children got admitted to a good school in Mumbai, he came on board.

The lesson from this was that the best place to source a key person for your company is often outside the boardroom. You could find them at seminars or at sports meets, where their skills, thought processes and team spirit come to the fore.

One of Nair's first assignments was to set up our factory from start to finish—choosing location, acquiring land, building the plant and then setting up the systems to run it. That assignment stands proud even today—our Palghar factory. The factory manager Nair appointed still works there. Nair was with us for five years and did become CEO eventually. He did very well in operations and in tightening up things. He made sure that even after he left we'd have a very process-driven factory. He made sure that the protocols were in place.

Setting up the infrastructure and the systems, however, was just one part of the job, although a very challenging one. Marketing and selling the product was another animal. We now had a great scientist who had built the rocket and its launch pad. But we still needed to figure out how to fly that rocket right into space and plant our flag in the entire solar system.

49

Winning against All Odds

People say if you can make it in New York, you can make it anywhere. They haven't seen the FMCG market in India.

It is a walk on burning coals. Each of the twenty-eight states and regions, with their different languages and cultures, is like a different country. Ivy League MBAs struggle to survive in this price-conscious snake pit, where battles are fought as much on the street as in the boardroom. To emerge on top demands formal education, guerrilla tactics, thick skin, staying power and loads of cash.

Sometimes even that is not enough. No wonder even MNCs pack up or often curtail their India operations. Danone dairy products and grocery chain Carrefour are just two examples.

Our earlier CEO was a processes man. When he left the company for better prospects at an alcohol multinational, we started looking for someone with a marketing bent for the bloody phase ahead.

The search took a while. Some eight months later, we hired a person who headed a Colgate India vertical and had FMCG experience. We gave him carte blanche to enlarge our footprint in the market. Our brief to him was, 'Focus on the products and that they reach the customer. Don't worry about the rest of the company.'

With products, scaling up is easier than in a service. If you need to ramp up production, you don't need a complex mix of additional hands. In the clinic, on the other hand, we'd require doctors, nurses and skilled technicians. And we'd have to train them.

Besides, the clinic offered personalized or case-specific services, so our reach was limited to patients. Products, on the other hand, could take you into millions of homes. 'Think BIG' was our mantra and we wanted to extend our reach to become a household brand. We felt that we should have offerings within the Rs 199 price range, which everyone could make use of. And that's how the idea of products came along, and with it the possibility of people from all economic strata to benefit from our expertise and experience.

Our new CEO, the marketing man, followed the brief given to him. After a while, our products started to pop up in all parts of the country, including the border areas. We had some 20,000 outlets or vendors nationally. Some of our highest sales were among university students in Itanagar, Arunachal Pradesh. I'd like to believe our shampoo and acne creams helped the teenagers go on some memorable dates. The Itanagar example showed once more you can't predict a market until you experience it. You have to dive into the Ganga. And get washed away or come out blessed.

The flip side was that the CEO went on a hiring spree. He made 450 new recruitments in one year. In all, we had about 1,000 people on our payroll in the product company alone. The net result was that despite our growth, our profitability went down.

I asked a bright chartered accountant who had recently joined us to go to the field and look at the ground realities. He found out that there was primary sale, but not much tertiary sale. Goods were sold but on credit. There was no money coming in. However, on paper, our sales grew from x to 4x, when in actuality, they hadn't. And then we were paying GST on 4x. So we were losing double the money.

Not only that, the CEO was also giving merchants other incentives, like promising them an assistant or health adviser who'd pitch the products to customers. Health advisers are the people you see at stores wearing the uniform of a brand. At one point we had 400 health advisers. They don't come for free. You have to give them incentives worth Rs 15,000–Rs 20,000 a month. Health advisers are a good concept and some of them did translate into sales. But we certainly did not need 400 of them. And not all of them had brand loyalty.

And though the advisers weren't initially on our payroll, we incentivized our partners to pay them. Then we found out they weren't being paid on time.

It was time to take a decision about the CEO. We had to ask him to leave. After all, margins and cash flows are more important than growth for the sake of it. You cannot sustain a business that is bleeding continuously. This is why professional management doesn't work unless it is supervised till a point where it is aligned to the company's values and goals.

Another search for a CEO began. When we found one, his brief was the exact opposite of his predecessor's. He had to trim the flab, which he did. From being in nearly 20,000 outlets, we are now in a lean and manageable 2,000 outlets. We have about fifty good health advisers who are on our payroll, are well trained and supervised, and have developed a great brand loyalty about our products. We have also cut down to around twenty-five to thirty core products, which we know that the market wants.

Aggressive cost-cutting was the way forward to sustain the product vertical. It is often the little changes that make a big impact. I am reminded of the example of Southwest Airlines, which saved $40,000 a year in 1994, by reducing just one olive from every dinner plate served during flight, and $300,000 a year by not printing the company's logo on rubbish bags! Similarly, United Airlines in 2017 reduced one ounce of paper in the weight of their in-flight magazine, *Hemisphere*, saving 170 gallons of fuel a year and $290,000 in cost.

We too did our bit by negotiating prices with existing vendors of raw materials and packaging, to bring down the cost of goods, or replaced them with newer vendors who had the same quality but lower pricing. We replaced the super stockists with direct distributors, wherever possible, thereby saving another 5–7 per cent in margins.

Margins for retailers were fixed and extra claims stopped. Prices of fast-moving products were increased (this had not been done for three years). Staff travel expenses were rationalized. Salaries were moved to pay for performance. Every little change helped to break even, especially during the difficult Covid period.

There were other challenges too. The supply chain and market disruption during Covid, together with a reduction in the sales team and health advisers, meant that unsold goods over a few months were lying in the market. This meant going to each of the 200 distributors and agreeing to change unsold stock with fast-moving products. This led to further financial losses which were not anticipated.

We now work only on advance payment.

Through all our problems, we continue to innovate. We launched new products, some of them necessitated by coronavirus, like alcohol-based hand sanitizers. We also developed, researched and launched at least ten new products every year. This not only increased our product portfolio and excited the marketplace, but also added to our turnover and profitability. We continue to do this.

A few years ago we launched our first food supplement, Nutrigood. It is a hair nutraceutical you have with milk or water, like a protein shake for your scalp. There is a huge demand for it from our clinic patients as well as from the outside market and it has a healthy annual turnover. We are now coming out with similar nutraceuticals for skin, women's health, children's health and some other conditions.

We also have exclusive manufacturing tie-ups with international manufacturing houses like a natural hair colour under our brand which is manufactured in Italy and is doing very well in India. Our hair fibre is manufactured and imported from China (currently stopped after the border skirmishes with India, as part of our company's nationalistic pride). 'Atmanirbhar Bharat' has helped us to develop and manufacture this in India.

It was always a goal of mine to make homeopathy products available over the counter (OTC) at regular chemist outlets. This would increase the reach of homeopathy for the common consumer and change it from being merely doctor-driven. In the USA alone over 25 million units of homeopathy (OTC) products are sold every year. The market for OTC homeopathic medicines is expected to be $20 billion by 2024. In chains like Boots in the UK, and almost all over Europe, you can get homeopathy medicines OTC.

In the last few years, the Ministry of Ayush has made it possible to sell homeopathic medicines OTC in India too. We recently launched our first OTC product and homeopathic immunity builder, with an entire OTC range to follow. We plan to make these available to around 1200 chemists across the country. We are also presently in discussion with one of the largest homeopathy OTC chains in the world to bring them to India.

I will now explain a little more about the distribution of our products. Budding entrepreneurs will find many lessons in our arduous journey into the market, our experiences with different partners and the challenges of different channels of sales. Creating a distribution system, after all, is one of the hardest parts of trade.

Our primary channel for distribution is our 200-plus clinics, including 70 franchisee clinics. More than 50,000 brand-committed consumers visit our clinics every month and they form the bulk of our product sales. Even after offering discounts to our patients, it still leaves us with enough margins to make us profitable. Avenue number two is modern trade, which comprises supermarket chains. These are not easy to get into. They already have so many brands that you have to wait for a place to open up. It's like the Indian cricket team. You may be very good but you have to wait till there's a vacancy.

Once you get in, you have to pay the supermarkets a listing price for your product. Sometimes you have to pay separately for two sizes of the same product. Then you have to give them a good price, pay for shelf space and a health adviser, if you want one. Most of our modern trade stores which had a health adviser did well in terms of sales, but were not profitable due to increased costs.

We got into one major Indian chain even though they offered us low margins. The more we sold the more we lost. After a couple of years, we moved out.

Institutional dealers such as the government-run Khadi Bhandars and army, navy and police canteen stores are our third channel. We are doing well in some of those. But again, you need a lot of investment, not to mention navigate a web of rules and regulations. We have had cases where they didn't pay us our share of income. Getting them to do so took a lot of time and energy, and eventually we walked out. Currently, we are only in the navy and police stores.

Then there is general trade, which is the most difficult channel. You have to go through stockists and super-stockists, and many layers and commissions.

The final channel and the one where all the action is moving is e-commerce. It is our aim to strengthen our online presence. Currently we are selling across twenty e-commerce platforms like Amazon, Nykaa, 1mg, Netmeds, Paytm and, of course, on our own website—www.drbatras.com. Also on the agenda is increasing our use of modern promotional tools, such as influencers and social media. We have ramped up our visibility on online platforms and we have embraced modern ways of marketing. Traditional PR is almost dead with the advent of paid media, which is more expensive than regular advertising.

Tenacity is the lesson we learnt from our products vertical. Despite failing multiple times we kept bouncing back. And after ten long years of experimentation, our products vertical has finally turned profitable. Perseverance is the key to success in entrepreneurship.

50

Franchising for Fast Growth

FRANCHISING IS A LEGITIMATE METHOD OF GROWING YOUR BRAND without having to be hands-on yourself. However, the step needs to be thought through well. It's fraught with headaches, like franchisees installing their family members at the clinic or shop. Surely you have encountered, and been gypped of change, by a lady in casual clothes at a Dunkin' at Penn Station or Newark.

Here's the first rule of franchising. You have to time it right. Your brand has to have recognition and there must be demand for it. When we took the plunge some six years ago, we had 100 clinics around India and systems in place. Now we have over seventy franchisee clinics in sixty-four cities. A person in Jharkhand, aware of the brand story, is now likely to think, '*Dr Batra ka international brand hai. Abhi woh Jharkhand mein hain* (Dr Batra has an international brand and now he is in Jharkhand).' Such a person comes in with trust and does not mind paying for the treatment.

You also need to be clear about why you want to start franchising. We did it to provide professional homeopathy to smaller cities in India. Two, we wanted to increase the reach of the brand. Three, we wanted to leverage the brand as we had built it over almost forty years.

One of our key franchising protocols was (and still holds good) that the doctors would be trained by us. We also provided them the software, so the process was standardized everywhere. The medicines would be ours too. This meant branches had to have enough inventory. We didn't want someone saying, 'We ran out of medicines and had to use local ones.'

But even after taking due care, there is no guarantee that a clinic hundreds of miles away is being run properly. Measures like mystery shoppers, customer feedback and surprise visits are therefore non-negotiables. At times I've been tempted to mystery shop myself, in disguise like Hercule Poirot or Karamchand, but decided against it.

There have been several challenges along the way. The grand franchisee tradition of making Bhabhi or Jeeja or Didi or Bunty sit on the front desk is one such. When asked, the dealer usually replies, '*Wo ghar par baithe the, toh clinic mein bula liya* (They were just sitting at home, so I called them to sit at the clinic).' At times, they aren't even this polite. '*Mera paisa hai* [it's my money], I'll hire who I want.' The problem arises when Bhabhi/Jeeja/Didi/Bunty start telling the doctor what to do.

There are other issues such as the staff not being paid on time, because the doctor is depending on the franchisee partners to pay; or when the franchisee does not sell a particular product because it has a lower margin. There have even been cases when a franchisee has taken an irrational dislike to a doctor and treated him or her rudely.

A more serious issue arises when the franchisee sells the clinic to a third person. Swayed by the brand name, that person pays a premium price, but struggles to recover costs due to the market size in that region. For example, we had a clinic in Latur, Maharashtra. Suddenly we found that the partner had changed. The latest buyer had overpaid for the clinic there. In a small market like Latur, he could never recover the cost. He was stuck and so were we, while the original partner laughed his way to the bank (and then the bar).

Let me share a few other case studies. Don't always look outside for franchise partners. Look within and nurture entrepreneurial skills of people in your own organization. One of our smart entry-level staffers who joined us seventeen years ago in Gurgaon, learned the business so well that he opted to become a franchise partner in 2013. Today he is a proud franchise partner of four clinics—Greater Noida, Aligarh, Haldwani and Rudrapur—all doing very well.

Another way to build the franchise model is to select a good franchise partner and help him to grow from a franchise to a master franchise. Most people do this the other way round. Our Jabalpur partner grew from one clinic to seven clinics covering the entire state of Madhya Pradesh. You don't need too many partners—a few right ones are good enough.

Sometimes, unexpected tragedy strikes. A franchise doctor in Solapur passed away suddenly after successfully running the clinic for two years. Her father was a retired school principal, a very simple man living a retired life in his village. He requested us to let him run the clinic as he wanted it as a remembrance of his daughter. However, he had no experience of running any business leave aside the running of a clinic. Slowly the business started declining and suffering losses. We moved in, took charge and turned it around, making it profitable once again. Sometimes as a brand owner you need to be the go-to person and help your partners in need.

We also learnt that the skill set of a partner for every business is unique. He may be good in one and not necessarily in another. Our partner who was doing very well in Varanasi did poorly in our new venture of pet-care clinics (Dr Batra's® Pet Care). This impacted the relationship and the clinic's business.

Then there were occasions when the business of the franchise went down. That is when the partners start getting upset and unpleasant and you have to manage the situation. The lesson here is that your partner cannot just be someone who has money, but is also someone who is aligned with the company's purpose.

What the top leadership needs to communicate to the franchisees is that in a field like healthcare they should take into consideration the blessings and goodwill of patients. Franchisees often have multiple businesses. They may be selling electronics, for instance, but when they are also making a difference to people's health, it gives their existence new meaning. It may even burnish their reputation and help their other businesses.

And we did see doctors and franchisees, at least those with a heart, getting a great deal of job satisfaction when they cured patients. For example, they'd be touched when someone said, 'My mother was sick and I took her to the new Dr Batra's® clinic in town. Now she is so much better.'

Sometimes the location of a franchise proves to be a challenge for the owner. One of our franchises was near Naxalite territory, in a place called Jagdalpur in the Bastar district of Chhattisgarh. We were in the city and reasonably far from the base of the insurgents. But many of our doctors refused to go there. Freshers, however, were willing to take up the assignment. We provided them accommodation and travel allowance, so that they were comfortable. Besides, most of them were young and unmarried, not yet bogged down by the demands of grown-up life. Unfortunately, we had to eventually shut down the Jagdalpur clinic. But as long as we were there, the locals were happy.

Everybody needs doctors and medicines. We didn't always know who we were treating in Jagdalpur, whether it was a civilian or a guerrilla rebel. Our job was to heal them. They'd walk away grateful that there was, at last, someone to look after them. Rich and powerful patients have been arrogant at times, but the less fortunate have almost always been gracious.

Jagdalpur taught us that every city had to be carefully studied before entering. Some places may have the potential for multiple clinics, some for none. Even in the case of the former, it is best to test the waters with one and then launch another; and if, in some cases, the needle does not show movement, then the relevance of the city needs to be re-evaluated and a decision taken.

We also understood that what we could do in the metros would not work with franchises in the smaller cities. In 2016, we made a strategic shift from above-the-line (ATL) marketing to digital marketing. This was good for some markets, but had a huge impact on the franchise business, which so far had been thriving mainly on the company's central marketing. To cope with this we devised smart, city-specific marketing plans involving local newspapers and awareness programmes. It was effective and we built a self-sustainable business.

To summarize, franchising *does* work. Consistent losses, cheating, or, equally worse, indifference about the brand are the only reasons to end the franchise relationship. At the end of a working day, owner and franchisee should both be able to say what the painter Vincent Van Gogh said, 'I put my heart and my soul into my work, and have lost my mind in the process.'

51

Evenings in Paris

When I saw the *Munnabhai* films,[6] I laughed a lot. I didn't know that in 2011 I would be in a situation similar to the protagonist's. I'd be the oldest boy in a class. It started with my son Akshay going to ISB, Hyderabad, for a course. He was impressed by the school and what he learnt. In fact, he met two of our senior-level hires there.

When Akshay came back, his head was full of ideas. One of them was for me to apply to Harvard for a short but intense medical excellence course for doctors and hospital administrators. It wasn't an easy course to get into. You applied, and if invited, you went.

Harvard held a special place in Akshay's heart. It was his ambition to go there for a full two-year programme. But he had already gotten into practice and had also become a father and it did not happen. Now he wanted me to go. Normally, it is a father

6 *Munnabhai MBBS* (2003) and *Lage Raho Munnabhai* (2006).

who wants his son to do what he couldn't. Here it was the other way round.

On the other hand, I was comfortable where I was. Approaching sixty, I felt on top of my game and in control of my enterprise. But now my son was thrusting a school bag in my hands. This wasn't some Mickey Mouse course you chilled through and got a Harvard certificate at the end. It involved months of coursework, followed by a week of the actual course, with day-long classes and nights spent studying.

I expressed my reservations.

'No, you have to register.' Akshay was adamant.

My life had never followed a traditional script. So after some thought, I said I'd go.

Akshay filled up my application. Perhaps he praised me too much to impress the jury. I signed and we sent it off.

After my file sped through the cables and landed in the mailbox of the admissions office in Boston, we went on a holiday to Himachal Pradesh. We stayed in a small bungalow with a garden. You could see the Himalayas every morning, their peaks looking as if dusted with white talcum powder. Akshay and my grandson Hriman were with me. It was a lovely time, spent doing family activities and also enjoying the stillness that nature provides.

A mail from Boston then raced back through the cables and dinged on my phone in Himachal. I had been chosen for the course. Had Circuit from *Munnabhai* been there he would have screamed in the echoing valley, '*Bhai Harvard jare le.*'

It began to sink in. This was really happening.

To remind me of the rigours of what I had signed up for, Harvard sent me substantial course material. It wasn't possible to download it in Himachal, so I asked my assistant in Mumbai to do so and send me the printouts. After a few days, some 300 pages arrived at the bungalow. They were case studies and what not, which I had to read up before I started the course. My holiday was over. Goodbye lazy afternoons.

Initially, it seemed beyond me. Just the act of sitting down to study felt odd. It had been over thirty years since I left college.

'Akshay, I can't understand a single case study. Please explain it to me,' I said.

'Don't worry, Papa. You'll learn on your own.'

'You have been to ISB. Help me out.'

'It's not as difficult, just stick with it a few days,' Akshay said.

I gave the syllabus another shot. Gradually, the fear and rust dropped, and I started to understand some parts. The more I read, the more I grasped. And then I was ready to fly. The course involved a week's stay in Paris—not Boston—for day-long lectures and discussions. The rest of the programme could be completed online from home.

Our group had forty-six people. I was the oldest. Most people in class were in their early to mid-forties. There were two Indians—a doctor from north India and I. Many of my classmates were doing interesting work. One lady was a vice admiral in the American Navy. She was in charge of 300 base hospitals all over the world. There was a group from Singapore that had been sponsored by the government. I learnt from them that healthcare in Singapore is so important that it can be an election agenda. If a person complains about the quality of a state-run hospital, the government can change. So they do not spare any effort or expense to get their employees trained at the best institutions.

We stayed at the Hilton on the stunning Rue de Rivoli in Paris. However, hotel rooms in Paris were like their cuisine, small. You could either fit your family or your bags in one room. But there were beautiful shops and restaurants and museums nearby, not that we had much time to enjoy anything. The lectures were held in a cream-walled seminar room at the same hotel. We had two instructors, one male and one female. They hand-held us through the first steps, and then divided us into groups.

Analyses of organizational successes and failures were a big part of the course. One of the cases we discussed in detail was the Columbia space shuttle tragedy in 2003. The spacecraft had disintegrated due to a malfunction while re-entering the earth after sixteen days in space. All seven astronauts on board, including Kalpana Chawla, the first woman of Indian origin in space, were killed. The US National Aeronautics and Space Administration (NASA) was criticized for its handling of the Columbia space shuttle. The case study stressed the need for the kind of emergency management you should ideally have in your company.

The style of learning was interactive, with teachers and participants animated and engaged. Our day would start at about 8 a.m. and end at about 6 p.m. Some of the participants would then step out and enjoy Paris's nightlife. There were a few who had been sponsored by their company and were not really serious about the programme. I would step out for some fresh air in the evenings, then go back and study. As an owner who had enrolled in the course on my own dime, I wanted to make the most of it.

The week went by quickly. I remember that the course ended on my sixtieth birthday. The teachers gave me a small slice of chocolate cake with a candle in class, and complimented me on my participation.

I remember looking at the cake and saying, 'How do I share it with everybody?' The moderator said, 'Dr Batra, it is your birthday. So you get to eat the cake and nobody else.'

I had proved that no age was too old for learning. Job done and goodbyes said, I could at last enjoy the country. A couple of my friends joined me from India. That night we went to Lido. From Paris, we went to the South of France for a ten-day holiday. One morning at lunch, we raised a toast to my son, without whom this wouldn't have happened. Except instead of champagne glasses, we clinked baguettes.

52

Practising Customer Delight

'*Atithi devo bhava* (The guest is God).' This is one of the principles of Indian hospitality. Doesn't matter if deep within you want to throttle your guests as they raid your bar or fridge. Our attitudes to guests may be a mix of truth and artifice, but in work there is no such dichotomy. Our guest, the customer, truly is God.

Sometime ago, there was an article in *Forbes* magazine on the world's top 100 companies. It said that being customer-centric is more than just offering a good product or staffing a call centre. It is about this approach being the way of life for the company. Respecting the customer should be in its DNA.

Take Trader Joe's for example. It consistently scores high on the American Customer Satisfaction Index (ACSI). How does it do this? By selling quality products, for one. Two, Trader Joe's employees go to great lengths to make customers happy, such as opening a new packet to offer free samples.

Another great example is that of Amazon. Jeff Bezos is known to be a customer-obsessed leader. His empty chair story is famous amongst those who have read about the company. During board meetings, Bezos would leave a chair empty in the room. He'd tell the executives to assume that it belonged to the most critical and crucial member of the company—the customer. Bezos would then encourage his employees to make all their decisions keeping the customer in mind.

Such practices have a direct bearing on the bottom line. According to a study, brands that have a superior customer experience bring in 5.7 times more revenue than their competitors.

At Dr Batra's® too, we follow a patient-first philosophy and that transcends every facet of our enterprise. We believe that putting patients first comes in many forms—be it adopting new technology or getting real-time feedback. We pride ourselves on not just addressing our patients' needs but on building relationships with them, and for that trust is integral.

At the very outset of creating this brand, I made sure that every employee understood that we would always be transparent with our patients. Every decision taken by the doctor would be in the patient's interest. In fact, in cases of hair loss, we have got feedback from patients saying, 'I went to your clinic and the doctor told me that my hair loss was too severe and therefore they will not be able to treat me.' This is because we do not push patients to get unnecessary treatments.

Convenience also plays an important role in generating higher customer engagement and satisfaction. To give a basic example, at Dr Batra's® we have analysed the daily engagement patterns of our patients and found that they prefer appointments that are after office hours and on weekends. Therefore, our doctors conduct consultations for longer hours on weekends. In any case, all our clinics are open till 8 p.m. daily. To provide ease of access to patients, we also conduct online consultations and courier medicines to those patients who cannot visit the clinic.

There is no fury as that of a customer scorned. According to the USA's White House Office of Consumer Affairs, a dissatisfied customer shares a negative experience with at least nineteen other people, and 13 per cent of dissatisfied customers tell more than twenty people about it. On the other hand, a satisfied customer can become your most loyal brand ambassador.

We have developed a strong feedback system to monitor patient satisfaction. To strengthen the feedback system, an one-time password (OTP) is sent to the patient and negative patient feedback is sent to a senior doctor who then handles the case going forward. This feedback is also channelled to the senior management team to make sure that changes are implemented.

In addition, over the last fifteen years, we have undertaken regular third-party patient audits with reputed firms and also performed a mystery patient audit in every clinic at least once in a quarter. The overall experience, including the quality of the doctor's consultation, interaction with front-line staff and hygiene of the clinic are some of the components assessed.

In current times, having a robust and quick digital service has become non-negotiable. According to the International Data Corporation (IDC), transformation to digital is the first step to becoming more customer-centric. This includes adopting new technology and adapting to changing touchpoints. Covid-19 made it all the more important, as everything is tackled online as far as possible.

Globally, the social media era began around 2004 and started growing in India about a decade later. We were the first amongst the medical fraternity to partner with Google and Facebook in 2014, so that we could reach out to our patients in convenient and relevant formats. Today, we have a significant social media presence with six lakh followers on Facebook, Instagram, Twitter and YouTube.

As leaders in the field of homeopathy, we don't just look to provide medicine and treatment, but also try to: educate the patient about the efficacy of homeopathy; and ensure the knowledge of its treatment outcomes and benefits is available to the community at large. Be it Facebook, Instagram or YouTube, we create content that is bite-sized and in regional languages for wide and easy consumption. We also create informative content like our social media series, '*Good Health and Homeopathy*'. It garnered twenty-five lakh views and was even taken to the UAE market. Our social media and digital efforts also helped us win accolades, including the top rank in the Homeopathy Category in terms of traffic and followers on Alexa.

Customer studies show that they favour brands that offer an efficient self-service customer portal. As a strong believer in providing patients the right to choose, we give them platforms to talk about their ailments and share their treatment outcomes. We also provide self-evaluation through algorithm-based ailment tests available on our website. This helps them understand their health concerns and gives them a clearer picture about possible treatments. Additionally, we have developed a strong 'online reputation management' (ORM) module through which we monitor the ratings for each of our clinics and also incentivize doctors to create patient delight through every engagement.

Through our mobile app, we have M-powered our patients to connect with doctors at the click of a button. Patients can reschedule appointments, give feedback, get information about their ailments, learn about new developments, and avail of a plethora of offers. Our hyperlocal search system and the use of artificial intelligence (AI) in the form of chatbots across our website make engagement with the brand quick, simple and efficient.

Years of practise has taught us that just exceeding patient expectations doesn't make them more loyal to our brand. It's our transparency, trustworthiness and delivering on our brand promise that has increased our patient loyalty and retention.

Lastly, we make sure that it isn't just how we say hello to our patients that is important, but it's how we say goodbye. Through better interactions comes better patient approach, which is also an important part of improved patient outcomes. We therefore strive to ensure that every interaction with our brand is as sweet as our homeopathic pills.

53

Labour Pains

'If you be my bodyguard, I can be your long-lost pal'

— 'You Can Call Me Al', by Paul Simon (1986)

THERE WAS A TIME I HAD A BODYGUARD, THOUGH YOU COULDN'T call us pals. A couple of policemen were also stationed at my office. It's not as if I had become the sarkar. In fact, it was due to self-styled sarkars of the city and their thugs that I needed protection.

We were having union problems. If you watch gangster movies, this was a sign you had arrived. Big shot tycoons had union problems. But this wasn't *Deewar* (1975). This was real life in a small health and wellness company. We had sacked some employees for misbehaviour, after which they vindictively formed a union and made life hell for us for some years with the help of a Mumbai-based political party.

We were in London on a family vacation when the problems began. Our CEO called and briefed me about it. He was a tough-looking, moustachioed man, who had been the COO of a steel company. In all probability he had tackled major labour issues before. But here, he functioned like a 'bada saab' and was not quite hands-on. Besides, he was non-Maharashtrian. He didn't know how to deal with a uniquely Mumbai and Maharashtra problem. So he called me.

'Mr Chairman sir,' he said, 'so-and-so in the store department misbehaved and was aggressive, what should I do?'

Handling staff is one of the biggest challenges for an entrepreneur. Employees come in all shades. Some make you proud, others can be a headache. But I have zero tolerance for lack of ethics.

'Please throw him out,' I told our CEO.

This was not easy to do, especially with me being away, and I understood that. The CEO sacked a few of them but not the manager. However, after I came back, we got rid of him too.

Soon, however, a union was formed by the mischief-mongers and those whom they influenced and were still in the company. They gained further strength by joining a certain political party. After that, the gang went from one clinic to another, signing up more members. If someone did not wish to enroll, he was forced to. Soon, unions had formed in Mumbai and Pune, two of our top cities in terms of our numbers.

Goons, violence—we lived scenes from Bollywood, making me wonder why I was being punished for no fault of mine. But that is entrepreneurship. Van-loads of rogues would come with hockey sticks and iron bars and storm the office. Once, Dr Bindu hid in a dark cabin, scared and in tears. The HR head, a lady, did not find any place to wait it out. She found herself surrounded by the men and then threatened by them.

The union members were uncompromising. They wanted the sacked employees to be reinstated. It was plain dadagiri. Apart from destroying offices, they'd call employees, male and female, and say threatening things like, 'We know which school your kids go to.'

Our HR head and another female staffer eventually left the company, much to our chagrin. At this stage we let the police know. But with a local political party in the mix, they only paid us lip service. I realized I needed to escalate matters, and spoke to someone high up in the police hierarchy.

Meanwhile, some of the rowdy elements that hadn't been removed would deliberately hinder the work in our clinics. If they were dispensers, for example, they'd take forever to hand over the medicines to patients.

The ordeal went on for about six years. It was physically and mentally draining. We lost so much by way of energy and revenue due to these issues. At one point we even had to hire more people, as some of the existing staff wasn't working and neither could we sack them.

Then we employed a gambit that would have made a chess champion proud. One, we hired a manager from the same community as the union members and two, we stopped giving union members pay hikes. Everybody else in the company got a raise but union members didn't. Come to the clinic, sit, have tea, embarrass yourselves and go. No problem. But buddy, you aren't getting a rupee extra.

Of course there was a risk of serious retaliation involved with this move. But we weren't pushovers. Like I said, by now, we too had made some calls and got muscle to protect us. Gradually, we wore the union down. The manager explained to them gently that by continuing to go against the company, they were the ones missing out. Frankly, they too were fed up at not getting money when everyone else around them was. Can you imagine not getting a raise for five years or so? That can make anyone rethink their methods.

One by one, people started leaving the union. For a while, the defectors were threatened by the few that remained. And then the union collapsed completely, consumed by the leaping flames of its own greed and toxicity. But as soon as all this ended and we could exhale, some of our ex-employees joined another union, this one patronized by a party that had once dug up the pitch at Wankhede Stadium.

They would cross my path either through force or by pretending to be patients and say, 'We know where you live, your car number and when you travel. Next time, we'll harm you.'

I never changed my travel plans out of fear. But it was a difficult time. At one of our events at the Bhabha Theatre, M.S. Dhoni was the chief guest and I was sitting next to him. We were talking about philanthropy. Suddenly, in the middle of the show, a man pounced on me and demanded jobs for locals. It was embarrassing. Luckily, there was enough security around and he was taken away.

As a company we realized we had to invest in people who'd manage discord. We appointed a good labour consultant and then a chief people's officer. Together with Akshay, they resolved most of the issues. We also won a case that was filed in the labour court against us by the union. I think that's when they realized their khichdi wasn't going to cook in our pot.

In the last couple of years, we have settled everything and the matter is over. Also, we exercise great care and sensitivity when we let someone from the company go.

The lesson from this experience for me, and for all company heads, was that getting to the top is relatively easy, staying there is difficult. Conflict resolution, especially, is a big challenge. Luck can help you get to the top of the pyramid, but you need determination and guts to stay there.

54

Trust, but Not Blindly

There have been so many challenges and, equally, so many victories. One of our biggest wins was in the historic red building of the Calcutta High Court. A conniving employee and his accomplices had filed a case against me and our practices in our newly opened Kolkata clinic. But the honourable judge voted in our favour. I was not present at the judgment, but felt strong and vindicated when I heard about it.

I was also relieved. The preceding eighteen months had been among the worst of my life due to this employee and the nature of his accusations. My integrity was being questioned, even though all my professional life I maintained the highest ethical standards. Such was my passion for homeopathy that I would never do anything to bring it into disrepute.

This is how it happened.

In the year 2000 we launched our company and opened a clinic in Kolkata. It was in Minto Park, close to the serene Shahid Bhagat Singh Udyan. But there was nothing peaceful about the experience for us. For one, we had a lot of competition, as there were lots of legacy homeopaths in nearly every street in Kolkata. And then, one of our brightest doctors—whom we shall refer to as Milan—turned on me. Milan was good with patients. He was good with medicines. He was also Bengali, and was at home in the milieu. He just wasn't a good person.

Anyway, while Milan was still in our good books, we moved him to Delhi as we had a couple of good lady doctors in Kolkata who could handle things on their own. Also, we needed his skills and intelligence for our burgeoning scale in Delhi. The plan was that after a few months he could move back home to Kolkata.

As soon as Milan was transferred to Delhi, however, trouble started. There was a raid by the Directorate of the Food & Drugs Administration (FDA) on our Kolkata clinic. I was at a function when I received the shocking news. We had never been on the wrong side of the law. I respected my profession too much to do that.

Worse was to follow. One of the lady doctors in Kolkata was arrested for one night. This was outrageous. You don't just raid a property and put someone behind bars unless it is a hardened criminal. I felt responsible for the doctor, not just because she was an employee, but her father had personally visited me when she joined and respectfully told me, 'She is in your care now.'

Television, the same medium that contributed to my growth, now showed me its less alluring side. News about the raid played on loop. As we were blister-packing medicines we were told it was akin to manufacturing and we were accused of manufacturing medicines without a licence. I also bore the brunt of our media's legendary kite-flying abilities when some of them said I was 'absconding'.

The lady doctor was released the following morning. But the other problems continued. Every day there was speculation that some team or another was out to arrest me. We were told to change phones, stay in hotels, as if we were career criminals.

Within the company, it was becoming difficult to keep rumours under control.

One of my acquaintances mentioned a lawyer we shall call Lina. Her husband was a lawyer too. Lina was helpful initially, but she too started taking advantage of us. She'd travel at our expense to Kolkata with her husband and stay in luxury hotels. *Et tu*, Lina? My company and I were being emotionally and financially drained. The internal teams were affected as well. They were miles away from the goings-on, and therefore more prone to panic as they did not have accurate information. Papers and television were the only source of news at that time. There was no WhatsApp for an update, reliable or otherwise.

You may wonder why I, with patients and friends in high places, allowed myself to be hounded by relative nonentities. Why did I not reach out to my contacts, especially those in politics?

The only reason for that is I never took favours from politicians. It was my policy. I was a self-made man. I had appointed a lawyer and was fighting my own battle. Besides, I did not want to talk about the matter with the outside world. It was embarrassing enough, as it was.

It was time to take on the issue head-on. Milan played the good cop by suggesting he could approach powerful Kolkata lawyers. I okayed his suggestion, and we got some legal aces on board. After a long year and a half, the matter ended with the court ruling in our favour. But along with the satisfaction of victory was the disturbing realization that Milan himself had been behind the raid. For the longest time my style was non-confrontational. If something unfortunate happened I'd block it out and move on. Naturally, people took advantage of this.

Milan's shenanigans continued when he took all our secrets and started his own company. He also played me against my rival. True, we were competitors already. But Milan further poisoned our minds against each other.

In the meantime, another complaint was filed against me by a fake patient who said she suffered adverse reactions after taking my medicines from our Delhi clinic, when I had not visited Delhi on that day. Our Dadar clinic was also raided. Scared and insecure about their future, employees started jumping ship.

At such a time it is good to think boldly and make some advance moves, even if you have to swallow your pride. Unbeknownst to Milan, I met my competitor directly. The meeting was set up by a well-meaning friend. Over a cup of tea, we realized the full extent to which we were being played against each other by Milan. We decided it was in our best interests to call a truce of some sort and thereby neutralize Milan. We shook hands and parted, still not friends, but not enemies either. In fact, my competitor even asked me to introduce his son to Shah Rukh Khan and invited me to give the valedictory address at his college. Most importantly, we decided not to fall victim to Milan's plotting.

A tip to entrepreneurs: Ensure that you have a strong legal and administrative team when you start your company. Looking back at those years, while we had good doctors, we did not have enough legal, accounting and management experts to protect the company from troublemakers. Don't trust people blindly. The ones you trust the most sometimes stab you in the back.

55

Beware! There's Always Someone to Rob You

IN THE EARLY 2000S, WE HAD JUST STARTED OUR COMPANY AND I WAS working in the corporate office in Dadar. Outside on Tulsi Pipe Road, traffic laboured along, the stress of drivers apparent in their angry honking, the cars looking like caged pets snarling for freedom.

The phone rang. It was a call that was also like a timely horn, as it stopped me from getting run over by the crooked plan of a man I thought was my friend. We'll call him the Dark Side of the Moon (DSM). This potential usurper was also my patient, but more on our curious relationship later.

The phone call was from a famous boss of a bank, whom I had known for a while. In front of his desk was an application from our company for a loan of Rs 50 crore. The application was inveigled out of me by DSM and his broker friend. No doubt, they had plans to take a cut from the amount.

'Doc, I have sanctioned your loan,' the bank boss said. 'But don't do it. Don't grow so fast.'

When someone of that stature tells you something, you listen. I did not take the loan.

This peeved DSM and his broker friend. I had rained on their parade. They made life difficult for me, especially DSM. He was a vicious, cunning man. In his prime he had worked for a fabric company and had even taken on the textile king of India, the head of a rival company. He knew the rules inside out and he filed bogus complaints to different government departments, posing as a shareholder. Once, to humiliate us, he sent a peon to attend our annual general meeting (AGM). But I gutted it out. I made a lot of mistakes in my career. Getting influenced by this man was one of the worst. But every time I came out wiser and stronger.

How did I let this snake coil around me in the first place? Well, he was a patient. He lived nearby. So we spoke often. He appealed to my ambition to grow homeopathy. 'You should aim higher, do this, do that.' And due to his corporate stature and intellect, I was a bit in thrall to him. I thought he would help me come up with an IPO. It would have made us the first listed homeopathy company in the world and would have helped monetize our brand for growth.

My wife was noticing this, as most wives do. She wasn't comfortable with DSM. Her feminine intuition told her he was a man best left at arm's length. But at the time I believed people who are bad with some can be good to others. DSM was a jerk to the world at large, but might be nice to me, more so since I was his doctor, neighbour and a sort of a friend. DSM sold me big dreams like multiplying the number of clinics I had and coming out with an IPO, a sign of success and ambition at that time. 'I can help you do it,' he said.

Being ambitious, yet having no experience or knowledge of building a company, I fell for the idea and brought DSM on board for a hefty retainership fee, not to mention perks. Blinded by my dreams of a splashy IPO and a rapid climb up the corporate ladder, I even gave DSM a small percentage of my shares in the company. My wife was furious, and it strained our relationship.

Another person who felt DSM wasn't bringing much value to the set-up was our chartered accountant. He would have meetings with DSM and I would ask him how things went. Out of politeness, he didn't say much initially, but later on he did suggest DSM wasn't telling him anything new, and that we were wasting our hard-earned money on him.

DSM's demands and excesses kept increasing. 'There's an investor I know in Zurich we should meet,' he told me one day. 'He recently put in money in a big Indian group and wants to do more in India.'

I gave him the benefit of the doubt and gave the trip the green signal. DSM only flew first class, so our tickets weren't cheap.

Once in Zurich, we freshened up and went to see the investor, an eighty-plus gent who obviously came from old money. He sat in a large wood-panelled room with chandeliers, across a giant table on which we could have played ice hockey. In true Swiss tradition, the man was polite. We were offered refreshments. But in true Western business tradition, he also told us bluntly we were too small a company for him to bother with. The Indian group he had invested in was a corporate giant. He was clearly not interested in small change.

The next day DSM and I sheepishly took the flight back home. Now I was irritated. This interaction could have been done on the phone. Instead DSM had found an excuse to go to Switzerland. It was a waste of money and I let him know that. Chastened that his gambit didn't work, DSM said to me, 'Don't worry. I know a very good broker in India who can get us Rs 50 crore.'

I consented and DSM and his accomplice then applied for the loan, after which the bank's boss alerted me. 'Don't grow too fast.'

As soon as I changed my mind about the loan, the dam of tension burst between me, DSM and the broker. I told them I did not want them around any more. But they fought for every little scrap of money. With the broker I could sever ties with one payment. With DSM it was more complicated. He held shares in our company, and I had to pay him for those at a value inflated by him.

In all, we worked together for a year and a half. In this fairly short period DSM made a tidy sum for himself out of my company and gave very little in return.

Oddly enough, he continued coming to me for treatment. I don't hold grudges, and I discharged my doctor's duties. But I kept it strictly professional and did not say a word beyond what was necessary. I lost a lot of money due to DSM. But I learnt I could grow from one clinic to over 200 on my own. And I did it over the next twenty years, my way, with dedication and honesty.

There is a lesson here for entrepreneurs. While it is good to be ambitious, never get so carried away by your dreams that you don't do your due diligence. Aim for the skies, put your head in the clouds, but keep your feet firmly on the ground. Reaching for the moon is safer when you are your own person, untethered from devious partners.

56

Learn to Cut Your Losses

Being vertically challenged, no one appreciated the joy of growing vertically more than me. When you grow vertically, your feet are no longer on the ground. And thus, just when you are having your best run, you are most liable to imperil your growth. Young entrepreneurs would do well to remember this.

There was a period when we were growing at 30 per cent a year. We were not merely staying on the treadmill, the treadmill was trying to keep up with us. We thought we could diversify and had the resources to sustain our new ideas. We were wrong. We should have stuck to our core competency and not lost focus. Read on to know why.

One of our innovations was Dr Batra's® Pet Care. I had been an animal lover since childhood. It pained me to see animals being subjected to injections and the sort. I thought homeopathic medicines, which veterinarians often use in the UK, would be easier on them. Waffle, my Labrador, laps up her sweet pills from my hand. And all these years if anyone asked me for homeopathic medicines for their pets, I gave them free of cost.

Pets also have some conditions which are difficult to treat with allopathy or traditional medicine. Certain skin problems, arthritis, kidney problems and so many other things can be treated with homeopathy. Also, people in India were getting increasingly caring about their non-human friends, and that was the idea behind starting the pet care division. After all, we had the infrastructure and the experience. It was a matter of transferring it to animals.

At the time, Maneka Gandhi had a three- to four-storeyed animal hospital in a small lane in Yusuf Sarai, Delhi. Some international veterinarians performed the day-to-day duties there, and they were capable. But after a while, they had to return to their home countries. Suddenly, a prime property with lots of potential was rudderless, with hundreds of whimpering, helpless beings left to their own fate.

We took over the animal hospital and refurbished the property, both in terms of décor and equipment. We hired vets and paid them more than the market rate. But not everything is in our control. One of our better doctors got pregnant and another young and capable doctor went back to Kashmir, where he came from.

The hospital had built a good reputation but for some reason or another we were unable to settle down; cash was burning too. Then one day, the doctor from Kashmir who had since returned and rejoined the organization, stepped out of the clinic and had a fatal heart attack. Barely thirty-five years old, he just collapsed on the street and died. We thought this was some kind of an omen and after running it for almost three years we moved out.

Concurrently, we had started a couple of pet care clinics with partners. The clinics were all very nicely designed, animal friendly and had good vets. However, since there were other priorities for us to focus on, the pet division was gradually going to the dogs, literally. After three years of ups and downs, we decided to shut down the pet care vertical.

We also tried our hand at the media business. A division named Dr Batra's® Media was opened. It published a magazine called *Homeopathy and You*. We followed due process, like registering the title with the Registrar for Newspapers of India (RNI). We hired a small team of subeditors and writers, and the magazine was inaugurated by Shashi and Sunanda Tharoor. The editor was a doctor and friend named Raj. In any field there is no dearth of people who want to be the next Salman Rushdie or Pritish Nandy. Raj was one of those people. He was dying to unleash the power of his keyboard on various issues, including cricket, about which he was crazy. We also got into a tie-up for distribution with *TimeOut* magazine, owned by the Ruias.

The decline of print had already begun. But as usual, if I was doing something, I wanted to do it well. We used the best paper and content. For a while, the magazine worked for us, as it gave us visibility in bookshops, cafés and airport lounges. It popularized homeopathy as well.

And then *TimeOut* itself shut down. We kept the magazine going on our own, selling it to patients, among others. But after a while we could no longer afford to justify the salaries of the team, not to mention the high expense of paper and printing.

Academia was our next foray. One of our doctors worked in a homeopathy college as its vice principal. He felt we should form an alliance with educational institutions, after which we entered into a public–private partnership with Bombay University.

We now run a one-year fellowship course on dermatology for homeopathic MDs, which is certified by Bombay University. We also have some of our own advanced courses on various homeopathic subjects, which are attended by homeopathic doctors from different parts of the world. Some of them come from as far as Brazil. We are happy to share our knowledge and expertise and spread scientific homeopathy to distant lands.

Looking back, the pet care and media experiments clearly did not work. But you can't blame an entrepreneur for trying. Once your brand reaches autopilot, your mind is freed up to move the goalpost to a more difficult position. Besides, as a famous quote attributed to Churchill goes, 'Success is not final, failure is not fatal: it is the courage to continue that counts.'

57

Lessons Learnt from Covid

THE WORLD CHANGED IN MARCH 2020 AND WE WERE NO EXCEPTION. Coronavirus, which we initially viewed as something restricted to distant Wuhan, crept up on every country in the world, including India. Almost overnight, there was a global lockdown.

Our initial reaction was shock and awe. Questions swirled in our heads. The administration and the police were very strict regarding the movement of people and vehicles. There was no clarity on whether homeopathy clinics would be allowed to remain open. Since all public transport was stopped, it was difficult for staff to reach the clinics, including all our doctors. Hence, our 100 per cent retail and walk-in-led enterprise came to a sudden halt. But we realized quickly that we could either sit holding our heads or adapt. We did the latter. When I did my medical excellence course at Harvard in 2011, we were always reminded by our instructors that change was a constant.

Adaptability to change is what brings success.

Once we accepted the situation, we focused on problem-solving. Doctors couldn't go to clinics. Fine, we took the clinic to them. We sent computers to nearly a 100 of our doctors and got our enterprise resource planning (ERP) system working. This way the doctors could be safe at home and at the same time connected with work. If you fight together as an organization, your bond with colleagues strengthens. You have a common purpose and you build a stronger organization.

Patients couldn't visit us either. Fine. We started reaching out vigorously to them. Soon, we were doing a few hundred video consultations a day. Also, the security of our systems was redesigned to enable staff to work from home while protecting the confidential databases of patients.

One of the challenges of the situation was that people were wary of touching couriered medicine packages. Patients suffering serious conditions couldn't afford to discontinue medicines. Again, we explained to them how they could safely handle packages and resume treatment. Simultaneously we convinced the authorities to allow one or two clinics per city to open, so that we could use those as centres for medicine preparation and subsequent couriering. Within no time, we were delivering almost a 1000 medicine packets per day by courier.

Leadership is most important in a company at such times. You have to set an example to others and also be generous. Akshay and our group CEO Sanjoy Mukerji did not take a salary for three months. I also made a donation from my personal retirement fund towards an emergency pool that could be used by staffers if needed.

Also, Akshay and I moved to Goa when a lockdown seemed imminent, so that we could protect ourselves and operate the company in peace. During a pandemic, everyone's health is important, especially your workforce. You need to focus on your top leadership. If something untoward happens to them the whole company could collapse. Boris Johnson made this mistake and almost paid for it with his life. This wasn't a time to be macho.

I was also frequently videoconferencing with our doctors, keeping their morale up. Even a routine conversation with seniors in times like these goes a long way. We set up counselling facilities for staff and covered them under health insurance. And while some kept track of the data, others avoided watching the barrage of demoralizing Covid news.

Once the complete lockdown was relaxed, Akshay wore a personal protective equipment (PPE) kit and went to the clinic in Goa. It showed employees and patients that the family had not abandoned them while Rome burned. In Mumbai, our medical director Dr Bindu, who lives in Andheri West, went to far-flung clinics in Nerul, Thane and Virar for the same purpose. Such actions inspire loyalty. And loyalty counts most during crises. Everyone puts their hand on the wheel. This was a situation where we needed all hands on deck. If cancer is the big C, so is Covid. And we focused on 4Cs to deal with this C.

Communication was one. We kept talking to employees and patients. Continuity was another—as much as possible we saw to it that there was no break in treatments. The third 'C' was cost-cutting. From growth and top line, the emphasis was now on the bottom line and sustainability. We also negotiated with the landlords of our clinics in India and abroad and secured a 30 per cent reduction in rents. There is no shame in asking for relief at times like these. In the long run, it helped the landlords and us. They did not lose rents on unoccupied property and we got continuity at a discount.

Compassion was the last 'C'. For instance, we had to lay some people off in the company. But we were sensitive in the way we communicated this shattering bit of news to them and we helped them find other jobs. We also reached out to society at large by providing ten million doses of immunity-boosting homeopathic medicines free to the Maharashtra state police and their families, front-line workers in hospitals and people in containment zones or at a subsidized cost for others.

Once everyone is taken care of, you again think of growth. Adversity throws up opportunities. You have to spot them and seize them. Most leaders build an organization that is 'built to last' but equally important is to have organizations that are 'built to adapt'. In adverse times, an organization which adapts will survive. Companies that are quick to change are the companies that will last. Among other innovations, we sent out immunity questionnaires for children. Their answers gave us a clue on whether they needed to shore up their immunity or not. Based on this feedback we sent their families our recommendations. We also increased our focus on communication about mental health, as cases of anxiety and depression rose significantly during the pandemic.

After an agonizing, topsy-turvy four months, most of our clinics reopened in phases. Again, our approach was one of thoroughness. Every hour, the alarm on the hygiene manager's phone went off, so that the clinic was cleaned again. Mystery shoppers were also sent to see if standard operating procedures (SOPs) were being followed. Covid was everyone's common enemy, and we were prepared to go to uncommon lengths to fight it. As they say in Mumbai, '*Dadar ke aage seat hai, dar ke aage jeet hai* (Just as you'll get a seat beyond Dadar station, beyond fear lies victory).'

58

Leadership Is Responsibility

IT WAS LONGFELLOW WHO SAID, '... LEAVE BEHIND, FOOTPRINTS IN the sand of time'.[7] Footprints can be washed away. A good leader leaves behind *imprints* which stay with the organization even after he leaves. Amongst the many lessons I learnt at my Harvard course on medical excellence, the most important one was on the dimensions of leadership. I'm happy to share some of my experiences with you.

From the viewpoint of running an organization, leadership has three key components—vision, culture and structure.

I will start with vision.

Vision was the initial fuel behind one of mankind's greatest achievements—the moon landing. In 1961, with the US in an intense space race with erstwhile Soviet Russia, the newly elected John F. Kennedy set a goal of sending an American to the moon

[7] Longfellow, Henry Wadsworth (October 1838), 'Psalm of Life', *Knickerbocker Magazine*.

within ten years, and did it in just about eight. Kennedy did not live to see his dream come true. But the near miracle was achieved. Three men flew in a cramped rocket for about three days and landed on the moon. The moon! A nation started to believe it could do anything. That is what good leadership can achieve.

When it comes to vision, a leader must also create a shared urgency about an opportunity or performance gap. He must evoke an aspiration among staff that appeals to emotion as well as to reason. Take the concept of Atmanirbhar Bharat, which Prime Minister Modi has popularized. It immediately appealed to the public's sense of self-respect. Overnight, Indians began to think, 'If I learn to do something myself, I don't have to depend on others.'

It's not like no one knew the importance of self-reliance before. But when a leader says it, it makes an impact.

We too have a vision at Dr Batra's®. It is, 'Dr Batra's®—Har Ghar Mein (to reach every household)'. Is it a tall order? Yes, but so was launching humans to the lunar surface.

Culture is the next element of leadership. A good leader creates a culture of psychological safety in their company. It means that someone will not be punished for asking questions or speaking their mind. It means failure will not be stigmatized. At Harvard, we were told about the 'failure parties' at Eli Lilly, the pharma company. The logic behind the parties was that, hey, we tried something which could have helped millions of people. It is disappointing it did not come to fruition, but we gave it our best and learnt a few things. And now that we have closed the project, we will save some of the crucial research funds. So let's celebrate our spirit of wholesome experimentation and our hard work with a little cake.

In the end the parties were curtailed, as teams had mixed feelings about them. But the message from the company was noble. Failure is not a bad thing.

According to Amy Edmondson, Harvard Business School's professor of leadership, failures are of three broad types—preventable, complexity related and intelligent.[8] So while some failures can be cheered, some others have to be taken very seriously. This is why the 2003 Columbia space shuttle tragedy was discussed in detail in our class. The space flight burnt to bits during its high speed re-entry into the earth's atmosphere, killing all seven astronauts aboard.

This is what happened. During Columbia's lift-off at the Kennedy Space Center, a suitcase-sized chunk of foam from the shuttle's external tank broke and slammed into its left wing. For two weeks, the astronauts peacefully went about their job in space. But there was always a risk. Down on earth, NASA knew about the foam bit. They had enough time to do something about it. But they did not take the potential danger seriously. Harvard's Edmondson was among the many who believed that had NASA acted on time, the disaster could have been averted.

Also within the parameters of culture is the lesson that when good leaders are faced with staff resistance to systemic changes, the bosses use reason and not pressure to win them over.

Julie Morath, the COO of Children's Hospital and Clinics in St Paul in Minneapolis, implemented this method with sensitivity. As a nurse years earlier, Morath had seen a child in hospital die due to a medication error. The tradition then was to not openly speak about mistakes. Many years on, as COO, she worked towards a culture where errors were acknowledged, recorded and then eliminated.

When hospital staff was resistant to change, Morath did not coerce them into following the new system. Instead, she gently asked questions about cases. Gradually, her colleagues came around.

---

8 Edmondson, Amy C. (April 2011), 'Strategies for Learning from Failure', *Harvard Business Review*.

'A leader is one who knows the way, goes the way and shows the way,' said John Maxwell,[9] the leadership expert and writer. Morath's deeds fit the description.

At Dr Batra's®, we go the extra mile to maintain the company's ethos. For example, two months before a senior person joins and at least four to six months after, I make sure I meet them every day, or at least every week, just to ensure they are aligned with the company's culture and mission.

Also, a lot of companies work according to the ABC model—accuse, blame and criticize. As a leader, I made sure that this was not the culture in our company.

A leader responds to customer needs. Back in the 1990s, Commerce Bank launched penny arcades in their branches in New Jersey. Kids and families could exchange coins collected in piggy banks for notes. The idea was a hit. Millions of dollars worth of change was collected and exchanged. On weekends, when queues were long, jugglers would keep the children entertained. Sure the bank did not make any profit from the penny exchange, but more people lined up to open accounts with them. The organization also earned a priceless amount of goodwill and publicity.

I could identify with Commerce Bank because I'm fond of children too. At my Chowpatty clinic, I imported a bubble gum machine and filled it with imported natural gum. Kids loved it. Suddenly, going to Dr Batra's® became a fun outing. It's all a part of responding to customer needs. For example, we noticed that more people were coming to us for chronic problems, not acute ones, so most footfalls happened on the weekends. Therefore, for the last ten to fifteen years, we stay open longer on weekends.

Next up is the third pillar of leadership—structure. In simple words, you have to create a company where everyone has a chance to succeed and grow. It may sound easy, but is not always the case.

---

9 Source: www.brainyquote.com

Due to insecurities and politics, many companies have a structure where only a few grow.

Here's a classic example of a faulty company structure we learnt at Harvard, where the right hand does not know the challenges of the left. A person joins a bank at a high level. A few months later, they are not happy with the way things are functioning, and throw a tantrum—'Why are things not improving?'

This person is then sent to a branch to work. And now they see what the problem is. Customers scream at them. By the day's end, this person too loses composure and is raving and ranting. They realize the pressure that people in the branch face—there is no scope for them to succeed. So they are not motivated, and ultimately work and performance suffer.

Good leaders also tweak the goals of employees. If people have the same targets year on year, they will not develop. A good leader keeps raising the bar for employees. He sets them not only efficiency targets but also learning ones.

Lastly, there is the human touch. Every leader must have it. In our clinics we do not turn away needy patients for want of money. We also do small things like holding the door for patients and finding them a taxi. It goes a long way, for our patients and for us too. As Peter Drucker said, 'Leadership is not rank or privilege, title or money. Leadership is responsibility.'

59

What Goes Around Comes Around

'LIFE IS AN ECHO, ALL COMES BACK/ THE GOOD, THE FALSE, THE true/So give the world the best you have/And the best will come back to you.'

My mother always said this when I was a child: if we are in a position to help, we should do what we can. And I strongly believe it, but we have to be strategic to make a greater impact. Philanthropy binds everyone to a common cause. We measure success not by money or time but the impact we make in the lives of the people we touch or heal. 'Healing people changes lives', is the philosophy of our company and we live by it.

I have seen poverty at close quarters since my early days as a doctor. I spent a lot of time in Dharavi treating patients. Later, in my own clinic, I treated some people free of cost as they had next to nothing. Sometimes I also gave them some money along with the medicines, as I did with a patient who had three eligible daughters but was desperately low on funds.

As a company we worked with schools for the visually challenged for about thirty years and also for old-age homes, where despite their misery eighty-year-olds sometimes broke into song or danced, their skin withered but their eyes still catching the twinkle of yore for a few moments. Some of them were left behind by children who had migrated. It was heartbreaking to see them. It was also inspiring. They were not in their own homes, or among their own people. Yet they managed to find joy in what little they had.

The very nature of medicine is to provide service. A good doctor anyway spends most of his life spreading himself thin for others. It was the same with me. I believe the best way to give is to give a little of yourself. When I turned fifty on 1 July 2001, I thought I needed to bring some structure to our philanthropic activities. That's when we started Dr Batra's® Foundation.

Vilasrao Deshmukh, the Chief Minister of Maharashtra at that time, and also my patient, came for the inauguration despite his busy schedule. The function was held at the Crystal Room of the Taj in Mumbai and the Chief Minister was kind enough to donate Rs 5 lakh from the Chief Minister's Fund. Karisma Kapoor was also present, among others.

But celebrity presence alone did not make it special. The ceremony acquired substance due to the presence of some 200 patients of ours who had battled various illnesses. I always felt that the best ambassador of hope for a patient is another patient, someone who has staged a recovery. So, when a fit-again cancer patient stands in front of another cancer patient and says, 'There is hope, my friend. A few months ago I was weak and near death, flimsy as a shuttlecock. Today, I am playing badminton. Can you believe it?', then the other patient gets motivated. He feels he has a chance at not just survival but a full, active life.

Among the guests was a person who had cerebral palsy and yet made a career for himself in medicine. We also had an individual with epidermolysis bullosa dystrophica (EBD), an almost impossible thing to treat. She was now a lawyer in Canada. They told their stories and many people went home that day with their hopes reignited.

The experience of the inauguration—where the patient was the star—led to the Positive Health Awards, a marquee annual event in Mumbai. Initially, we honoured just our patients who had overcome health adversities.

Two or three years later, we opened up the Positive Health Awards to everybody who had shown spirit in the face of serious health setbacks. Around that time, Rajiv Bajaj was my patient. The concept of the Awards appealed to him, and he came on board as a sponsor. We then formed a board, comprising Rajiv, R. Balakrishnan (Balki), Vivek Oberoi, Maneka Gandhi, me and (for a time) Anu Aga.

Six people from various fields who had surmounted huge odds, were awarded every year. They received Rs 1 lakh each. Often, they came from small towns and villages. Many were running their own NGOs, and the cash award helped them in their mission. Like Kousalya Periasamy who overcame the society-inflicted stigma of being HIV positive, to found the Positive Health Network in Tamil Nadu. She helped over 400 HIV positive women get vocational training, gainful employment and financial support. Noori Saleem—the third person to be officially declared HIV positive by the Indian government as far back as 1987—was another exemplar. A trans woman, she overcame many difficulties before accepting her identity and starting a shelter for abandoned HIV positive children.

There were other hugely inspirational stories. Like Sai Kaustuv Dasgupta, whose body had suffered more than fifty fractures due to a rare brittle-bone disease called osteogenesis imperfecta, which rendered his body 90 per cent disabled, but only the body, not the mind. Kaustuv is a singer, graphic designer and motivational speaker, happiness coach and a wheelchair warrior. Twenty-five-year-old Latheesha Ansari, another awardee, who similarly has osteogenesis imperfecta, has suffered over 1000 fractures. Latheesha helps other children with osteogenesis imperfecta get admission into school.

There was Major General Ian Cardozo who stepped on a landmine in the 1971 Indo-Pak war and had to cut off his wounded leg with his own khukri (a form of knife). Later in a fitness test, Gen. Cardozo completed the physical course leaving behind seven officers (with both legs). When he climbed 6000 feet to meet the Vice Chief of Army Staff, his determination led him to become the first war-disabled officer to be given command of a battalion. A little later, he became the first such officer to command a brigade. He paved the way for other disabled officers to become army commanders. One officer who had both his legs amputated even became vice chief of army.

I am proud that we were the first to identify and honour achievers who survived great odds, like the Para-Olympian Deepa Malik. We also awarded Arunima Sinha, who became the first female amputee to climb Mount Everest. She did on one leg what most people can't do on two. Both ladies went on to get Padma Awards later. Laxmi Agarwal, the acid attack survivor, who was later portrayed by Deepika Padukone in the movie *Chhapaak* (2020), was also felicitated by us. These are just a few examples.

As the platform was noble, celebrities were happy to associate themselves with us. They did not ask for money. Shah Rukh Khan, Saif Ali Khan, Hrithik Roshan, Abhishek and Aishwarya Bachchan, Sanjay Dutt, Shatrughan and Sonakshi Sinha are among the stars who have graced the awards. M.S. Dhoni and Vidya Balan too have been chief guests.

We devised the 'one per cent deduction for causes formula' in our company many years before the 2 per cent corporate social responsibility (CSR) investment became mandatory. Not only did the clinics donate 1 per cent of their profits at that time, but even the employees would donate 1 per cent of their salaries. Naturally, it did not always work out. We then changed it to at least Rs 100 a month, which most people did not mind paying. Our philosophy of creating wealth to share wealth also helped us grow.

I also convinced the doctors to step out of their comfort zones and air-conditioned offices and go into the slums and chawls and help people. I had done all that, and I wanted everyone in the team to do that. Today, young doctors come from well-to-do families that can afford to pay their college fees. Then they join a recognized hospital or doctor, and have a ready-made line of patients, some of them VIPs. They are not always exposed to the real world.

Our doctors go by rotation to NGOs. And some become so attached to this work that they continue to do it for several years. I have a doctor who was going to a school for the visually challenged for fifteen to twenty years. They love him there. Some of the front desk people also go to help. The result is they become much more human.

We underestimate the power of kindness. All of us have experienced the feeling of well-being that goes with being kind to someone. This sensation is not imaginary, it is the result of a chemical discharge in our body. When we do an act of kindness, it releases oxytocin. Oxytocin is, famously, the happy hormone. Therefore, the kinder we are, the happier we will be. *Quod erat demonstrdum*—QED.

We also found other ways of helping. For example, every first Wednesday of the month the doctors and the staff come in three hours earlier and provide free treatment for life to anyone who needs it. Today, Dr Batra's® Foundation runs over 175 free clinics in all, providing medicines and consultation worth about Rs 3 crore a year. Whenever there is an epidemic, we give free treatment. We gave 900 doses for bird flu in Jaipur and Delhi a few years ago. During Covid we gave one crore free doses through NGOs like the Rotary Club, including to the families of nearly 80,000 police personnel in Maharashtra.

It's also important to do good in your neighbourhood. In Palghar, where we have our product factory, we work with an old-age home. Helping local people helps you sort out local problems.

We also give to education. Some years ago, the Dr Mukesh Batra Scholarship was instituted in some of the top universities and colleges in India. One of them is my alma mater. Through the scholarships I hope to inspire young doctors towards excellence. The scholarship also provides financial aid and recognition to medical students. There are no conditions attached like work bonds. Recipients are free to practise when they graduate.

If a young student gets Dr Batra's® medal for academics, he is liable to boost his career chances and confidence. It also motivates others to work hard. We have six such medals or honours in every college, three for academic merit and three for disadvantaged students.

Often, the students are overcome with emotion, and so are we, as few things compare with the joy of helping a deserving person make a life for themselves. Once, when Akshay presented a scholarship to a student in Pune, she was in tears. She said her father was a rickshaw driver, who would be relieved to receive our financial aid and feel very proud of his daughter. In truly meritorious cases, we even pay the fees for the entire five-year course.

There were some other heart-rending stories. A student's farmer father in Jaipur had mortgaged land so that his son could become a doctor. There was a medical student whose mother had mortgaged the family jewellery to the local goldsmith. The scholarships helped them to repay their loans and free their families from the bondage of the local moneylenders.

A brand's EQ—emotional quotient—is as important as its financial quotient. It creates goodwill, which may not be measured, but impacts consumer decision. I have also used my passion for singing and photography to generate funds for the foundation. Our musical show 'Yaadon ki Bahaar' and my photography exhibitions have raised a substantial amount of money.

It was Helen Keller who said, 'I cried that I had no shoes until I came across a man who had no feet.' This is a line I often quote to people. We all have intrinsic talents; can we use them to fulfil the world's needs and to create a better world? There is so much we have, really, and it must be shared so that someone somewhere will walk again.

60

Succession Planning

SUCCESSION PLANNING IS A BIT LIKE A DAUGHTER'S BIDAI. YOU HAVE to let her go, but you also want to do everything to ensure she is in the right hands. Similarly, there comes a time when an owner must abdicate the throne in a company, but see to it that the next person in charge is capable.

Lots of organizations, particularly those that are family led, rightly spend a lot of time and effort on succession planning. Some even hire highly paid advisers. Choosing the right successor is not easy. The management guru Ram Charan once wrote, 'In CEO succession, it takes a ton of ore to produce an ounce of gold.' It took General Electric's Jack Welch seven years to just narrow a shortlist of twenty potential successors to three, according to Charan.

In my view, the best model for succession planning is the Rotary Club. I was the president of the Rotary Club of Bombay, one of the largest in the global Rotary network, so I know how they function. Their succession process is almost a four-year exercise.

First you become president nominee, then president elect, and finally president. After your term ends, you cease to be president. But worry not, you are still immediate past president, where you are a mentor and adviser on the board. If the movie *All the President's Men* (1976) was made on the immediate past presidents of the Rotary Club, it would have had a rather long title.

If the process takes so much time in an NGO, it has to be even more thought out in a professional organization, where business worth millions is at stake. I find that a lot of families quickly thrust their next generation into the hot seat. I was clear I wasn't going to paratroop Akshay into the office, with a cabin and secretary waiting for him. He may have been my son and destined to take over at some stage, but he had to work his way ground up.

I have treated many billionaires and found that while their companies are run by great professional managers, the next-gen is actively involved in the business as well. That is a lesson I have learnt.

Thus, when Akshay graduated as a homeopath in 2000–01, we had a corporate office in Dadar, with a boardroom and a small clinic below. I did make a cabin for him, but told him he was not going to occupy it yet. He was sent to the clinic instead, where he immersed himself in the nitty-gritty. Only after ten years of apprenticeship was he allowed to move into his cabin. It was the same with boardroom access.

Once Akshay was seasoned, he was made deputy MD. I was still CMD, chairman and managing director. I was never one to give him corporate fundas. He was qualified enough. For the rest, I asked him to learn on the job.

But on the day there were sixty-five candles shaped like swimsuit models on my cake, I decided to step down (kidding about the models). It occurred to me that the four stages in a man's golden years are ill–pill–bill–will and I should respect the passage of time.

Akshay was ready to take control, and I wanted to do other things in my life. I had become the president of the Rotary Club, which, believe me, was a full-time commitment. There were 325 members and 100-odd projects. Every day there were three or four events.

I passed on the baton to Akshay as he wanted to protect me. We had a lot of envious rivals. Some of them even tried to malign me with underhand tactics. Akshay wanted me to be unencumbered in my retirement years. I am no longer on any board of the company. I don't draw a salary, though I remain the founder and chairman emeritus and hold the bulk of the company's shares.

That brings me to the next point. I see a few cases around me of successful businessmen who, either out of naiveté or excessive generosity, gave everything away to their children or other family members. They thought they'd be well taken care of. Instead, they were neglected. They struggled for dignity, when actually they should have been kicking back on a beach sipping cocktails and wearing Tommy Bahama shirts. So it is essential that before you cede control, keep enough money for yourself so that you can live without compromising on your lifestyle. Two, losing power and relevance is not easy to get used to. So you must have some role or some purpose identified for the rest of your life. It could be your foundation or your Rotary Club.

In the initial days after I resigned, I felt odd and useless. I would still go to office, and I could see loyalties changing overnight. From being the most wanted guy in the organization to sitting in some corner, doing nothing in particular, took getting used to. It was a bit like when your children start driving the family car. All these years, whenever you went for a picnic with your family, you were driving and the kids were at the back. Now your son is driving and you are sitting in the rear, aware that any back seat driving will be met with irritation, just like it was for you.

From the company's viewpoint, it helps to have clarity on who's the boss. There cannot be two people in one chair. So you have to make sure that you are out, because I have seen the mixed messages and confusion that can happen if two perceived bosses are in the same office.

When we were in the old office, I had my room and Akshay had his. He was the deputy MD and I was semi-retired. But as long as I was there, people would come to me with queries. You can't be an unconstitutional head. Since the last few years, I don't go to the corporate office at all, I have my own office which is located at Nariman Point. I speak or advise only when I am asked. And I daresay that on such occasions my word is followed.

Another important factor when you are handing over the reins to somebody else, whether it is your CEO or your own son, is that they must be aligned to your values and vision. In lots of companies, the new boss wants to do something totally different. It creates confusion and angst. Luckily, Akshay, our group CEO and our leadership team are value-based people like me. They share my vision for the company.

Family conflicts should be avoided, or at least anticipated. Often in business families things are okay till the children get married. When the spouses come into the frame, equations and priorities change. Friction between cousins is also common if their fathers or mothers have run a company. Therefore, it is important that the conflicts don't reach a point of no return.

Lastly, power comes and goes. But the goodwill you build and respect you earn stay. Goodwill is not just among customers, but also employees. You may leave, but your legend and your stories will be a part of the office for years. Every company has its stories, like the Mahabharata or Ramayana. Over time, they get exaggerated too. But their essence remains. That's your legacy. I always say this. Nobody hears or sees the Phantom, but he is still the Ghost who Walks.

61

Padma Shri

One day one of my patients in Delhi, an influential person, came up to me and said that I should get a Padma Shri.

'You've treated Prime Minister Manmohan Singh for forty years, and many others. You've done a lot for homeopathy. Why don't you send me your bio,' the man said.

I was surprised, and a bit chuffed.

The selection criteria for the awards was: 'While no rigid criteria or trenchant formula for selection is applied by the Padma Awards Committee, it looks for lifetime achievement of an individual while making a selection. It should not be merely excellence in a particular field, but the criteria has to be "excellence plus".'

I didn't know if I was 'excellence-plus', but I felt I met the other requirements. It had been a lifetime with a considerable amount of public service. I thought it was worth sending my résumé to the gentleman. It would mean a lot for homeopathy. So far, only two or three homeopaths had been awarded the Padma Shri in seventy-odd years.

I sent my bio and got on with life. I never made a follow-up call to anyone in high places. I had access to Manmohanji, but I'd never pollute our relationship by asking him for a personal favour. The only thing I ever asked him for was to come as chief guest for an event or two.

Did I want the Padma Shri? Yes. Was I going to lobby for it? No. Someone suggested I try for it. I did. That's all.

A few weeks later, the list of awardees came out. My name was among those who were considered, but not selected. I felt disappointed, despite my philosophical approach towards the whole thing. But I shrugged my shoulders and accepted the committee's verdict.

In a few days, I'd be fine, I knew. But I thought I must at least inform the VIP well-wisher who had suggested I apply for the awards.

When he heard what had happened, he was upset. He felt I merited the honour.

'This is unfair,' he said.

'Don't worry about it,' I said, and quoted Harivanshrai Bachchan. '*Mann ka ho toh achcha, naa ho toh aur achcha* (If what you wish happens, that's good; if that doesn't happen, it's even better).'

He wasn't in a mood to give in. It was common for people to miss out for some reason or the other on their first attempt.

'I appreciate your attitude, but I feel you must try again this year,' he said.

With nothing to lose, and by now familiar with the process, I entered the fray once again when the applications started for the following year.

Some weeks later, far away from the goings-on in Delhi, I went to Goa with my family during Christmas 2011. I was driving through the tree-lined, winding roads around Benaulim, humming '*Dil chahta hai*', when my phone rang. It was from someone in Delhi.

'We need more information on what you've done for homeopathy and society,' said the man.

I called up my trusted assistant Louisa in Mumbai.

'Louisa, sorry to make you work during Christmas, but we need to send some documents to Delhi.'

Over the next couple of days, before the committee's second meeting, we sent them information about my various initiatives towards homeopathy, charity and society. And then again, I adopted the Bhagavad Gita attitude—do your work without expecting rewards.

New Year's Eve came and we watched fireworks going up from Vijay Mallya's Kingfisher Villa, although, thankfully, we ourselves were in a much quieter spot far away from the hyperactivity of Candolim. A couple of days later, we went back to Mumbai. The air still carried a nip and a holiday mood. We did have one more celebration coming up. January 25 was Akshay's birthday. It's also the date when they usually announce the award winners.

Later that day, I was in the office with Akshay. I got a call from the home ministry saying that I was getting the Padma Shri. They wanted me to confirm if I would accept it, as they didn't want an award wapsi incident that would embarrass them.

I was confused and excited both.

'Are you sure? Is this some prank?'

The person at the other end assured me it was a genuine call.

'Okay. Thank you so much,' I said. 'I'll be honoured to attend the ceremony and accept the award.'

I have won a few things in my lifetime but nothing came close to the euphoria I felt when I got the Padma Shri. When you get such a big honour from your own country, your entire family feels proud. Every Indian knows the Padma awards. It also puts your name in the history books, and makes you feel your life was worth something.

The awards were held at the Rashtrapati Bhavan in March 2012. The winners were divided in two groups, and each batch was felicitated in two ceremonies held ten days apart. We were called a day in advance and put up at the Ashok hotel. There is a limit to the number of people you can take with you for the ceremony. But there are times you can, and should, ask for a small accommodation. In this case, I wanted just one more pass, and got it. It was for my youngest brother, who had helped me revise my application when we got the call in Goa.

The day before the awards, winners had a rehearsal. We were packed in white buses and taken to Rashtrapati Bhavan, many of us giggly and pleasantly nervous like new lovers. The protocol for awardees is very specific. You cannot turn your back to the president. You walk exactly a certain number of steps up. You bow to the president, accept the scroll and look at the camera. Then you go back to your seat without crossing anybody else's path.

D-day arrived. Dressed in a dark bandhgala, I walked up the red carpet towards the hall with my companions. A band played and tall men in uniforms and turbans stood in position. When my name was announced, memories and emotions engulfed me. I imagined all the key people in my life sitting in the hall—my grandparents, parents, friends, my immediate family, my patients, my spiritual guides, my pets. And then I, a man who made homeopathy his mission, walked towards President Pratibha Patil to receive the biggest honour of his life.

62

In Favour of Homeopathy

There is a famous story about Sachin Tendulkar. One night at a coaching camp, a young Sachin was not getting sleep. So he started practising. As the knocks of the ball against the bat echoed in the midnight hour, his coach got up and asked him to go back to bed. Such was Sachin's passion for cricket.

It is the same with me. My passion, though, is homeopathy. Luckily, homeopathy pills would not make as much of a sound as a cricket ball in case I entertained myself with them on a sleepless night.

Every waking hour of mine is spent thinking about some aspect of my profession. I read about new plants or natural minerals being used in medicines. I think about our products and patients. Just like Sachin would travel miles in buses or local trains for a chance to play, I go to great lengths to help people or promote homeopathy. In my younger days, I had the same approach. That is why I did not mind changing three buses to go to a clinic in Dharavi, and then return and work some more. I did all this for little or no money. Today, all these years later, I cannot imagine what my life would have been without homeopathy.

It has given me recognition in India and overseas. It has brought me a Padma Shri. Even more importantly, it has given me an opportunity to change so many lives for the better and alleviate suffering. That is what a doctor strives for.

Now as I reflect on things, I would like to take stock of homeopathy. To make things clear and concise, I have divided my thoughts into things that are working for homeopathy, and those that need to be tweaked so that this gentle, often misunderstood branch of medicine grows further. I will discuss the latter in the next chapter.

Perhaps the biggest point in favour of homeopathy is that it has no side effects. Fine, so some of you do not believe in it. And yet, you can try it without worrying about adverse effects. Isn't that wonderful?

The world is ravaged by opioid crises and drug dependency, which leads to side effects. According to a survey done by Pandol in the UK, one in three people did not know the difference between aspirin, ibuprofen and paracetamol and popped in whatever was nearest to them.

Antibiotic resistance and adverse drug reactions (ADRs) are other concerns from allopathic drugs. According to the USA's Food and Drug Administration (FDA), studies estimate that there are over 106,000 deaths caused by ADRs annually in the USA. And in many cases, trigger-happy doctors who dole out prescriptions are to blame.

Speaking for India, drugs banned elsewhere continue to be sold here sometimes. And people take them and set themselves up for dangerous side effects. As per a 2013 article in *Mint*, India was still selling over fifteen globally banned drugs. And in 2018, the health ministry started deliberations on banning over 300 drugs that were potentially harmful.

In such a scenario homeopathy, made from plants and natural minerals, is a boon.

The next point in favour of homeopathy is that despite naysayers, it is popular. It is prevalent even in first world countries with no dearth of the best in conventional medicine. Switzerland, famous for its exacting quality controls and high standard of living, rates homeopathy equal to conventional medicine at many levels. The Swiss government described it as 'effective, cost effective and safe'. The Swiss make the best watches. Who better than them to know what makes something tick?

In Asia, India leads in terms of number of people using homeopathy, with 100 million people depending solely on homeopathy for their medical care. There are over 200,000 registered homeopathic doctors in India currently, with approximately 12,000 more being added every year. In all, around 500 million people around the world use homeopathy. Surely, all of them can't be wrong.

Hippocrates, the father of modern medicine, himself endorsed the principle of curing through a treatment that was like the problem itself. He said: 'By similar things a disease is produced and through the application of the like is cured.' A system as universally endorsed as vaccination has its roots in this idea.

The healthy homeopathy market size is one more win for the field. According to Transparency Market Research's latest market report, the global homeopathy product market was valued at US$ 5.6 billion in 2018. Beginning with just forty to fifty drugs during (founder) Hahnemann's time, today there are more than 2000 clinically tested homeopathic medicines in practice.

A clear indicator that homeopathy is not just tiny disco balls is its effect on plants and animals. And in case you brush this off as something not concerning humans, do remember that the well-being of flora and fauna has a direct bearing on us, the air and the environment. And homeopathy goes a long way in ensuring this well-being. It is widely used in livestock, especially in order to reduce the use of antibiotics.

Where plants are concerned, agro-homeopathy has yielded encouraging results. Indian start-up Agpulse Organics, associated with the prominent Nexus Incubator programme, is using the technique in its work. A couple of years ago, agro-homeopathy helped some farmers in Italy grow exotic fruits.

Another positive is that the Indian government realizes the importance of alternative medicine. It developed Ayush, the Department of Ayurveda, Yoga and Naturopathy, Unani, Siddha and Homeopathy to develop education and research in these fields. A true testament of the government's belief in the science of homeopathy was witnessed at the onset of the Covid pandemic, when it issued a directive prescribing Arsenic Album 30 as a prophylactic to boost immunity.

Moreover, homeopathy can be an alternative when healthcare systems the world over are overworked. India's per capita expenditure on health remains among the lowest in the world. Its health spend is only 1.15–1.5 per cent of the annual GDP. India has 0.5 hospital beds per 1000 people as opposed to the 5 per 1000 as recommended by WHO. While India has the recommended number of at least one physician per 1000 patients, this includes the number of alternative health practitioners.

Every medical doctor who graduates takes the Hippocratic Oath. One line in the pledge is, 'I will neither give a deadly drug to anybody who asked for it, nor will I make a suggestion to this effect.' It is possible that back in those days, 'deadly' meant 'death-causing'. That doesn't change the deeper meaning of the statement, which is to be responsible while prescribing or giving medicine. Had he been alive, Hippocrates himself would have had an open mind towards homeopathy. That's one more point in its favour.

63

What Needs to Improve

AS MUCH AS I LOVE HOMEOPATHY, THERE ARE SOME THINGS ABOUT it that need to be addressed. Topmost on the list are aggressive clinical trials that prove the efficacy of homeopathy.

Secondly, we need to give a fitting answer to the biggest criticism of the field, which is that it is a placebo effect produced by medicines which are too diluted to have any impact. 'Oh, homeopathy is just a placebo.' This one line has haunted homeopaths for years. It is a label that has stuck despite considerable evidence to the contrary. For example in 2015, a team of experts led by Dr Jayesh Bellare, head of department, chemical engineering, IIT Mumbai, and featuring scholars from reputed organizations such as the Haffkine Institute, Bhabha Atomic Research Centre and the Tata Institute of Fundamental Research, proved that homeopathic medicines contained nanoparticles of medicinal molecules.[10]

10 Chikramane, P.S., A.K. Suresh, J.R. Bellare, S.G. Kane (2010), 'Extreme Homeopathic Dilutions Retain Starting Materials: A Nanoparticulate Perspective'. *Homeopathy*, 99: 231–242.

Dr Bellare said, 'While earlier it was thought that homeopathic medicines do not contain medicinal molecules, high resolution microscopes used in the IIT-B lab to observe the medicines found that the molecules do exist in nano sizes.'

There have also been double-blind trials that proved the power of homeopathic medicines. The most robust data on this came from a 2014 meta-analysis of placebo-controlled, double-blind randomized trials which found that homeopathic medicines, when prescribed during individualized treatment, were one and a half to two times more likely to have a beneficial effect than a placebo.

In addition, Austrian molecular biologist Dr Michael Frass and Indian scientist Dr Gaurisankar Sa proved the anti-cancer properties of homeopathy in laboratory experiments on cell lines extracted from the human body. If nanotechnology, nuclear physics and other methods can further produce such findings, and if there are many more aggressive clinical trials, I think the biggest criticism of homeopathy will be buried.

Since the last ten years or so, we have been practising evidence-based treatment in our clinics. We have in the region of one million cases which are evidence based. And we have all the data regarding them, in case anyone wants to see it. For example, if a patient is diabetic his HBA1C levels over a period of time are lowered. This data is also vetted by a medical board which has MD doctors.

One of the things I often hear is, '*Doctor achcha mila toh homeopathy lagti hai, nahin to nahin* (Homeopathy is effective if one gets a good doctor, otherwise not).' In order to remedy this situation, standardization of homeopathy education and protocols is critical. It will lead to better doctors, and the feedback from patients will not be mixed any more.

The world over, homeopathy courses are vastly different. In India, it is a rigorous five-and-a-half-year course. But that is compromised by the inconsistent quality of Indian colleges, resulting in a mixed bag of doctors. There are some 186 homeopathy colleges in India churning out nearly 12,000 doctors in a year. But the colleges do not have the same facilities or quality of faculty members. So, there is a need to standardize medical education, if you really want to capture people's faith and goodwill.

We can further understand the inconsistency in the quality of doctors if we consider how varied the academic requirements for homeopaths are the world over. In the UK, the homeopathy course is a mere six months. In almost the time it took Harry and Meghan to pack up their belongings at the Palace, you were a homeopath. In the rest of Europe, an MD doctor can practise homeopathy without learning it separately. In New Zealand, there is no law. Even a sheep can become a homeopath. In America, it is state-wise. In Nevada, of all places, there is a proper course of four years to become a natural doctor and then practise homeopathy. Nevada may allow gambling in Vegas, but I'm happy to see they don't take chances with their medicine.

So this is why you will not get the same standard treatment from a homeopath across the world. The education is different everywhere.

The second part to standardization is the protocols of treatment. At Dr Batra's® we have strong protocols. If we have a female hair loss patient, but notice she has hair on her chin and irregular periods, the red flag goes up. To us, these are possibly signs of polycystic ovarian syndrome (PCOS). So we investigate that first and then prescribe medicines.

I believe the homeopathy world can learn a lot of lessons from the UAE, which is a standard-bearer when it comes to data standardization for diseases, signs and symptoms, abnormal findings, complaints, social circumstances and external causes of injury or diseases. Practising facilities also follow a standardized International Classification of Diseases (ICD-10) coding system. The UAE has regular compliance and surprise audits that ensure the quality and safety of patient care. Besides, all doctors and staff have to undergo a certain number of hours of Continuing Medical Education (CME) and training to ensure competency.

We also need insurance companies to cover homeopathic treatments, as in the UK, France, Switzerland and Luxembourg. In the UAE, homeopathy is covered by at least six major insurance providers. In India, while fifteen insurance companies provide cover for homeopathy, they do so only for hospitalization, and there are very few hospitals.

Lastly, integration into the mainstream can help homeopathy gain a rightful place as a reliable healthcare option. It is already happening to some extent in India. The Modi government actually turned to some leading homeopathy brands to perform clinical trials for Covid. We too were in the process of signing a memorandum of understanding (MOU) with the All-India Institute of Medical Sciences (AIIMS), Bhopal, to conduct clinical trials.

Also heartening is that AIIMS, Bhopal, has a homeopathic division. There is also integration of homeopathy in various national healthcare programmes, such as the National Programme for Prevention and Control of Cancer, Diabetes, Cardiovascular Diseases and Stroke, Healthy Child, and Swasthya Rakshan. This will not only see more recoveries in a gentle, safer and cheaper way, but will also result in a more satisfied patient population and lesser per-patient burden on the conventional health model.

No single system of medicine is complete in itself and therefore the best that every variant has to offer should be integrated for the betterment of humankind. So if you had to make a choice, you'd do well to choose the following combination—homeopathy, allopathy and, for some luck, Tirupati.

64

The Future of Medicine

If doctors today practised the way we did fifty years ago, we wouldn't need Seema Aunty from the Netflix show *Indian Matchmaking*. Back then, a doctor was a healer, family friend and even a matchmaker. Scores of families would ask 'the good doctor' to look for a suitable boy or girl for their eligible children. I have had such requests myself and was happy to help.

The very existence of the phrase 'the good doctor' was indicative of the physician's place in society—a person of decency who people consulted not just for health, but also family matters. A real mensch, as the Jews say.

Those days, a patient was born at home and died at home. Today, both birth and death take place in a hospital, with more strangers than family members for company. In most cases today, the doctor is no longer a friend, no longer an unassuming God, but a brusque professional who merely thinks he is God.

How did we get here?

An exploding population, a faster pace of life, consumerism, mobile phones and nuclear families have ensured that doctors are kept on their toes. When everyone has more money to make, another appointment to reach, when the phone is always buzzing, which doctor will sit down for a cup of tea and discuss cricket and alliances? No, she or he is Usain Bolt in a white coat. Always running.

Why blame him or her either? Many medical colleges have ceased being noble, service-oriented organizations and have become financial plunderers, often run by politicians. Of the nearly 2600 medical colleges in the world, the largest number are in India (479). Fees amount to around one million a year, which means five million for the entire course. A loan of that amount necessitates an equated monthly instalment (EMI) payback of approximately Rs 60,000 per month. No wonder medical students are stuck in a debt trap for years, and feel compelled to quickly recover costs.

Taking regional and global headwinds into consideration, what does the present and future hold for Indian healthcare? What are the key things that are going to play a big role in the years to come?

As a homeopath, I'm happy to say that alternative medicine is here to stay. People are better informed these days. They are fitness conscious, and have a healthy wariness towards mainstream drugs, given their chemical content and side effects. People are therefore more inclined to give alternative medicine a chance. Alternative medicine will not cure bullet wounds, but combined with activities such as yoga, meditation and exercise, it can help people manage many ailments without taking harmful medicines. Not for the first time, I will also mention the government's Ayush initiative, which will definitely make more people consider alternative medicine, including homeopathy.

This brings us to one of the drivers of the alternative medicine movement—mental health, which is going to be a key area in medicine. Earlier, health meant physical health, where you played football, showered and sang the Lifebuoy soap ditty: '*Tandurusti ki raksha karta hai Lifebuoy …*' Now there is a shift and people have realized health also means being emotionally strong.

According to the WHO, India is the world's most depressed country, with around fifty million people suffering from depression. Market Research Future, a data analytics firm, states that India holds a 20 per cent market share in the Asia-Pacific depression-screening market, a market that is globally expected to be worth $5,177.8 million by 2023. Statistics like these, coupled with an increasing number of celebrities raising awareness about mental health, are clear signs that mental health is going to be a big part of India's medico-wellness landscape.

Tele medicine is another game changer. If you can talk to a doctor from the comfort and privacy of your home, why would you go through the trouble of taking the offline route unless absolutely required? M-health also reduces the pressure on the doctor's infrastructure.

From the doctor's point of view, AI and wearables will lead to advanced and quicker treatments. A lot of AI is already being used by hospitals for duties ranging from scheduling appointments, digitization of medical records and reminder calls for follow-up. In various parts of the world robots are assisting in surgeries, intelligent prostheses are being used by the differently abled or wounded, and AI is also being used for many other tasks. This leaves doctors and their support staff free to concentrate on core matters.

People's tendency to go online for a diagnosis the moment they have certain symptoms is one more sign of the times that isn't going to go away. Moments after leaving the doctor's clinic, and after being told by him or her to avoid checking things with Dr Google, people do exactly that. Of all the queries Google receives in a day, an estimated 7 per cent are health related, according to Google Health Vice President David Feinberg.

The questions range from the sublime to the ridiculous. Some of the ones in the latter category are: Can holding my burps back make me a better saxophone player? If I swallow gum will it come out if I do a head stand? Why do my eyes twitch after I sneeze? How can you tell if you were born with a tail? Can my kidney explode?

Nonetheless, there are certain pros to Dr Google. Legible text is one. As per a UK study, patients saw the internet as a good supporting tool in their understanding of their condition. Dr Google, bless it, also helps you find advise from specialists. *Good Health and Homeopathy*, our series uploaded on social media, reached twenty-five lakh people and gave people access to qualified experts. The episode on depression alone got two million views.

Internet forums help you connect with someone who has a similar ailment as you. This way you find solace and a confidante. You find a support group which can guide you to navigate the challenge.

Dr Google has cons too, in every sense of the word. It can turn people into cyberchondriacs, worrying about every little negative thing they read online and thinking they are doomed. Also, as per one study, two in five people misdiagnosed themselves with serious diseases after consulting Dr Google. Things will evolve in the future, among them the patient–internet relationship. Maybe it will make working from home a viable option for doctors. A day might even come when doctors will go back to being matchmakers. The only thing is that the person having a cup of tea with you, discussing likely partners for your child, may not be a human but a robot.

65

A Life Well Lived

Waffle, my Labrador, ambles towards my chair in our house in Goa, her ears flopping. I know what she wants. I open my left palm, which has her homeopathy pills, tiny white and sweet pellets. She polishes them off with one long wet lick of her pink tongue. Her furry beige tail wags.

I remember Kaalu, my first dog and my childhood companion. He too got pellets, but of a different sort. He was killed with an air-gun, suffering a slow, agonizing death while I, his best friend, was at school. Even all these years later, the memory triggers anger and sadness within me. I wish I could have taken care of Kaalu as I do of Waffle. As my eyes moisten, I console myself that maybe there is a bit of Kaalu in Waffle. Or that, at the very least, he is happy watching us from above.

From one pet to another, from being a grandson to now being a grandfather, from getting hurt in various ways to eventually healing the sick, life has come full circle. I've been a doctor, entrepreneur, husband, father, grandpa, part-time singer and photographer. It's been a life well lived, with rarely a dull moment. If life was a bike ride, I rode fast. Sometimes I skidded and fell but then got back on the saddle. And I'm glad I could do my bit for homeopathy, which gave me everything.

Waffle sits beside me, barking at a cat in a photograph on the table. My family members walk in and out of the room. As I reflect on the years gone by, I remember an old Hindi song, written by the lyricist Asrar Suri, '*Manzil mile na mile iska gam nahin/Manzil ki justuju me mera karwan to hai.*' My interpretation of the lines is this: There is no regret about missing some goals. But in the pursuit of those goals, I found my people and my world.

Seventy years of existence on this planet teaches you a lot. I have dotted this book with lessons that readers and professionals can benefit from. And in this chapter, I will encapsulate the various things I have learnt from life.

1. Aim big, aim to make a difference: Listen to your instinct. Sachin Tendulkar, Virat Kohli and M.S. Dhoni were all middle-class kids. But they realized they had a talent for hitting a cricket ball better than most. And then they worked hard at it. Stop seeing dreams as something abstract and unachievable. With the right tools and attitude, they can become a reality.

2. Leave behind a legacy: Be a pioneer. There was a time when, at parties, people would hastily end the conversation when they found out I was a homeopath, and not an MBBS doctor. I went on to set up a brand and grow it, and put homeopathy on the map. We have our critics, but it is fair to say we wouldn't be where we are today without merit.

3. Lead a values-based life and inspire others to be truthful: Ideas create, values protect. Don't glamourize jugaad (makeshift work). It is a culture encouraged by the mediocre and the crooked. It may help you in the short term, but in the long run, your product and Indian business practices will be shown in poor light. Yes, you will make mistakes. At such times, it's best to own up to them. Remember, this is a world of social media and online reviews. Dishonesty can be flashed in seconds to a global audience.

4. Build multilevel leadership and understand the real meaning of leadership: Leadership goes beyond just a fancy office and speeches. Leadership means you are always being watched. Hundreds of employees will base their value system upon how you conduct yourself and the decisions you take, especially in a pressure situation. As for multilevel leadership, it will bring out leadership qualities in others, and they will always be thankful to you for that. You will be seen as someone without insecurity, and it will also help you ease some of your own work burden.

5. Trust but not blindly: The world does have devious people, and not all of them are in Nigeria sending scam emails. Some of them are right there in your company. Beware of their intentions, especially when you are successful. Never show all your cards to anyone. Learn to see red flags. If someone is selling you a story that seems too good to be true, it probably is. Do your own independent homework on a matter before committing your name or money to it.

6. Innovate: It will keep you ahead of the game. We were the first to have computer data and blister-packed medicines. At the same time, the timing of innovation is critical. It should be done when your existing range is stable, and when there is a need in the market for it. Do not launch a range of sunscreen in Cherrapunji.

7. Put your money where your mouth is: If you say all the right things about providing employee benefits to impress your friends or the media, but fail to actually do what you have said, you will lose the respect of your workforce and the corporate world in general.

8. Create not just profit but also goodwill: There will be financial highs and lows. But goodwill can set you apart from your competitor. In our company, we take care of the underprivileged and the less fortunate. Their blessings keep us protected and their prayers help us grow.

9. Be prepared for crisis and conflict management: Entrepreneurship can be first-class travel and champagne one moment, trench warfare the next. You will need a mix of patience, aggression and quick thinking to resolve matters. When Covid broke out, we sent computers to our doctors' homes and started video-calling our patients within days. Soon we were doing up to 1000 e-consultations a day. It was an unprecedented time and calamity, and we hit the ground running.

My teenaged grandson and his friends arrive. Youth radiates from everything they do or say. There is a bounce in their step and freedom in their voices. They take Waffle to their room. I get up from my chair and walk outside in my bright-coloured sports shoes. The clouds have cleared. It is humid, but everything around is green and fresh.

I think about my future, and realize that although I have almost retired from my company, I'm its founder and chairman emeritus. A part of me will always be involved in it, and in the spread of homeopathy. As I walk, a cool breeze ripples through the trees and hits my face. I feel charged. I remember, as I often do, the words of the poet Robert Frost: The woods are lovely, dark and deep/ But I have promises to keep/And miles to go before I sleep/And miles to go before I sleep.[11]

---

11 Frost, Robert (1969), 'Stopping by the Woods on a Snowy Evening', in E.C. Lathem (ed.), *The Poetry of Robert Frost: The Collected Poems Complete and Unabridged*, New York: Henry Holt and Company Inc. (The poem was first published in 1923.)

Index

Acknowledgements

THE IDEA OF MY AUTOBIOGRAPHY WAS SEEDED BY FAMED JOURNALIST and author Satya Saran. I thought that my seventieth would be an apt occasion to pen down and share my life's journey. With a hope that my ability to convert challenges into opportunities and failures into success would give budding entrepreneurs food for thought, which they won't find in any textbook or management degree. While not the Holy Grail, I've found cheat codes to make life's journey a little bit more pleasurable and fun as you go along it.

Ashwin Sanghi, bestselling novelist and the co-author to my earlier book *13 Steps to Bloody Good Health*, turned guide and mentor to me. Not only did he share his wisdom but also connected me with the literary agency Siyahi and the wonderful Mita Kapur who zealously took this book forward, championing its story to the best publishing houses in the business. *The Nation's Homeopath* finally found a home with HarperCollins and you are reading this copy thanks to the priceless inputs from Sachin Sharma, my publisher, who held my hand all throughout our publishing journey. To the team at HarperCollins – Akriti Tyagi, Shivendra Singh and Rahul Dixit – thank you for your dedicated efforts in the distribution and marketing process of this book even during this difficult pandemic period.

While the world around us came to a standstill because of Covid-19; I would wake up in the middle of the night with my mind racing excitedly to let thoughts flow to paper at a thousand words a minute, with my dog Waffle and her soulful eyes encouraging me through the night. The narrators, Reshma Jain, Alpana Lath Sawai and especially Akshay Sawai, who helped to bring out the wonderful manuscript that you see before you.

Our design partners Vandana and Ragini from Water Communications for their artistic inputs and constant support, no matter the hour. Our home team – Dr Batra's marketing and corporate communication team – for their integral support in getting the word out.

Louisa, my constant helping hand, for her invaluable support and attention to detail while proofreading the copy over and over again.

My think tank – Akshay, Farah, Hriman, Aara and Zoha – thank you for your critique during our after-dinner readings that helped to make the manuscript more reader friendly to the millennial audience.

To my family – my sons, brothers and their families – for their love, patience, support and encouragement. And to my extended family – my patients and my colleagues at Dr Batra's from whom I have learnt so much.

A big thank you to all of my friends who have been right by my side through my journey of a multitude of experiences, some of which I have recorded in the book. And finally to you my reader – thank you for choosing this book. I hope my misadventures bring laughter and joy to your lives and inspire you to lead more fulfilled lives.

About the Author

THE MAN BEHIND THE BRAND DR BATRA'S®, DR MUKESH BATRA IS a homeopath of international repute and Founder and Chairman Emeritus of Dr Batra's® group of companies—which encompasses the largest chain of homeopathy clinics, day-care aesthetic centres and health and wellness products. His journey as a doctor and entrepreneur has been both fascinating and challenging. His life has been full of opportunities and failures that he overcame successfully with great fortitude. As a doctor, he treated both, the who's who of India, such as various heads of states, celebrities, artists, as well as the common man. Dr Batra has authored six bestselling books on homeopathy. He has also published several research papers in journals and chaired scientific sessions at homeopathic conferences, nationally and internationally. He has developed new protocols for hair and skin diseases that will objectively and scientifically measure treatment outcomes, not only for homeopaths but also for doctors from other streams of medicine.

As an entrepreneur, Dr Batra set up the first state-of-the-art, branded homeopathy clinic in 1982. He faced many challenges along the way, but he never gave up. With his team of professional managers and over 400 doctors, he put homeopathy on the world map by starting over 200 clinics in seven countries and in 150 cities of India and other parts of the world.

He launched a product company dealing with FMCG products with over 100 different hair care, skin care, personal care and nutraceutical products.

As an academician, Dr Batra was professor emeritus at the Hahnemann College, UK and USA and has trained more than 500 doctors internationally, including MDs. He is also the only Asian homeopath whose research and clinical cases are the subject of a film shot in Hollywood, which is used today as course material for post-graduate homeopathy studies all over the world.

As a philanthropist, Dr Batra's® Foundation provides free homeopathic treatment to over 20,000 patients, through free clinics across 123 cities. The foundation also provides free lifelong homeopathic medicines to NGOs in different parts of the country with which it is associated. Dr Batra has introduced a set of annual awards that recognize and celebrate those that have overcome disability and have contributed to society.

Dr Batra's own personal interests that include photography and singing have led to over fifty exhibitions and ten concerts that raised funds for charitable causes.

Dr Batra is a patron of theatre and arts and has judged the Filmfare Annual Film Awards, twice. He has also been a book critic for the *Indian Express*.

Dr Batra has been honoured with the Padma Shri for Medicine (Homeopathy) in 2012 by the President of India for his contribution towards the field of homeopathy.